IMAGES
of America
WELLSVILLE

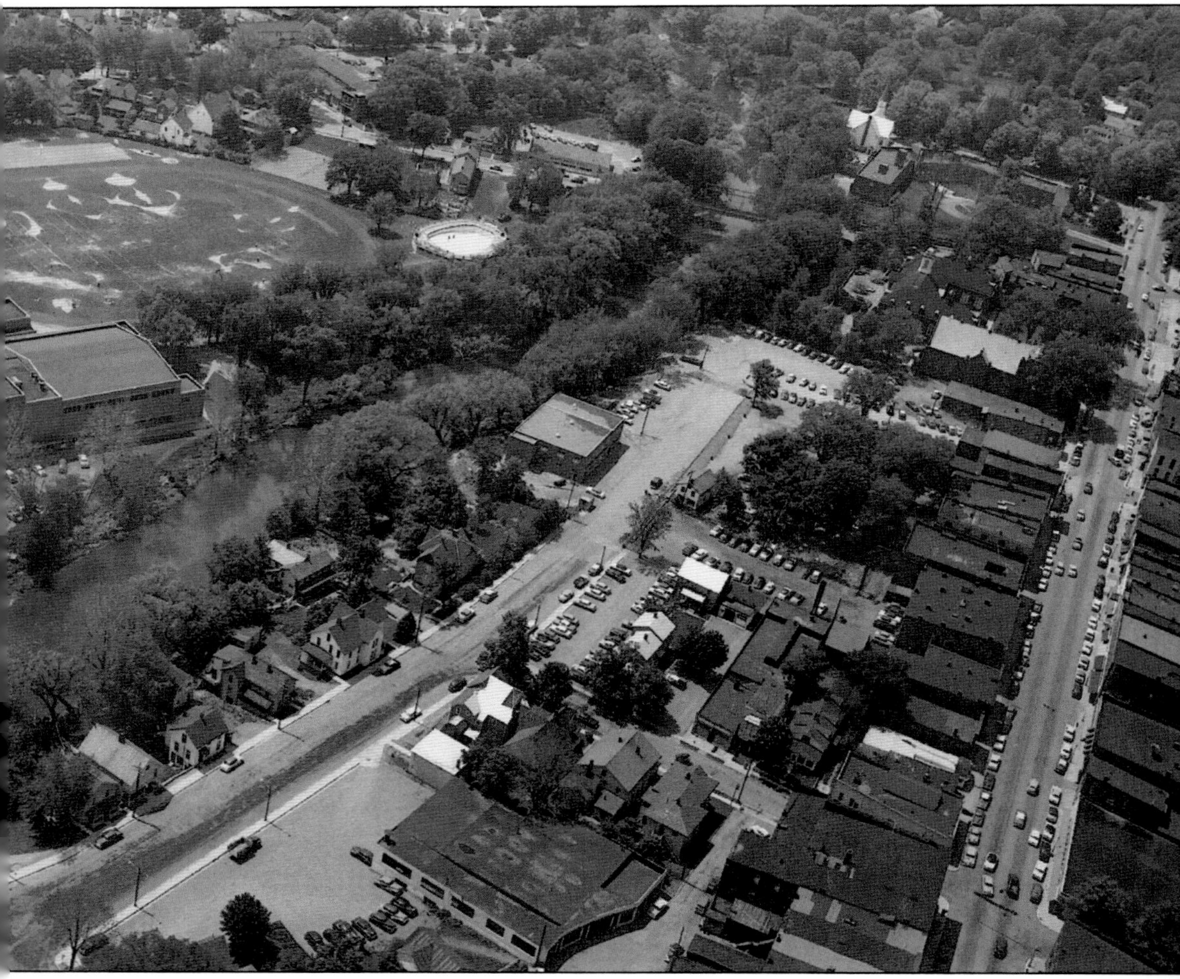

This aerial view from the 1960s depicts a section of Wellsville that has changed significantly in the last 40 years. A flood control project changed the course of the river, and a new state highway bypass took most heavy traffic off the narrow Main Street. The Genesee River can hardly be seen through the trees as it meanders northward past the high school and the Veterans Memorial Pool. (Donald Baldwin.)

On the Cover: The volunteers of Dyke Street Hose Company No. 2 are shown as they stand ready for a Fourth of July parade around 1904. The fire hall was constructed in 1899 to help protect the southeastern part of the village, especially the large tannery located just a block away. The building remained home to Dyke Street Hose Co. No. 2 for over 60 years before its need for a larger building was realized. The former fire hall was purchased by the Thelma Rogers Genealogical and Historical Society in 1966, and it has been the society's home since that time. (Cindy Bledsoe and David Helmer.)

IMAGES
of America

WELLSVILLE

Thelma Rogers Genealogical and Historical Society

ARCADIA
PUBLISHING

ISBN 978-1-4671-2350-1

Published by Arcadia Publishing
Charleston, South Carolina

Printed in the United States of America

Library of Congress Control Number: 2014955047

For all general information, please contact Arcadia Publishing:
Telephone 843-853-2070
Fax 843-853-0044
E-mail sales@arcadiapublishing.com
For customer service and orders:
Toll-Free 1-888-313-2665

Visit us on the Internet at www.arcadiapublishing.com

This book is dedicated to all residents of the Wellsville community who recognize the importance of preserving and sharing our history.

Contents

Acknowledgments

When I started this endeavor, I knew that I would need help in gathering additional photographs. The images of the Thelma Rogers Genealogical and Historical Society (TRGHS) are significant and growing every week, but many of the photographs the society holds have been published or frequently shared on social media. New historical photographs appeared when I least expected them! Thank you, to the many members and nonmembers who volunteered their images for this project. Our digital files have grown richer thanks to you. Special thanks go to Donald Baldwin, James Dello, Christina Wightman, David Hornburg, and Ann Comstock. You always think of TRGHS whenever you find new items or images, and we truly appreciate your thoughtfulness. A thank-you goes to Allegany County historian Craig Braack for sharing his office files as well as his personal postcard collection. Thank-yous also go to Jill Palmer, Donald and Micky Bohne, Mary and Joel Havens, Alice Stevens, Martha Fuller, and the L.C. Whitford Company for responding to my pleas for information. Thanks are extended to Kristen Kruger for digitizing the society's old glass negatives. Those images have proven most useful. Further thanks go to the wonderful people who work at the David A. Howe Public Library (DAHPL). You are the best!

Because one editor is never enough, thank you, Joanne Allen, Christina Wightman, and Dr. William Paquette for your time and advice.

Thank you, to Jane Pinney, who served as president of our historical society for many years. Jane's personal knowledge and her database of Wellsville information have been invaluable in this endeavor. Thank you, to my husband, Robin, who was denied the used of our computer while I worked on this project. Robin supported me in so many other quiet ways. Thank you, to Sharon McAllister of Arcadia Publishing, who responded quickly and clearly to my many e-mailed inquiries.

Unless otherwise noted, the images in this publication are from the files of the Thelma Rogers Genealogical and Historical Society.

—Mary J. Rhodes

Introduction

The story of how Wellsville was named is a simple one, perhaps too simple to believe. A group of pioneers met at Harmon Van Buren's Tavern in 1832 and decided to name the settlement Wellsville after resident Gardner Wells. Wells had come to the area only a few years prior and acquired extensive properties in the settlement. He moved downriver to Belfast by 1850, but he is honored every time we recount our history or say the name Wellsville.

In 1832, the settlement of Wellsville was part of the town of Scio, and the area was sparsely inhabited. The Van Buren family built a cabin, which developed into a tavern and a meeting place by necessity, as there were no other public buildings. Informal trade was conducted early by Silas Hills until Norman Perry erected a real store in 1835.

Pioneers put the Genesee River to use immediately. The river runs south to north, emptying into Lake Ontario, and was prone to flooding, but mills were built on the banks to cut wood and grind meal needed for everyday life. Lumbering operations used the river to move logs during times of high water, and, of course, the river was a source of food. Early settlers so relied on the area's abundant game for survival that later in the century it became a novelty to actually see a deer. Job Straight, Silas Hills, William Weed, Reuben Kent, Harmon Van Buren, Daniel Tuttle, Zenas Jones, Asa Foster, and Gardner Wells are names that will always be associated with the settlement of the town and village.

Early travel was difficult as the few roads in the area probably followed Indian pathways or deer trails. It was a challenge for a wagon to navigate these routes to bring products to market, and it was an investment of time counted in days. In 1849, a plank toll road facilitated the movement of lumber and supplies to and from the settlement. Wellsville, in the southern part of western New York, drew a slow, steady stream of settlers. As the Erie Railroad laid its way through the heart of the settlement, Wellsville's population began to swell with families who knew they could make a good life here.

Tanneries and lumbers mills were the community's largest employers. Hemlock trees grew in abundance in the woods around Wellsville and were lumbered for their wood and bark. The trees were cut, stripped of their bark, and sent to mills for processing. The hemlock bark was sent to the tanneries, where it was an essential part of the tanning process. Wellsville was dubbed Tanbark City because the Wellsville, Allegany, Genesee, and Hatch Tanneries had so many large piles of hemlock bark, called tanbark, lying in their yards. The Erie Railroad brought raw leather for processing from as far away as South America. The tanneries also attracted many German and Irish immigrants who stayed here after the United States Leather Corporation ceased its operations in the early 1900s.

In 1855, the town of Wellsville was created from the townships of Scio, Andover, and Willing, making it the second-youngest township in Allegany County. By 1857, there were enough residents to vote for the incorporation of the settlement of Wellsville as a village. The vote was 150 for incorporation, with only eight voters dissenting.

The Erie Railroad always called its station in Wellsville "Genesee Station" for the place where the railroad touched the Genesee River. A legislative act in 1871 changed the name from Wellsville to Genesee, but this proved confusing. There was already a town of Genesee in Allegany County, and a township of Genesee in Potter County, Pennsylvania, as well as a town of Geneseo in Livingston County. Another legislative act in 1873 legally changed the name back to Wellsville, and the railroad station officially became the Wellsville Station.

Wellsville was built and rebuilt as fire repeatedly worked its remodeling magic on the community's buildings. In the late 1860s, the village was swept by several large fires that ingested wooden structures faster than citizens could work the bucket brigades. The village mandated that newly constructed buildings in the business district be made of brick. It is surprising to see how many new buildings were erected in the course of just a few short years because of fire.

Orville P. Taylor came to Wellsville around 1871. His belief that oil could be discovered in the area changed the face of the county. Almost bankrupt from drilling dry wells, Taylor finally hit oil in 1879 and caused a rush of people to move to and invest in Wellsville. Many residents had no idea what oil was used for.

By 1902, an oil refinery was built in Wellsville to collect and refine the oil of the Allegany field. That refinery later became the Sinclair Refinery. Folks say that the people of Wellsville never felt the effects of the Depression because of the Sinclair Refinery.

In the mid-20th century, the need for automobiles became as much of a force in the remodeling of the village as fire had been in the 19th century. Municipal parking lots grew to accommodate vehicles, removing some neighborhoods completely. A New York State initiative to build a highway around the village created more changes to the landscape.

Today, as with many small villages across the country, Wellsville struggles to maintain its downtown character. In an age where people no longer barter face-to-face, Main Street has lost many of the small businesses that were the heart and soul of Wellsville's marketplace. The people of Wellsville are resilient; they will adapt over time and find new uses for their treasured buildings.

This book cannot begin to tell the whole story of Wellsville's rich history and interesting people. Many cherished photographs and wonderful stories cannot be shown or recounted here because of limitations of space. Perhaps the photographs and brief descriptions contained in this book will encourage you to delve deeper into Wellsville's history. There is so much more to learn about this amazing community.

One

WELLSVILLE TO 1880

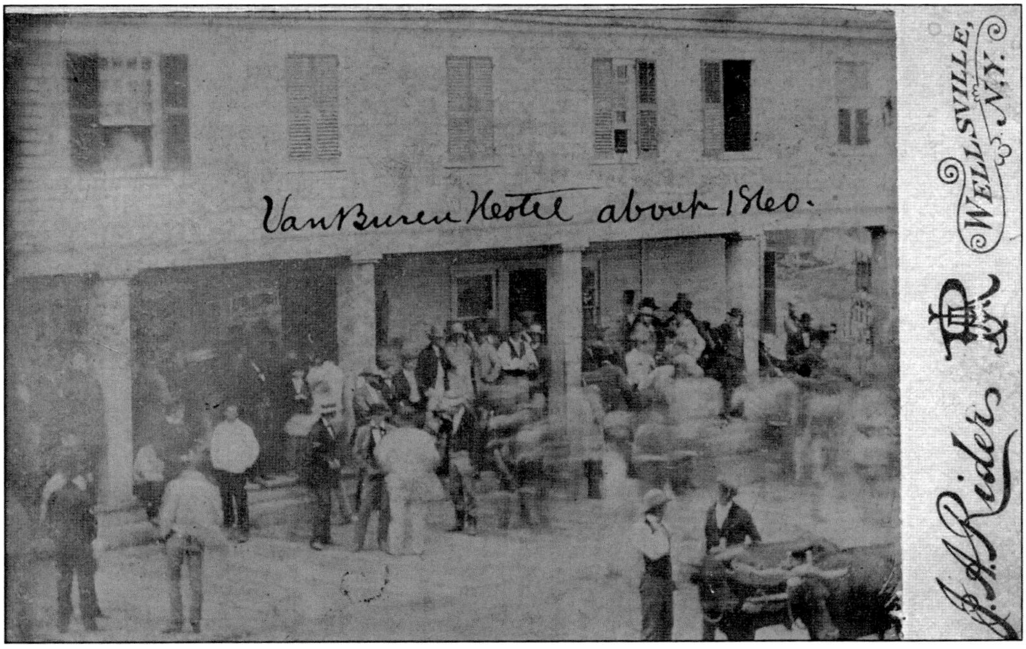

Van Buren's Hotel was the first commercial building in the village or town of Wellsville. The hotel was originally built of logs and was home to the Harmon Van Buren family. It was enlarged over the years to meet the demands of a traveling public. A fire in the fall of 1867 burned the hotel to the ground. (DAHPL.)

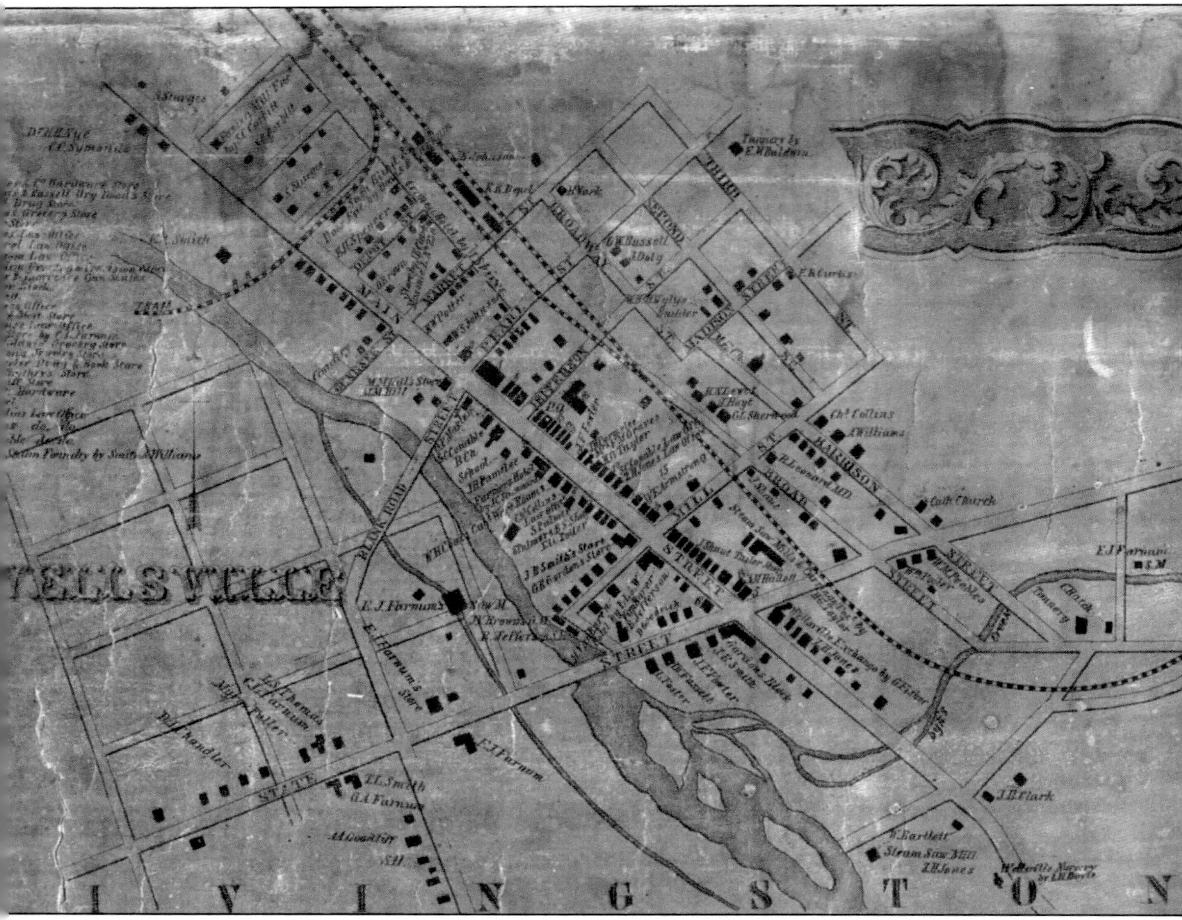

An 1856 map of Allegany County contains a small sketch of the village of Wellsville. The sketch shows the business district taking shape along Main Street, built entirely of wooden structures. (Map of Allegany County, New York, from Actual Surveys, G. Bechler, 1856, published by Gillette Matthews & Co., Philadelphia.)

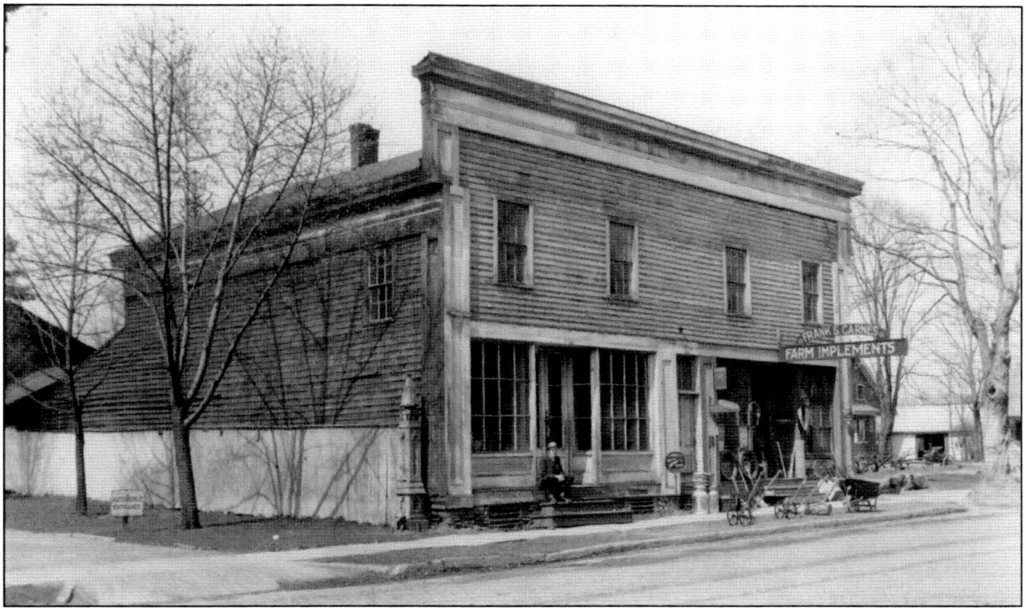

Brothers John and Samuel Carpenter established their store in 1856 at the northern part of the village. The store was known as the Carpenter's Store, and it endured into the 20th century, operated by John's sons Whitfield and George. The family never yielded to technology, operating the place by the light of a kerosene lantern and the warmth of a woodstove. Toward the end of its life, Carpenter's Store was more of a social gathering place, as depicted in the photograph below. This c. 1910 image shows (from left to right) John Lish, Ambrose Coats, Frank Richards, Whit Carpenter (standing), Henry Smith, Marion Marsh, and Delos Marsh gathered for conversation. (Above, DAHPL.)

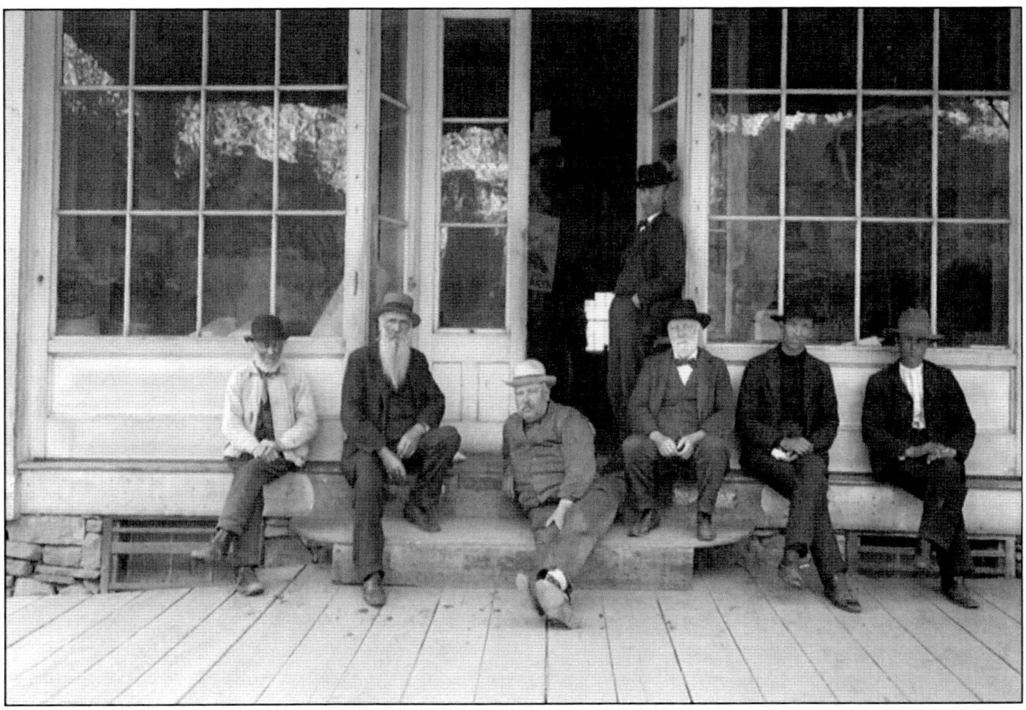

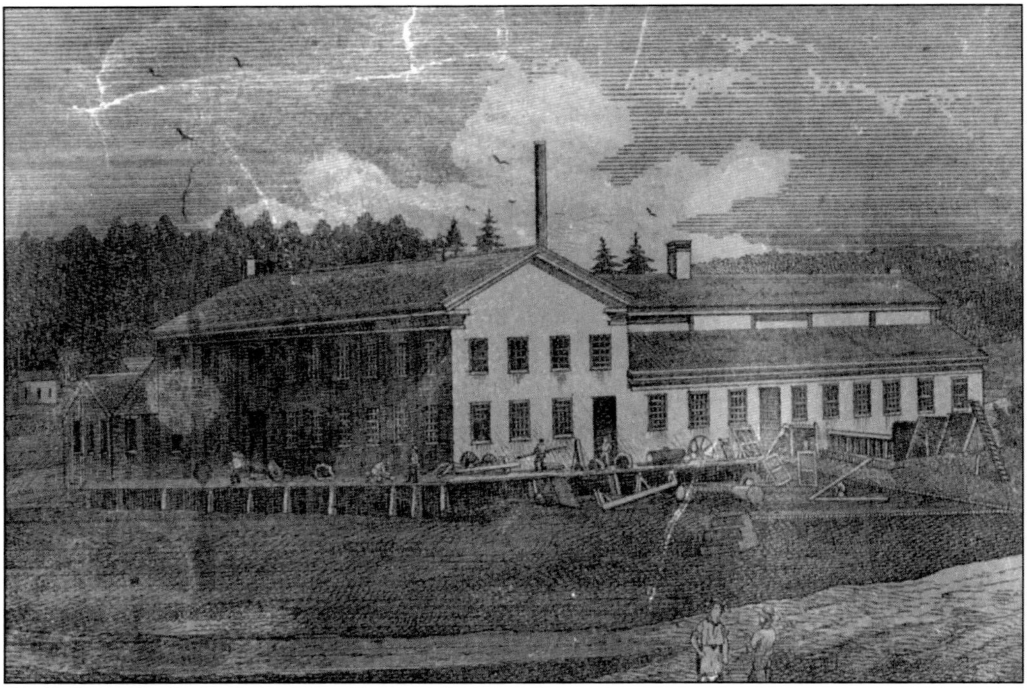

The Genesee Steam Foundry is shown on Bechler's 1856 map of Allegany County. Lebbeus Sweet and Nathaniel Whittaker formed a partnership in 1852 and developed the Genesee Steam Foundry. Located near the Erie tracks on Furnace Street (now Jefferson Street), the foundry manufactured steam engines, mill gearing, castings, and farm machinery.

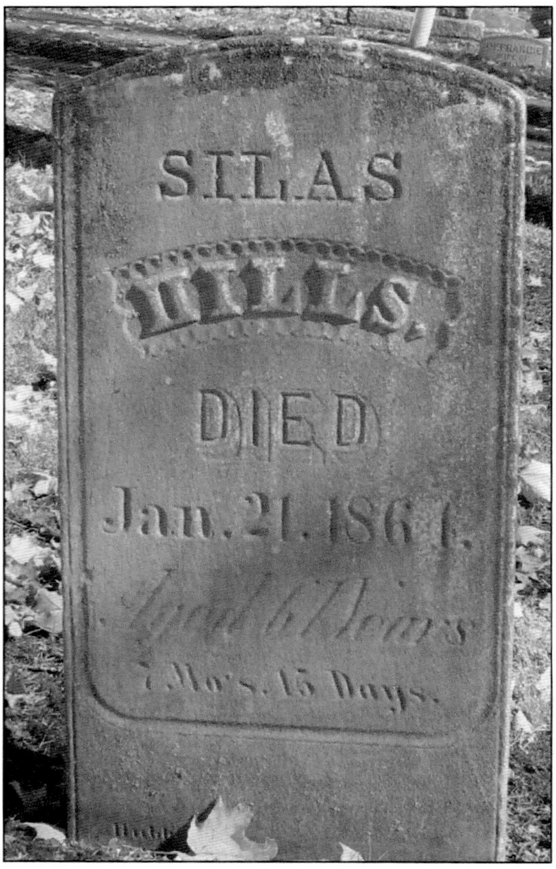

Silas Hills of Swanzey, New Hampshire, was an early settler in the village. Armed with carpentry skills and business acumen, he helped build the wooden homes and businesses of his neighbors. Hills is credited with being the first merchant in the village, selling goods out of Van Buren's Tavern in 1832, and was part of the group that gathered at Van Buren's Tavern and named the settlement after Gardner Wells.

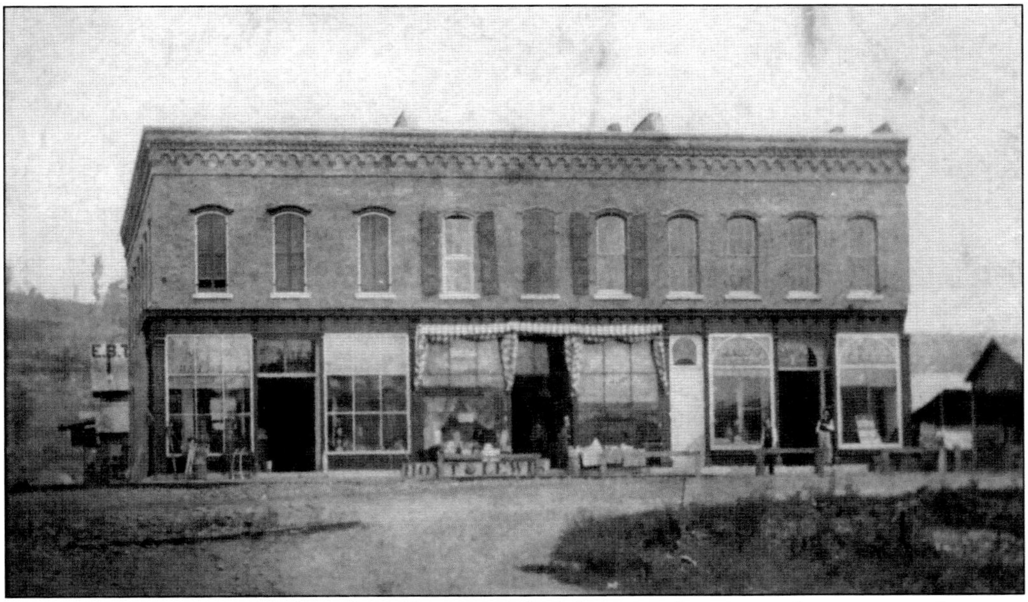

Several large fires occurred in the village in 1867. The most destructive began in a saloon on the west side of North Main Street. Flames spread from the corner of Plank Road (West Pearl Street) to the Baptist church. Strong winds carried the blaze to the east side of North Main Street, destroying almost everything from North Main Street to the railroad tracks. The brick Union Block was the first store to rise from the ashes and was occupied by the same businesses whose establishments had burned—E.B. Tullar's hardware store, Hoyt and Lewis Hardware, and E.B. Hall's drugstore. (DAHPL.)

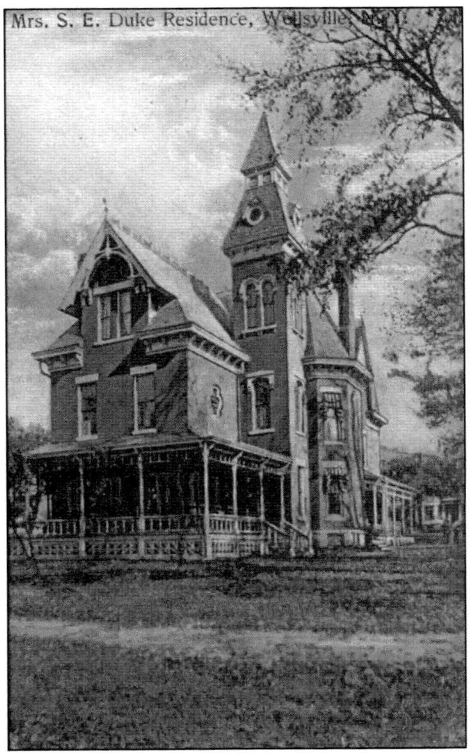

Lebbeus Sweet built his home in 1868 on a rise overlooking the village, not too far away from his foundry on Furnace Street. He built with brick to ensure his family's safety. Sweet included the modern convenience of gas lamps inside the residence, which were the talk of the town. William and Semantha Duke purchased the house in 1882 and remodeled it extensively, as shown in this postcard. This home on East Pearl Street became the lodge of the Benevolent and Protective Order of Elks in 1926.

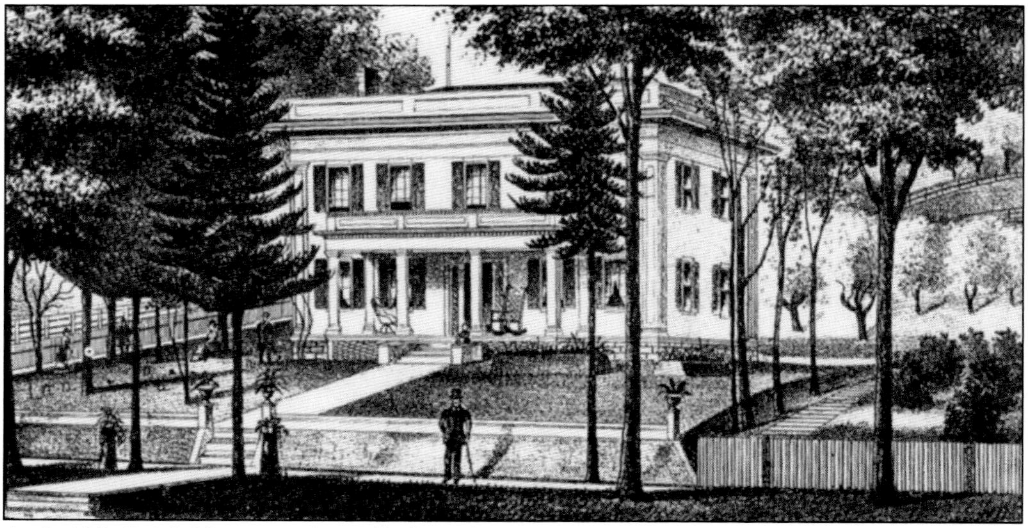

Asahel N. Cole's Home on the Hillside is shown in a sketch from the 1879 *History of Allegany County*. The home was built in the 1850s by William Pooler, who occupied it for a short period. Pooler sold the home to William Armstrong, making Cole the third owner of this house on South Highland Avenue. Cole was the editor of the *Genesee Valley Free Press* and was locally considered to be the father of the Republican Party. He often wrote of his Home on the Hillside in his editorials. (*History of Allegany County 1806–1879*, by D.G. Beers)

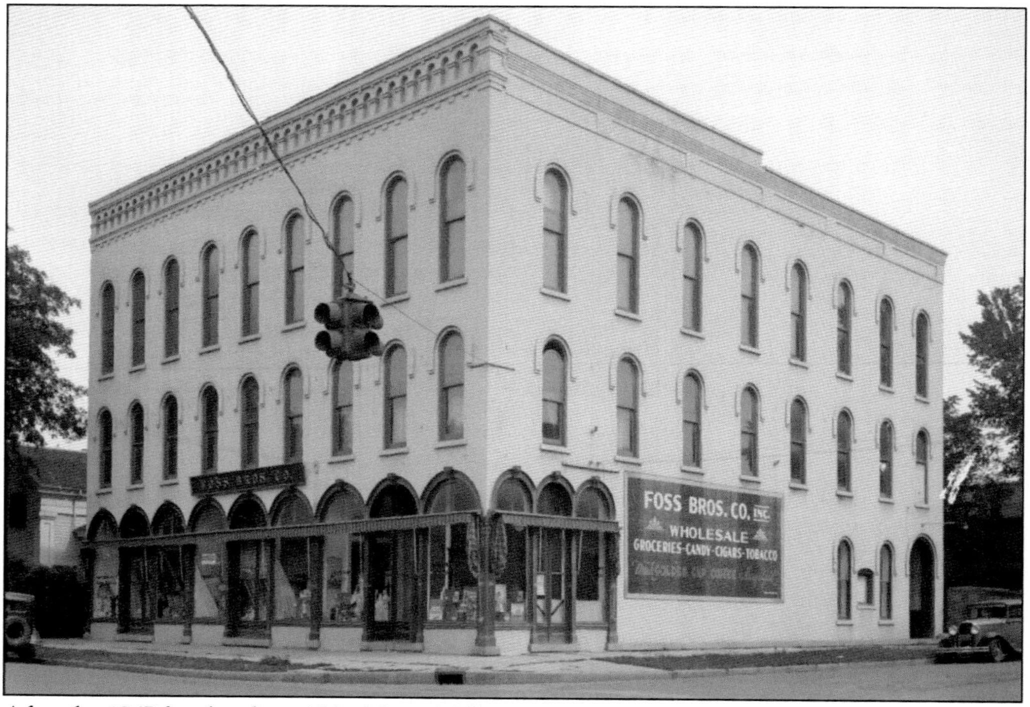

After the 1867 fire, brothers Alfred S. and Allen L. Brown erected this large brick building, which they named the Lincoln Block after Pres. Abraham Lincoln. The third floor held a community hall, which hosted many speeches and debates, including an 1870 debate on suffrage between Susan B. Anthony and the Honorable Horace Bemis of Hornellsville. The Foss Bros. Company occupied the store from the 1930s until it moved to Olean in 1964. (Kristen Kruger.)

It is probable that this old photograph is a view of the Bush and Howard Tannery on the Brooklyn side of the village. At its zenith, the tannery employed more than 75 men. The Healy Tannery purchased it in 1883, and extensive repairs were made to keep it in running order, but it closed by 1886. This area is now the neighborhoods of Earley and Stevens Streets. (James Dello.)

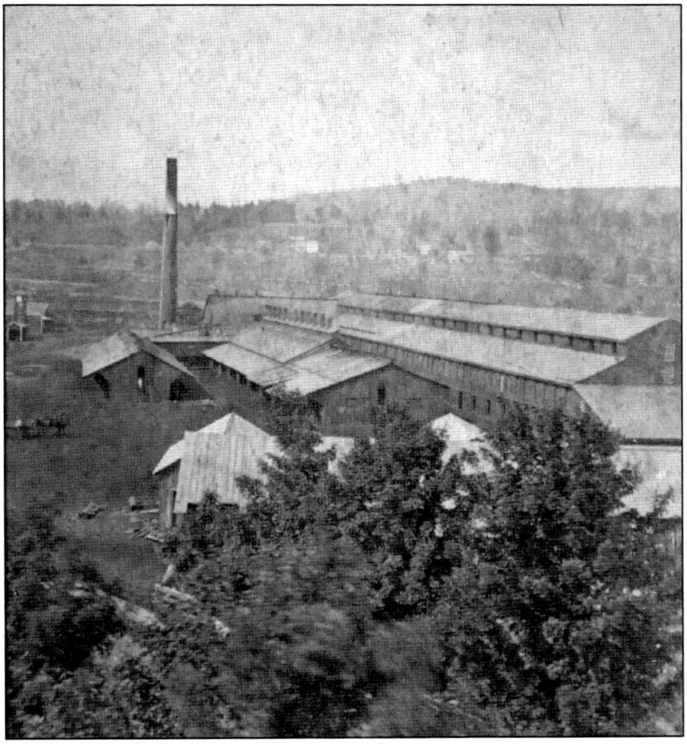

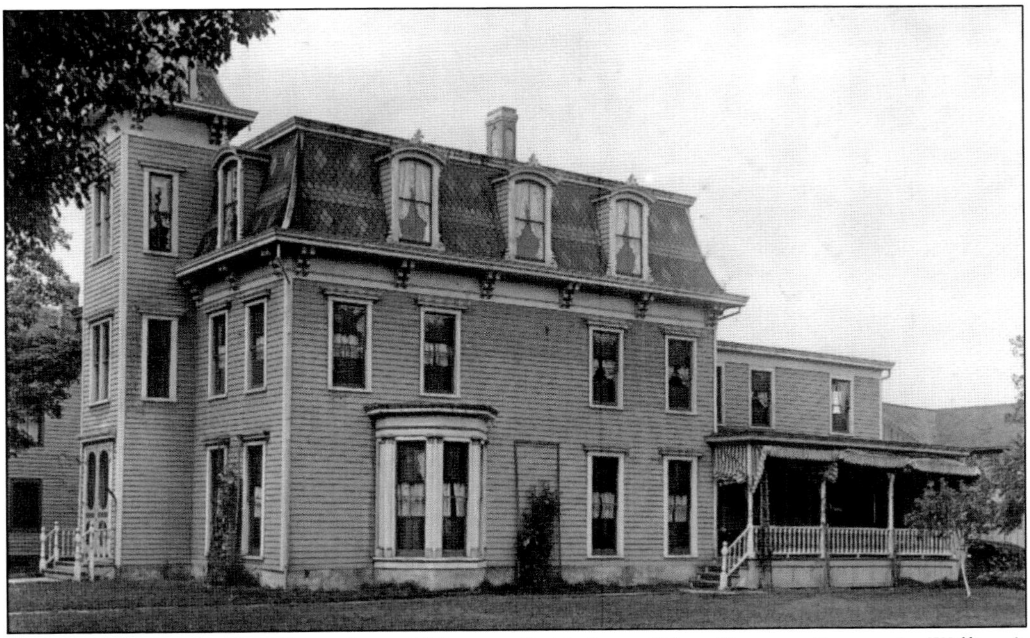

This was the home of William A. and Minerva Baldwin on West Genesee Street. At William's death, Minerva sold the house to Judge Clarence A. Farnum, who lived there for over 20 years. The Odd Fellows purchased the house from Judge Farnum for their lodge, and they hosted many stage shows there under the name of the Odd Fellows Temple Theatre. James Macris, the next owner of the building, added a large hall for movies and turned the grand old house into a real stop on the entertainment circuit. (Donald Baldwin.)

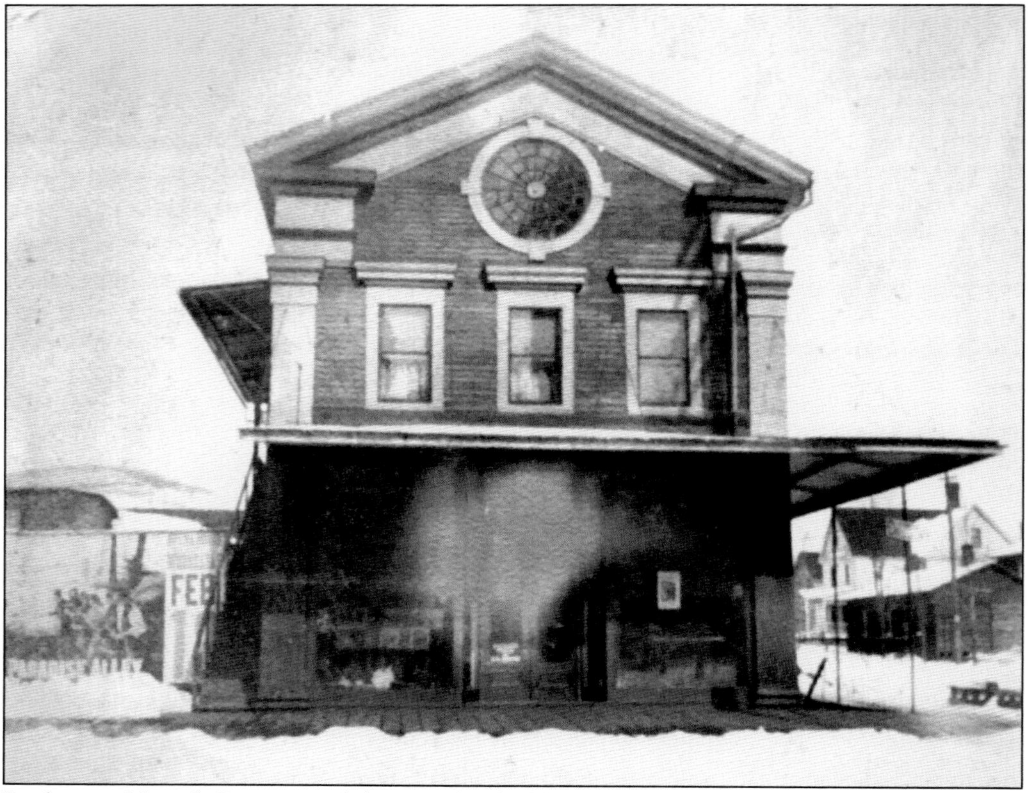

Reuben and Joseph Doty moved this wooden building from the west side of North Main Street to the corner of North Main Street and Furnace Street (now Jefferson Street) after the 1867 fire. The building was purchased by Fred Rice years later for the Mather and Rice Music Store. The land the building occupied was sold in 1907 to erect the first library in Wellsville, and this wooden store was moved again just a few feet north. Rice added a third floor and a new brick exterior to modernize and update it. The image below depicts the building, the Fred Rice Music store, around 1930, with Studebakers on display from Rice's car dealership at 26 Jefferson Street. (Above, Mather Homestead.)

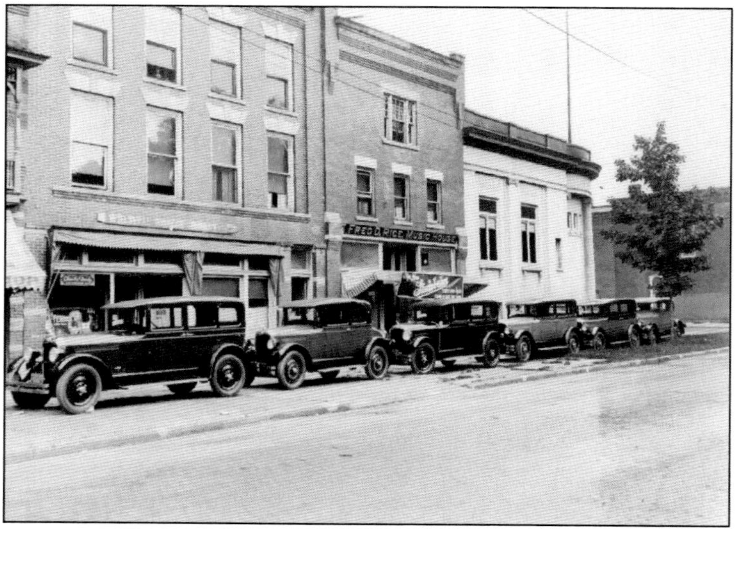

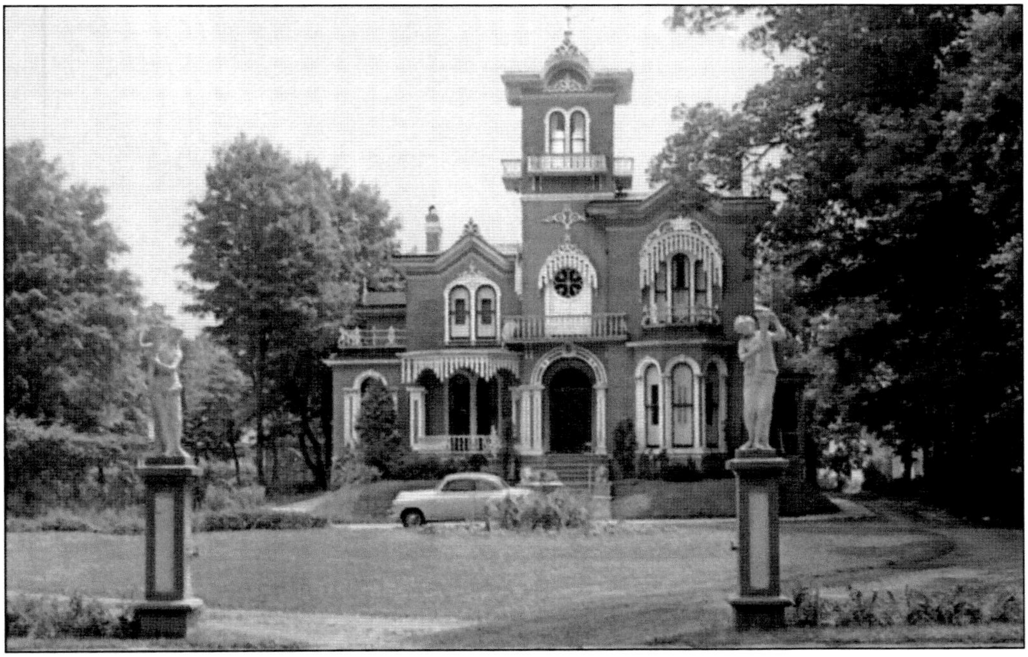

Edwin Bradford Hall of Bridgeport, Connecticut, came to Wellsville at the advent of the Erie Railroad and opened a drugstore on North Main Street. Hall married Antoinette Farnum, a daughter of Wellsville businessman Edward J. Farnum, and they built their home, the Pink House, in 1867. The Pink House was recently discovered to be almost a replica of a home built for Eli Thompson in Hall's hometown of Bridgeport. This beautiful residence has graced the covers of many books and magazines and is now occupied by the fourth generation of the Hall family. On the right is a photograph of Edwin B. Hall in 1904 at the age of 79.

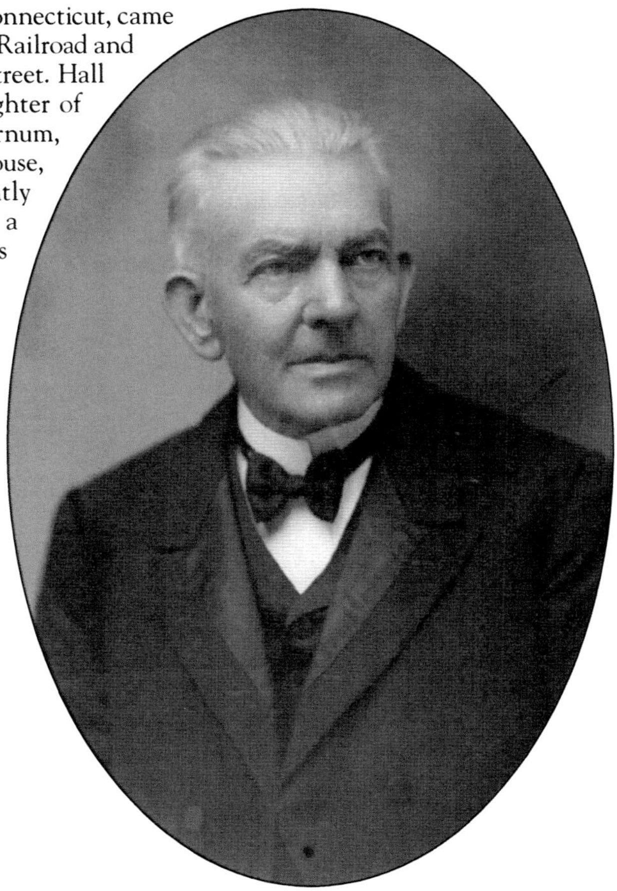

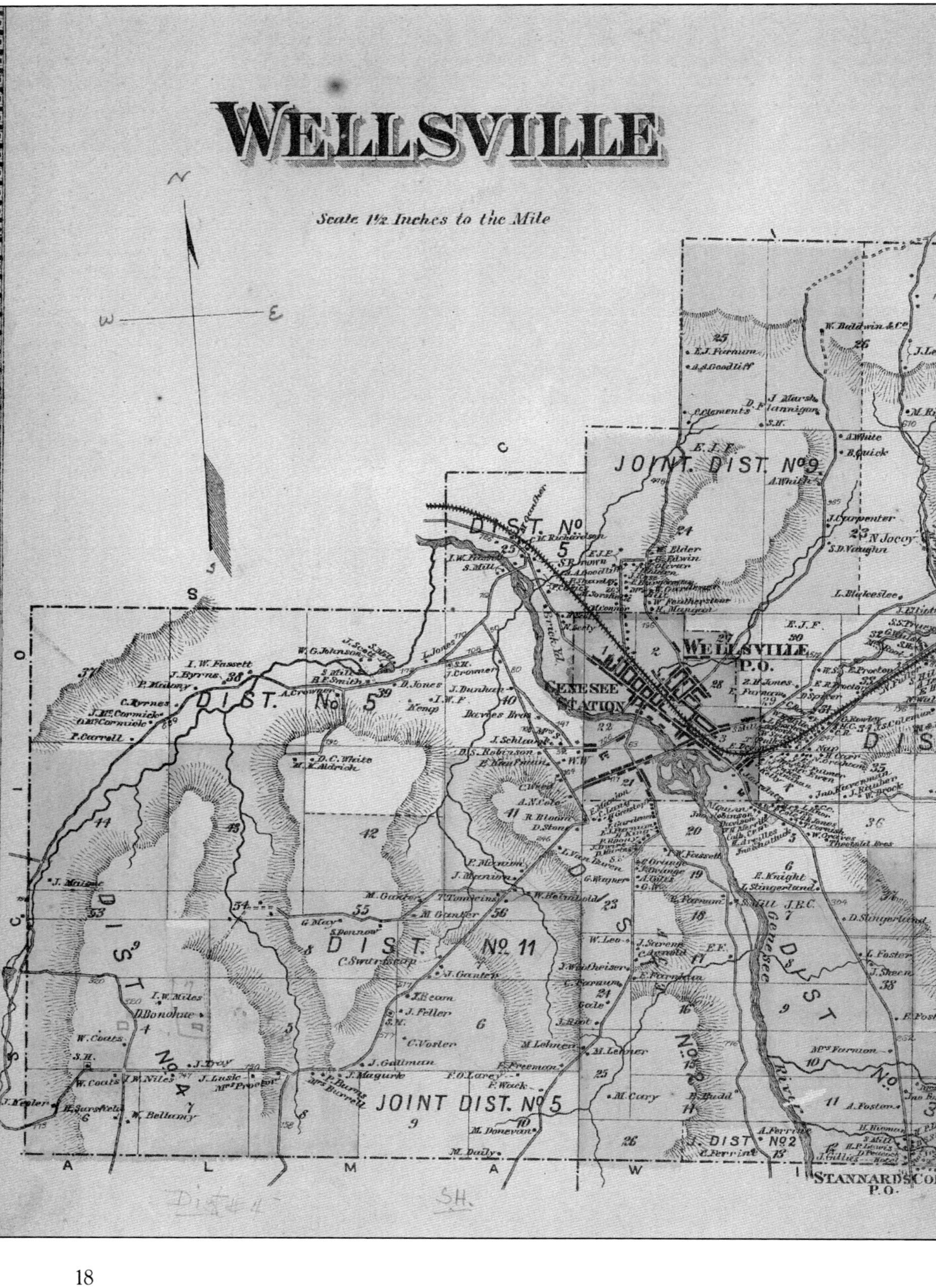
WELLSVILLE
Scale 1½ Inches to the Mile
N
E
W
JOINT. DIST. Nº 9.
DIST. Nº 5
DIST. Nº 5
WELLSVILLE P.O.
GENESEE STATION
DIST. Nº 11
JOINT DIST. Nº 5
J. DIST Nº 2
Genesee River
STANNARDS CO
P.O.
A L L M A W

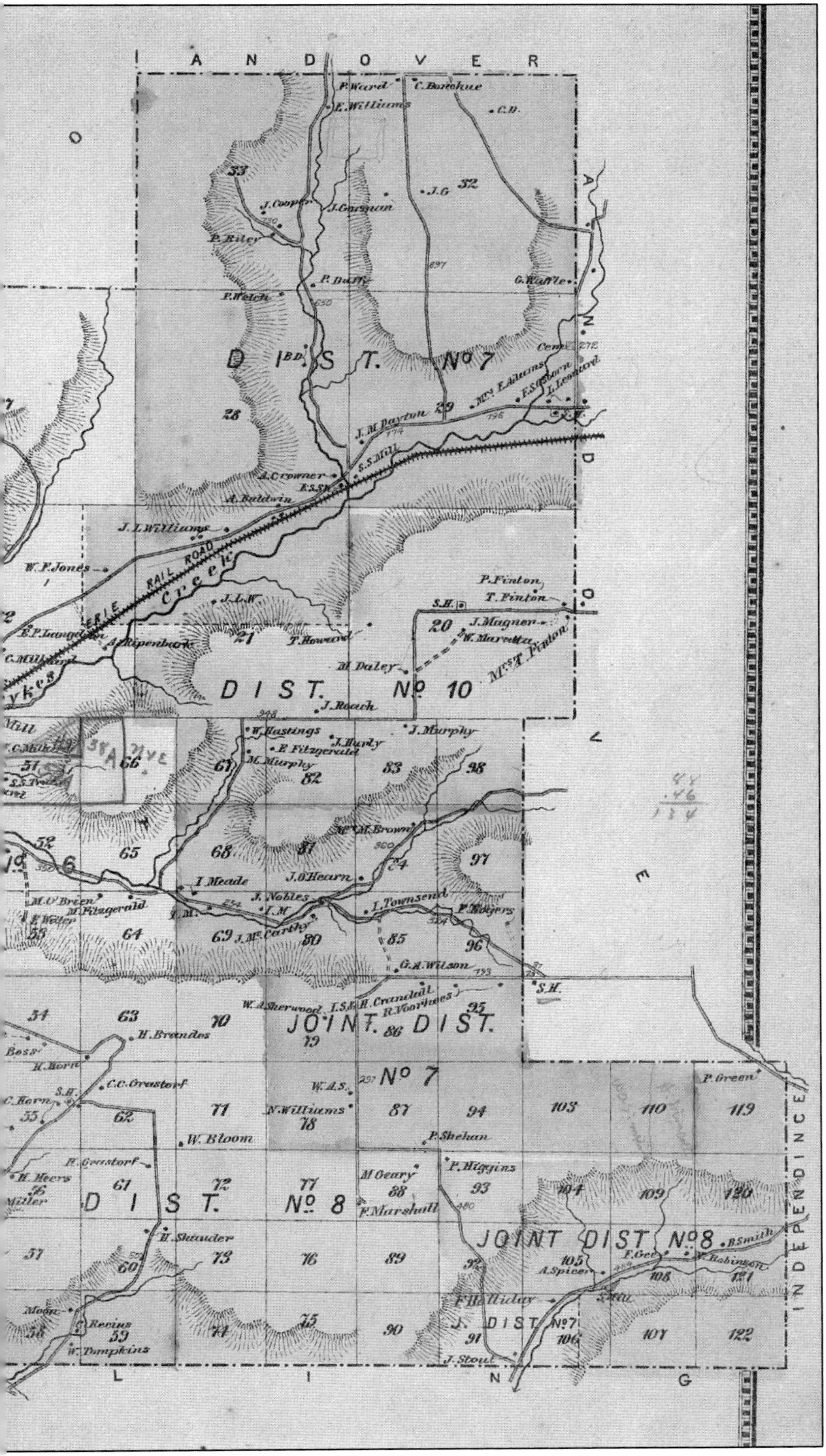

The town of Wellsville is depicted on this map from the 1869 *Atlas of Allegany County, New York*, by D.G. Beers & Co. The names of property owners are recorded on the map. The town of Wellsville, created in 1855, is the second-youngest town in Allegany County, with the town of Ward being the youngest.

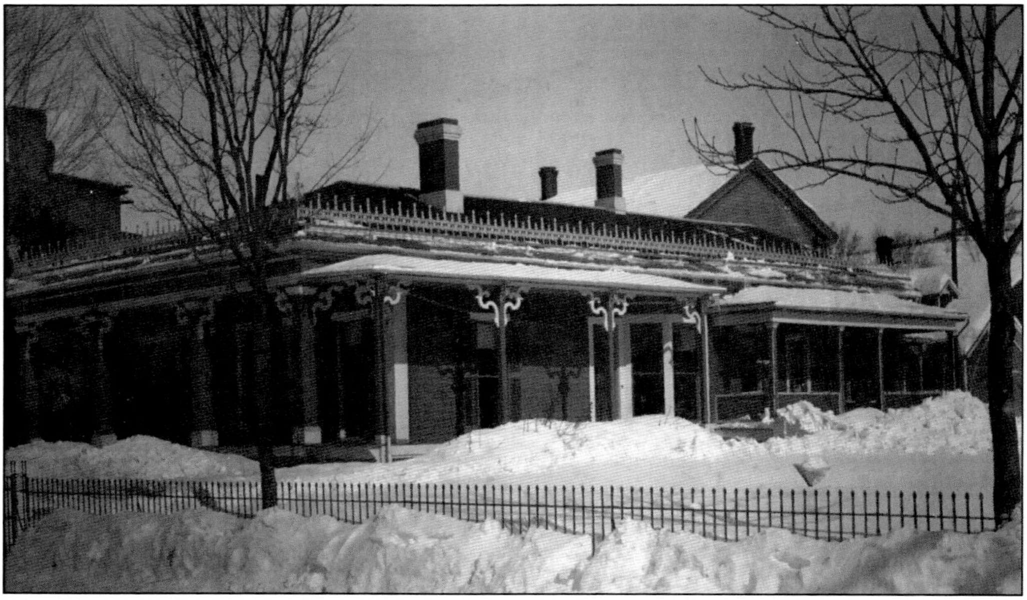

This house, on the corner of North Main Street and Fassett Street, was built in the late 1850s by William and Angelica Pooler and became the home of James and Mary Johnson Macken after their marriage in 1867. The Mackens lived their entire married life here. Dr. Fredrick McCarty purchased the property in 1920 and used it as his office and family home. The house was moved to Cummings Circle in 1954 to make room for the new J.J. Newberry Company store. Below are photographs of the Mackens in the 1880s. James was a veteran of the Civil War, a drugstore owner, an oil producer, and a former mayor of Wellsville. (All, DAHPL.)

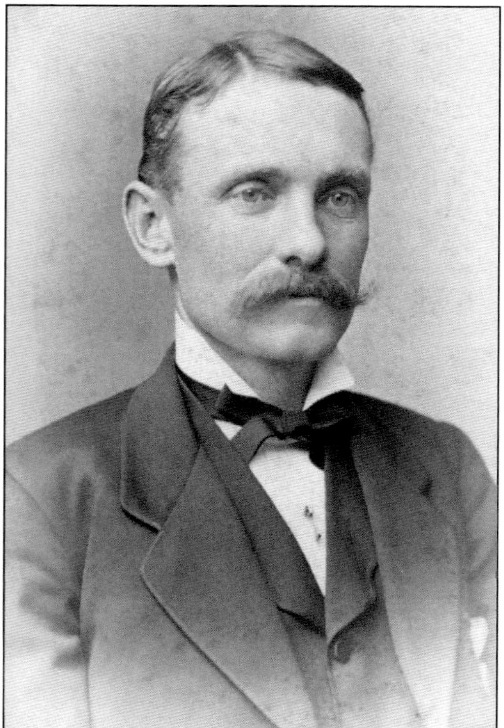

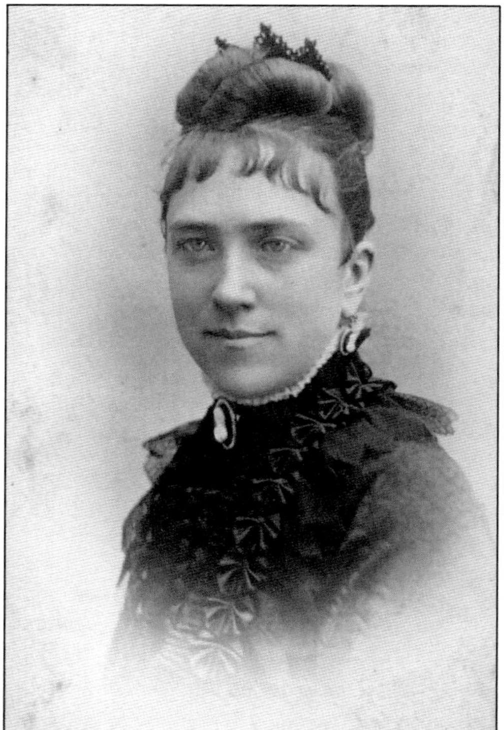

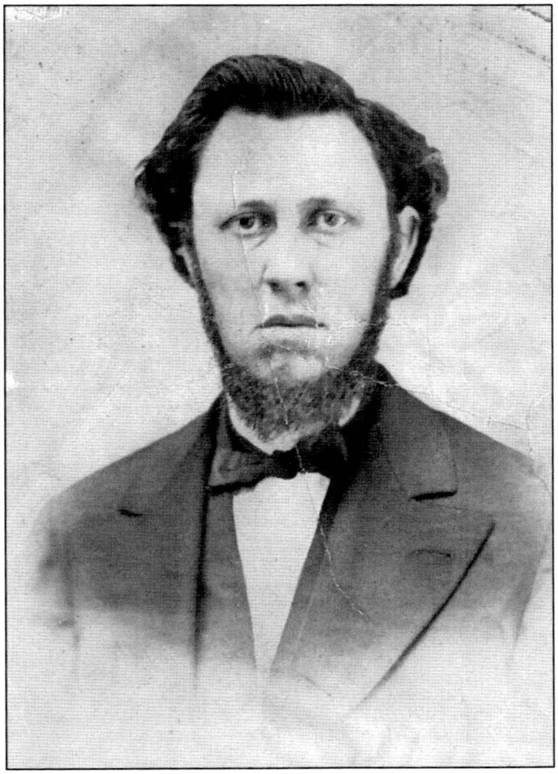

Charles H. Simmons arrived in Wellsville in 1864 and built his dry goods business in a store he called the Regulator for his ability to set prices with which other stores had to compete. Simmons is said to have built 17 brick stores and 15 private houses in his short tenure here. One of the first structures he built was the Opera House Block, located on the corner of North Main Street and West State Street. This was a three-story building with four ground-level stores, offices on the second floor, and a large hall on the third floor. Simmons Opera House opened in January 1871 with an exhibition of Milton's *Paradise Lost* in tableaux format. A fire in 1930 destabilized the building, necessitating its demolition. (Right, Virginia Wagner; below, James Dello.)

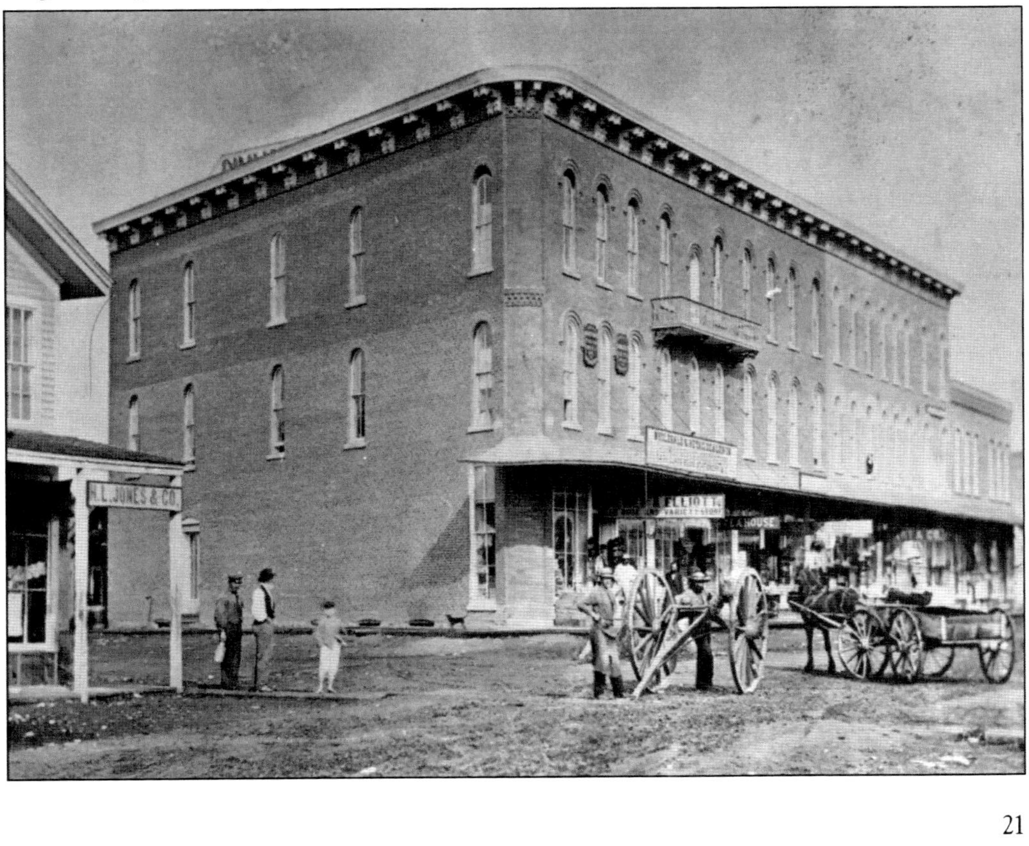

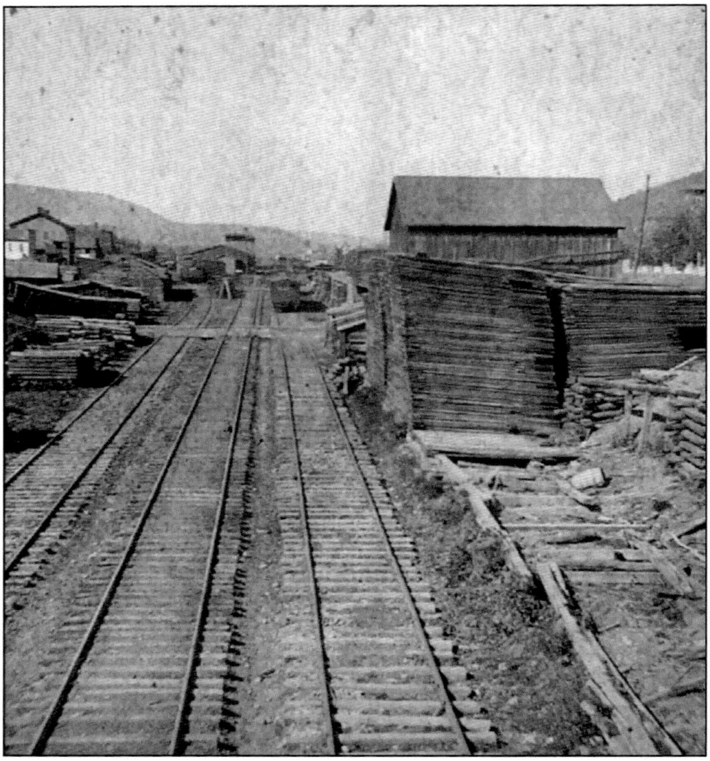

Early accounts of the village tell of great piles of lumber along the Erie Tracks from the heart of the village northward to Coats Switch. This undated view gives only one true landmark to definitively identify it as Wellsville: the top of the tower of the Lebbeus Sweet house on the hillside above the tracks places the date between 1868 and 1882. (David Hornburg.)

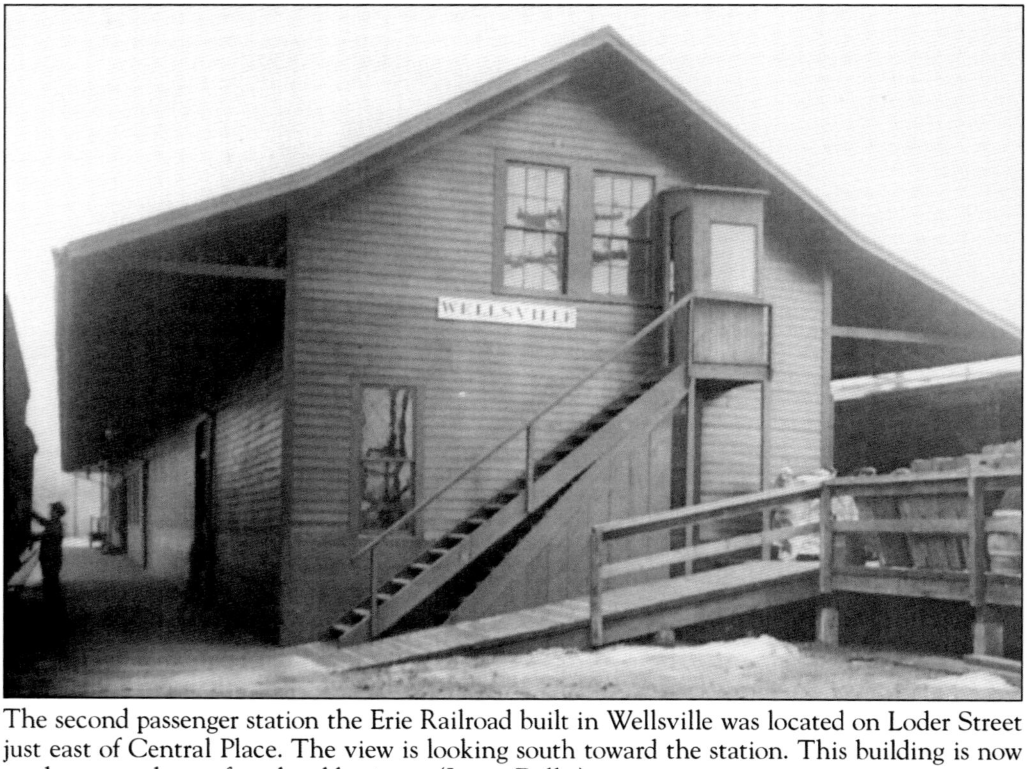

The second passenger station the Erie Railroad built in Wellsville was located on Loder Street just east of Central Place. The view is looking south toward the station. This building is now used as a warehouse for a local business. (James Dello.)

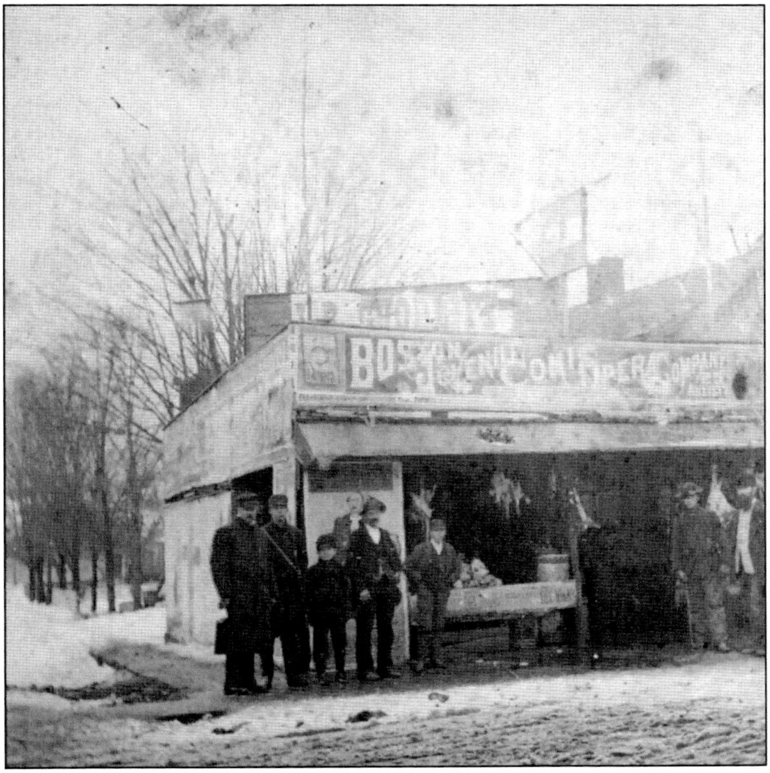

Joseph B. Goodliff operated a fish and meat market on the corner of Mill Street (Fassett Street) and North Main Street in the mid-1870s and early 1880s. The speed of the Erie Railroad made it possible for interior towns and villages to enjoy fresh ocean fish and oysters. In this photograph, Goodliff is advertising the engagement of the Boston Ideal Juvenile Comic Opera Company at Simmons Opera House, dating this scene to December 1882. (James Dello.)

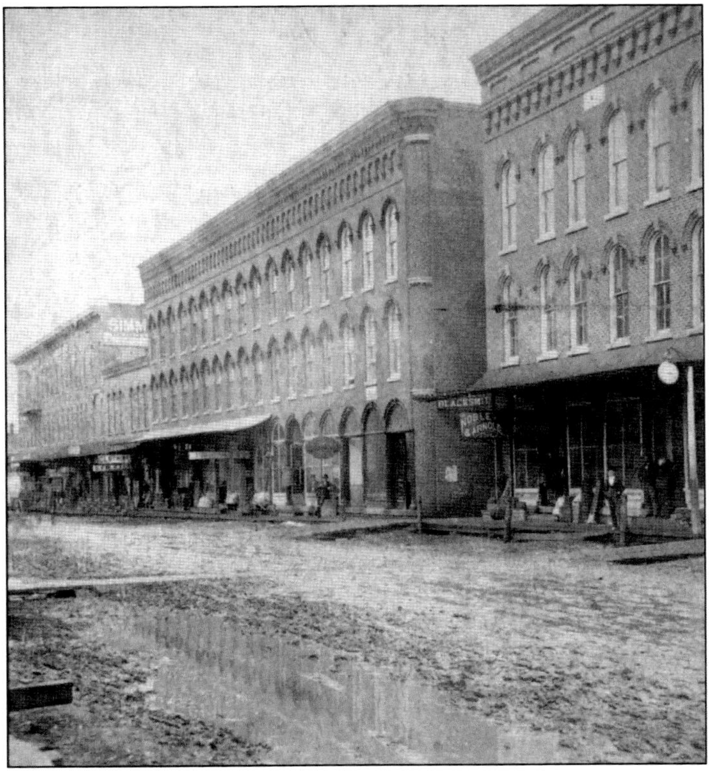

I.W. Fassett's Fireproof Block was built in the early 1870s, in a design very similar to his Fassett Hotel. This building has been redefined by fires, remodels, and partial collapses over the years. The photograph depicts the edifice as it was built by Fassett, with 17 windows across the upper floor. A 1901 fire in one of the stores forced a major remodel of part of the building, and a collapse removed the northernmost section in 1923. A small alley can be seen between the Fireproof Block and the Nobles & Arnold's Boss Grocery. This alley led back to several businesses, including the barns for the Fassett Hotel. (David Hornburg.)

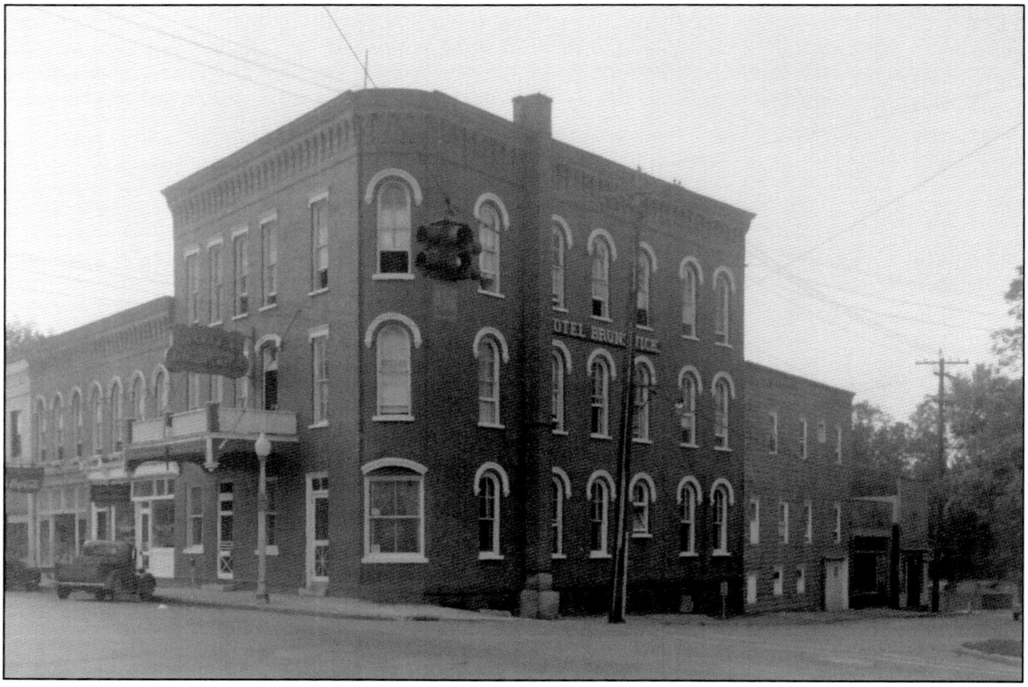

Henry Wilcox purchased the property on the corner of Plank Road (West Pearl Street) and North Main Street in 1870 and built an elegant hotel. A nameplate attached to the building reads "N. Johnston House," a misspelling of the name Johnson the local newspapers quickly noticed. They speculated that it was meant to honor Nathaniel Johnson, who was a friend to everybody. The hotel has had many names over the years, it is now called the Brunswick Building and houses several stores and offices.

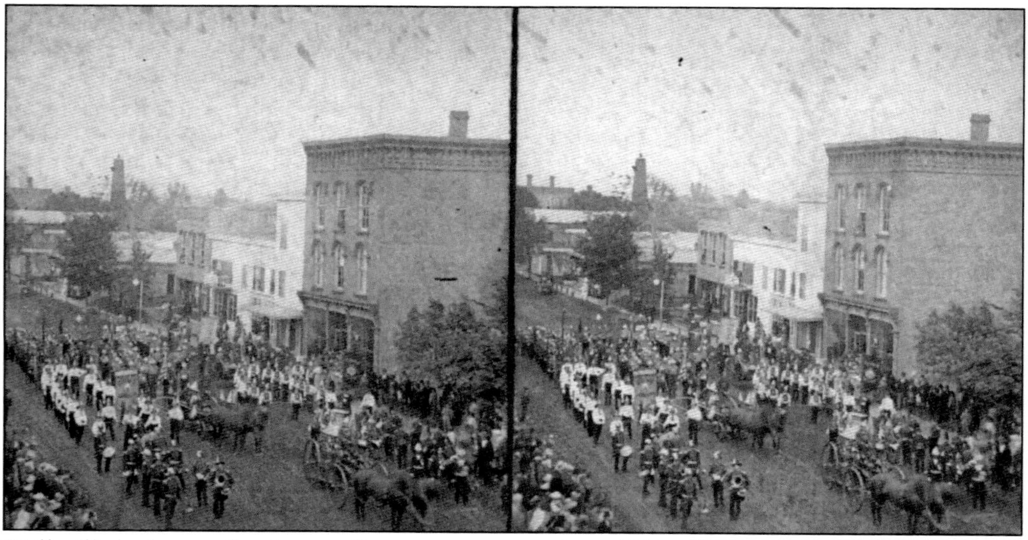

Wellsville had a small volunteer fire company as early as 1859 called the Pioneer Fire Company No. 1. The men did not have support of the merchants and so lacked funds to train and buy equipment. It was not until the early 1870s that support was given to the volunteers and the Wellsville Volunteer Fire Department was officially formed. This image is from one of the first inspections of the new volunteer fire department, in August 1876. (James Dello.)

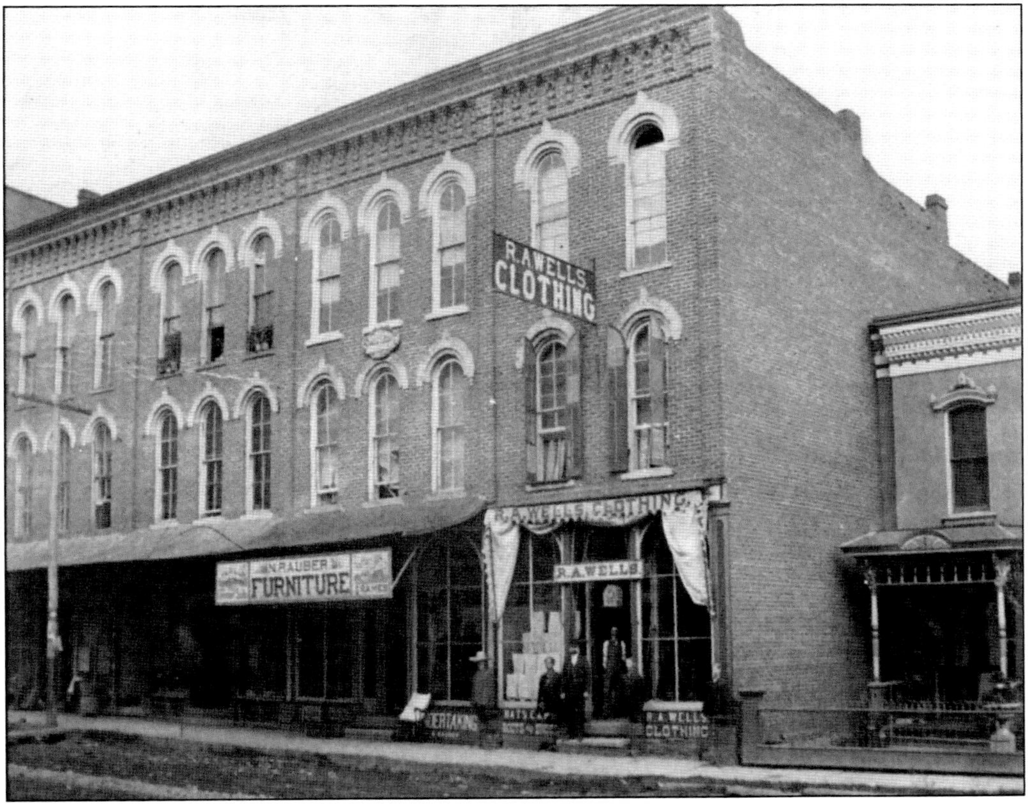

Rathbone A. Wells first had a livery in the back of this lot on North Main Street; then, in 1876, he opened this store in which he sold ready-made clothing. This photograph also depicts Nicholas Rauber's first store on North Main Street, in the Wells Building, around 1890. (Donald Baldwin.)

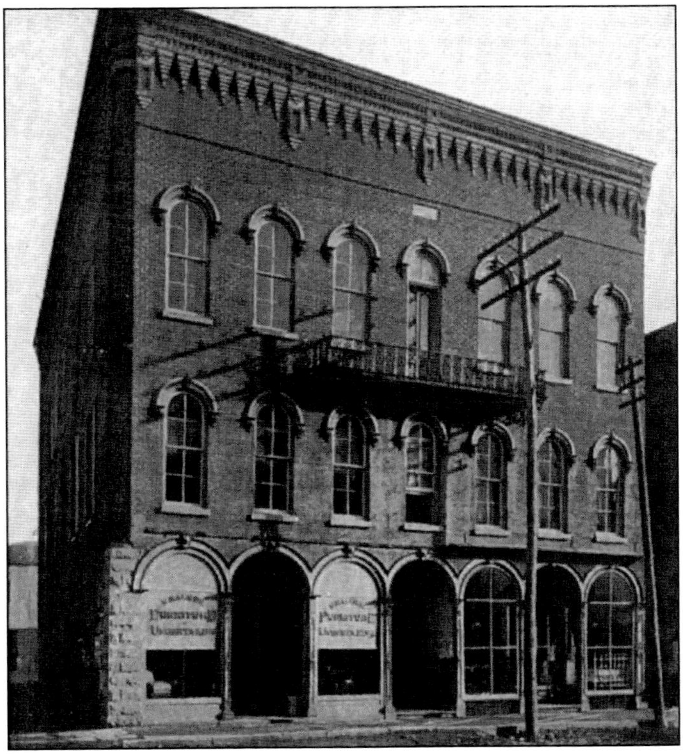

Thomas Pullar began building his new brick block in 1871, fitting up the third floor for a Masonic hall. Nicholas Rauber purchased the building in 1897. After renovations, Rauber moved his furniture and undertaking business here. The building still stands at 32-34 North Main Street, awaiting a promised remodel. (*Wellsville Illustrated*, 1898.)

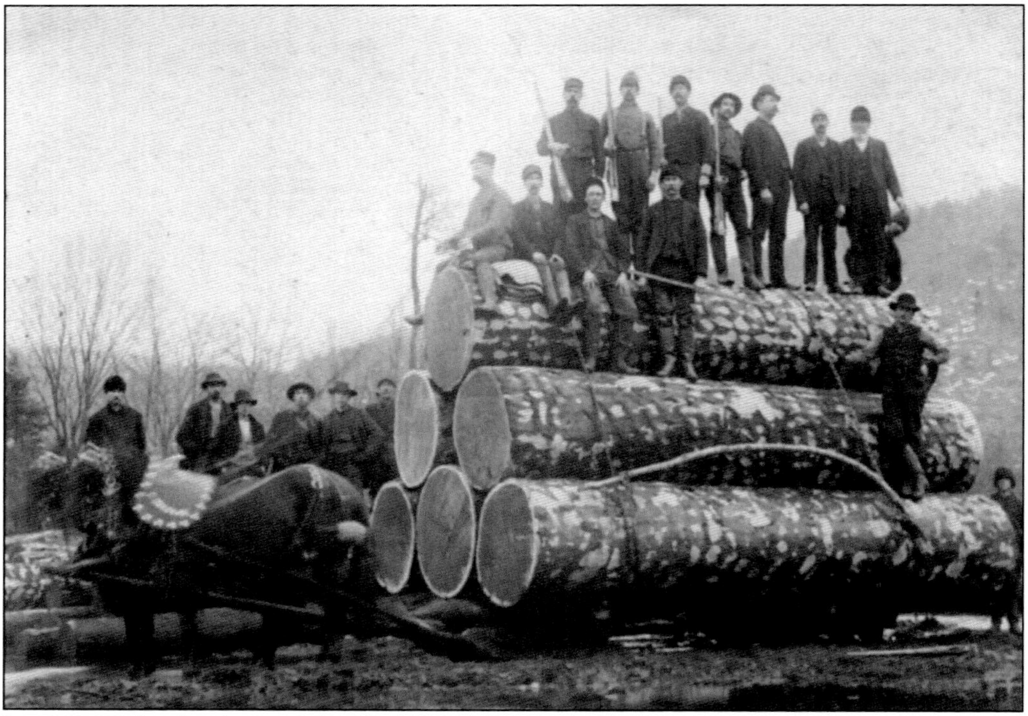

In 1887, Wellsville photographer Orin S. Wight captured this image, which shows a remarkable feat by one team of horses. James Shields of Alma hitched his team to a sled and drew the logs two miles to banking (an area where logs were stacked for transport). Wight's photograph depicts the largest load on record during the 1887 lumbering season, scaling (measuring) at 8,010 feet.

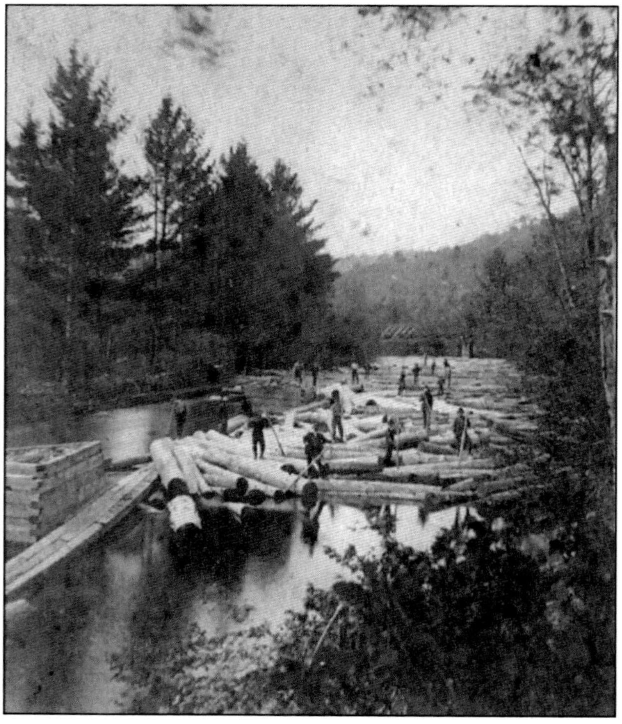

Duke's Mill was located south of the village along the Genesee River. This undated photograph shows log drivers upriver from the mill. An 1888 story reported that a log boom gave way during a series of severe storms, causing thousands of logs to dance on their way to Lake Ontario and costing the Dukes over $16,000. Duke's Mill also had a large millpond downriver from this photograph, located on property that became the Sinclair Refinery. (David Hornburg.)

Dickinson Clark opened a planing mill in the 1860s and took on partner Jesse Easton toward the end of that decade. Their mill near the corner of Stevens Street and (now) Brooklyn Avenue was known for its modern machinery and the excellent workmanship of its 16 employees. Clark and Easton supplied millwork for homes around the Wellsville area. Clark maintained the name Clark and Easton even after his partner passed away in 1880.

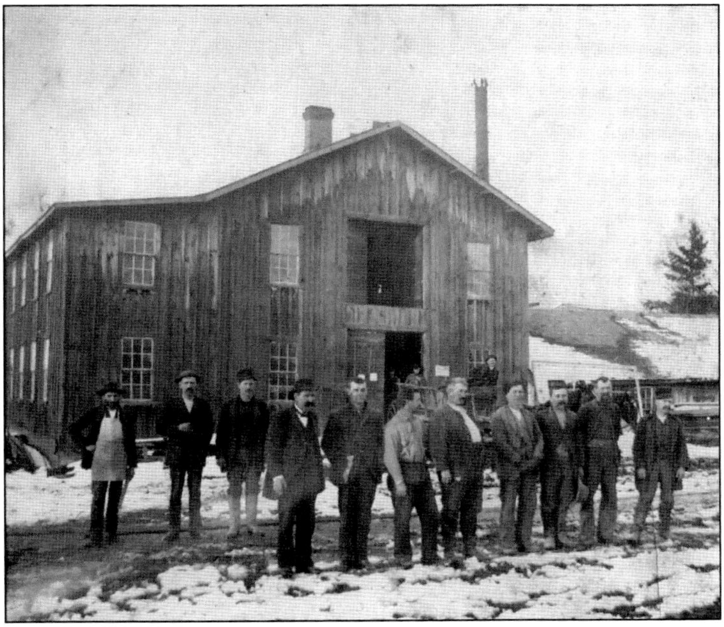

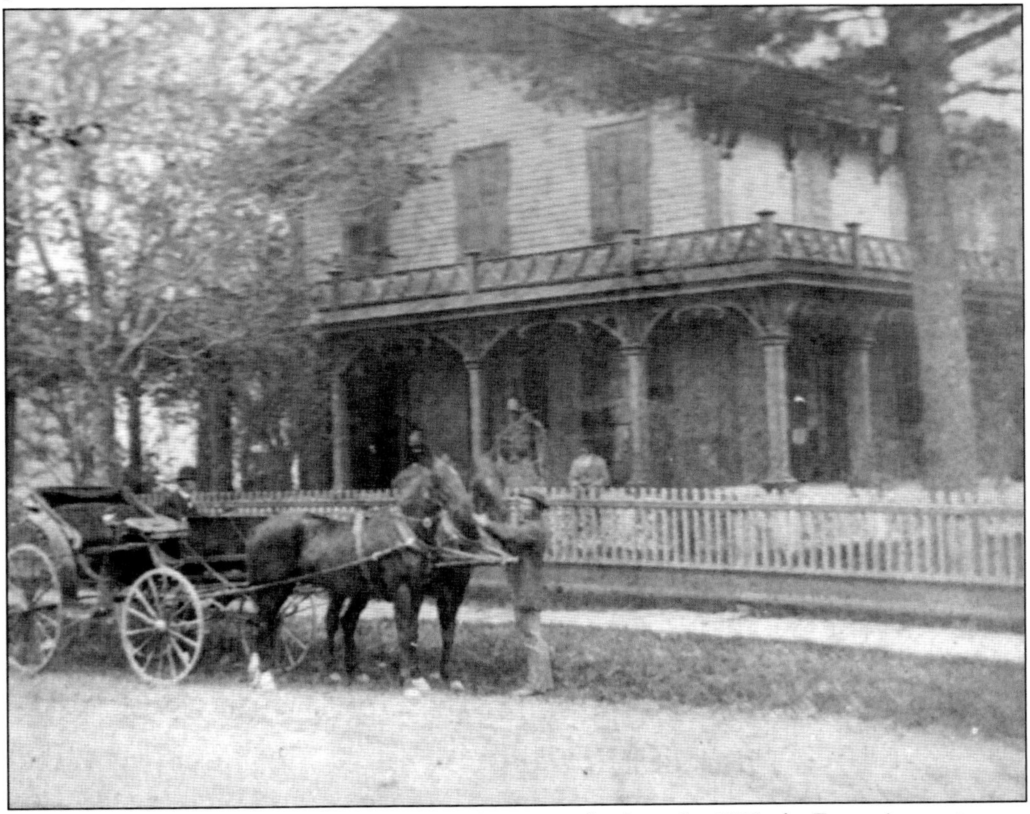

The Isaac N. Fassett home at 39 West State Street was built in the 1870s for Fassett's marriage to Cora Lee. Fassett grew up working in the lumber business with his father, Isaac W. Fassett, and later became a surveyor. The house became the home and office of optometrist Theodore Fleschutz and was eventually demolished to make way for a new highway bypass. (James Dello.)

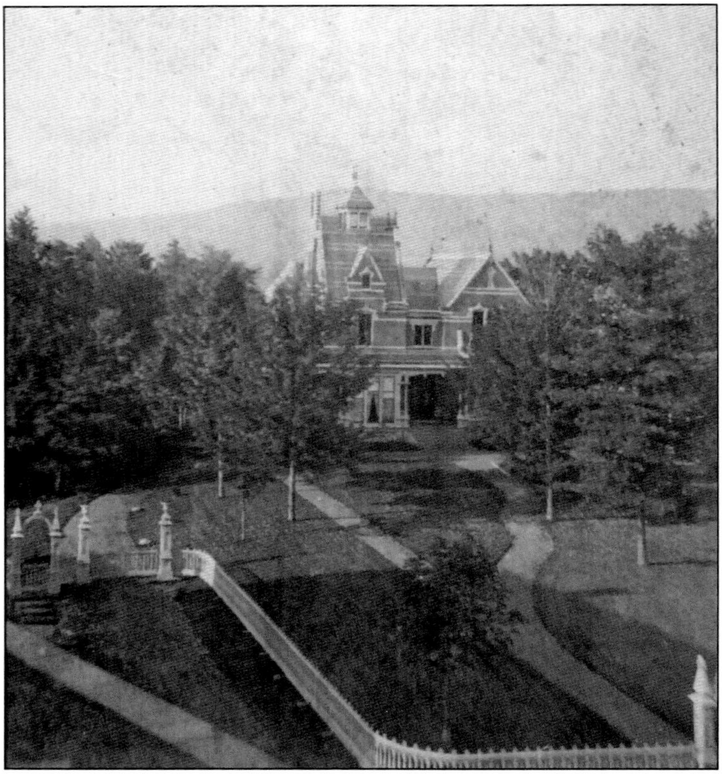

William and Gertrude Fassett Jones built their beautiful home on the corner of Plank Road (West Pearl Street) and North Main Street between 1871 and 1873. At Gertrude's death in June 1920, it came as a surprise to many that she had willed her home to the village for use as a hospital, if the village wanted it. A special election was called for taxpayers to ratify the village board's acceptance of the gift. Jones Memorial Hospital has grown and changed over the years and is a vital part of the town.

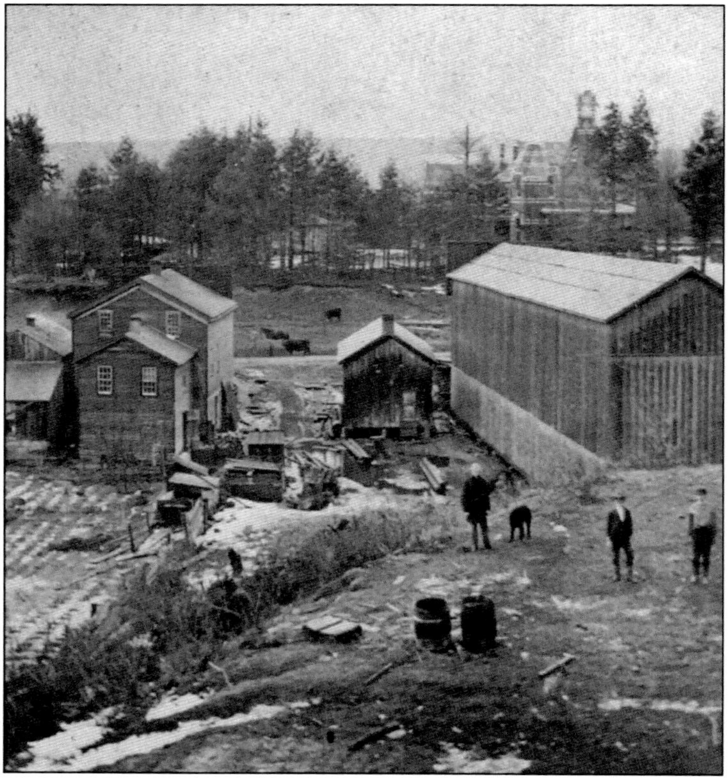

The photographer was most likely standing in a second floor window of the school on Main Street when he shot this scene of the buildings on Plank Road (West Pearl Street). The long building on the right is the Crane Livery, where E.C. Crane specialized in fine rigs, first-class horses, and a satisfactory price. Note the livestock grazing by Plank Road, a common scene in the village. On the hill in the background is the elegant William F. Jones residence. (James Dello.)

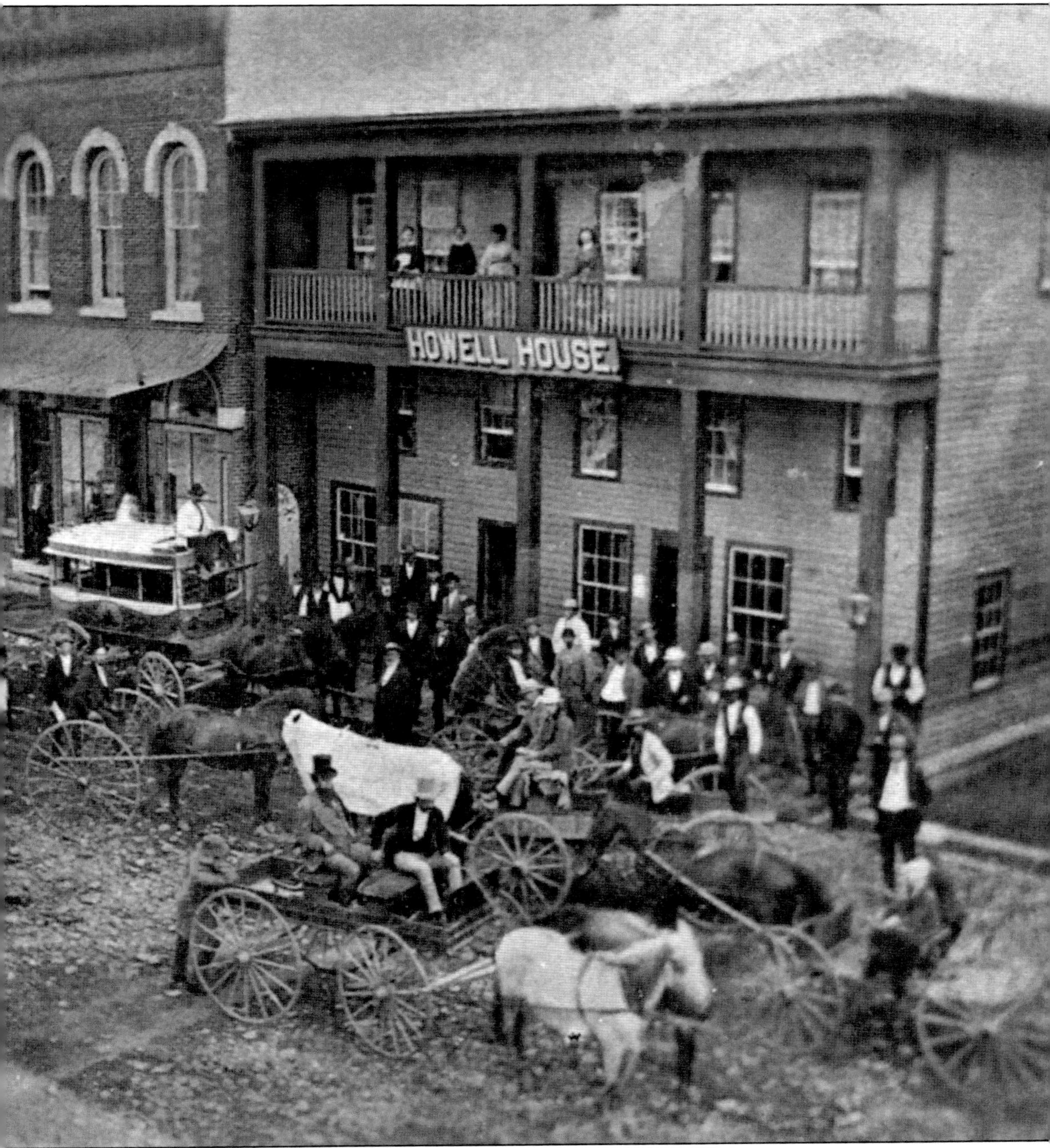

An undated view of the Howell House on Main Street appears to show a traffic jam of horses and carts on a very busy street. The old hotel was a fixture on Main Street, and it survived many fires that altered the buildings immediately around it. The hotel was run by William Spicer, who also operated a stage line out of his Spicer House. In 1868, Spicer sold the hotel to George and Eliza Howell. The building survived into the 20th century as a hotel, and in 1937, it was purchased by the Pickup family, who operated it as restaurant and hotel. The structure was destroyed by fire in 1961.

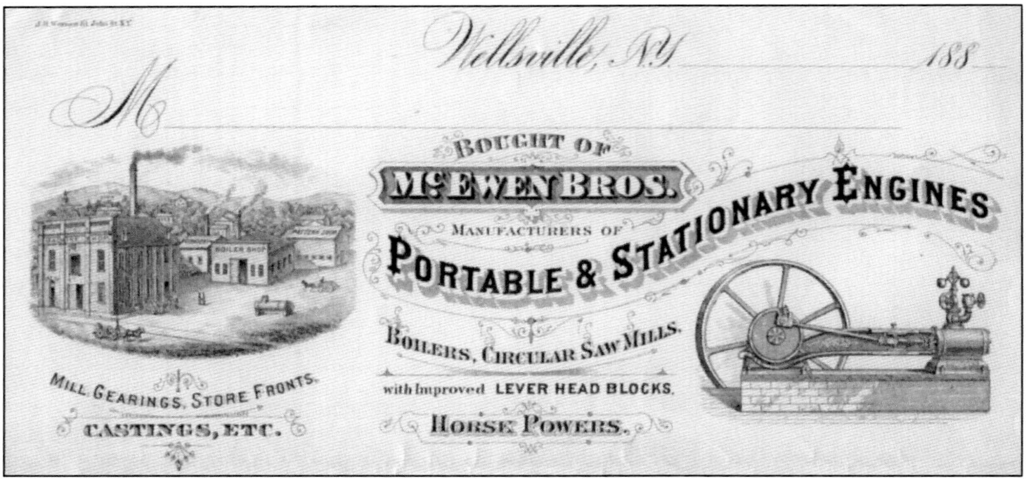

The McEwen brothers—John, William and James—carried on the family machining business after the death of their father, Duncan, in 1864. A fire destroyed their wooden foundry and machine shop, located near the corner of East State Street and Main Street in October 1876 with a loss of everything. The McEwens' new brick shop, shown below, opened almost a year later in October 1877. The brothers concentrated on manufacturing engines, boilers, shafts, and castings. Later, they manufactured specialized machinery for the oil fields. (Below, Kristen Kruger.)

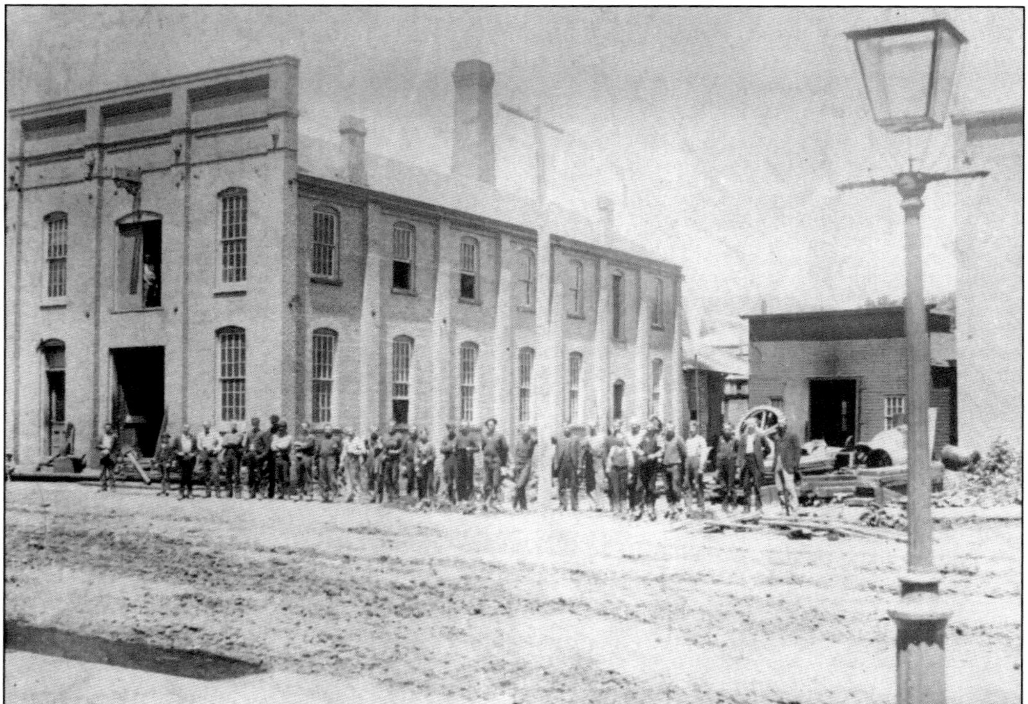

The McEwen Brothers Little Giant steam boiler and engine was wheeled outdoors to have its photograph taken by local photographer J.A. Rider. The McEwen brothers were possibly readying the Little Giant for display at the Cuba Mechanical and Agricultural Fair in September 1875. Information on this steam boiler was lost in the 1876 fire and few of them were manufactured. In 1950, William McEwen, son of John McEwen, speculated that the Little Giant was most likely a 10-horsepower, wood-fired steam engine.

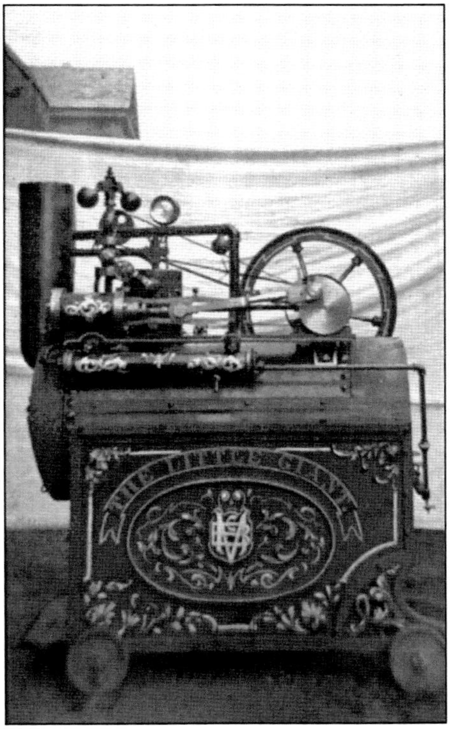

The McEwen family home on North Main Street was probably built just after 1860 when Duncan McEwen purchased the property. The home survived the 1876 fire that destroyed the McEwens' foundry and shop. After matriarch Susan McEwen's death, the house was converted to offices for the McEwen shops. A Quaker State gas station was built on this site in the 1930s. (Allegany County historian.)

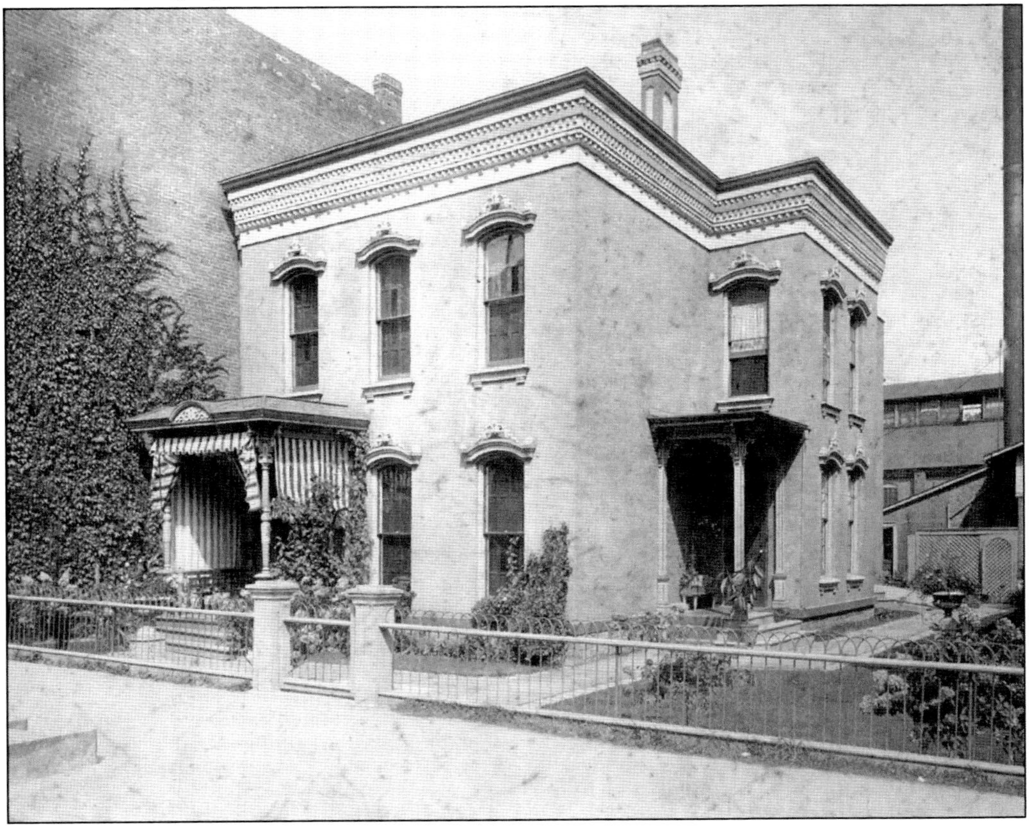

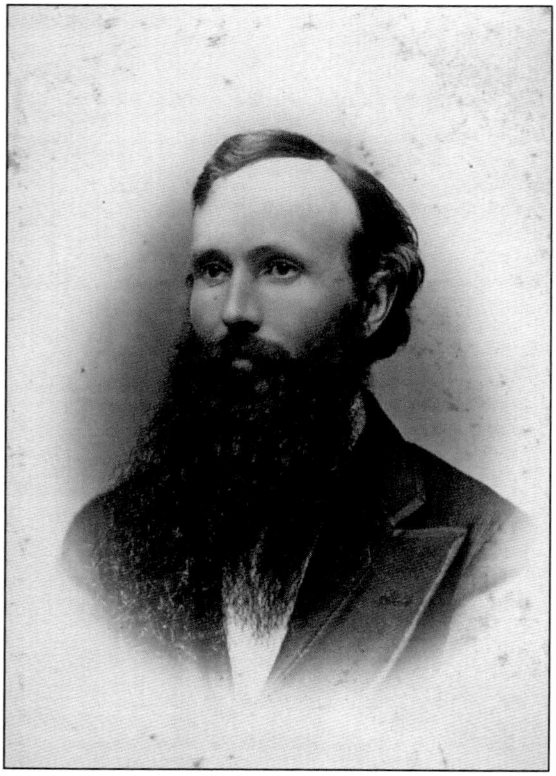

Orville P. Taylor had been a shopkeeper in Wellsville for several years when he formed a stock company to drill for oil in 1878. After several unsuccessful wells, he found himself almost bankrupt and ridiculed by many. Taylor struck oil in June 1879 with his Triangle No. 1 well in Scio, and his perseverance changed the economies of Wellsville and Allegany County.

William O. Taylor, son of Orville and Cornelia Taylor, is shown with the still-functioning Triangle No. 1 oil well in Petrolia around 1930. Taylor purchased a quarter interest in his father's oil business in 1890 and worked as an independent oil operator. He also held investments in gold-mining operations in Brazil.

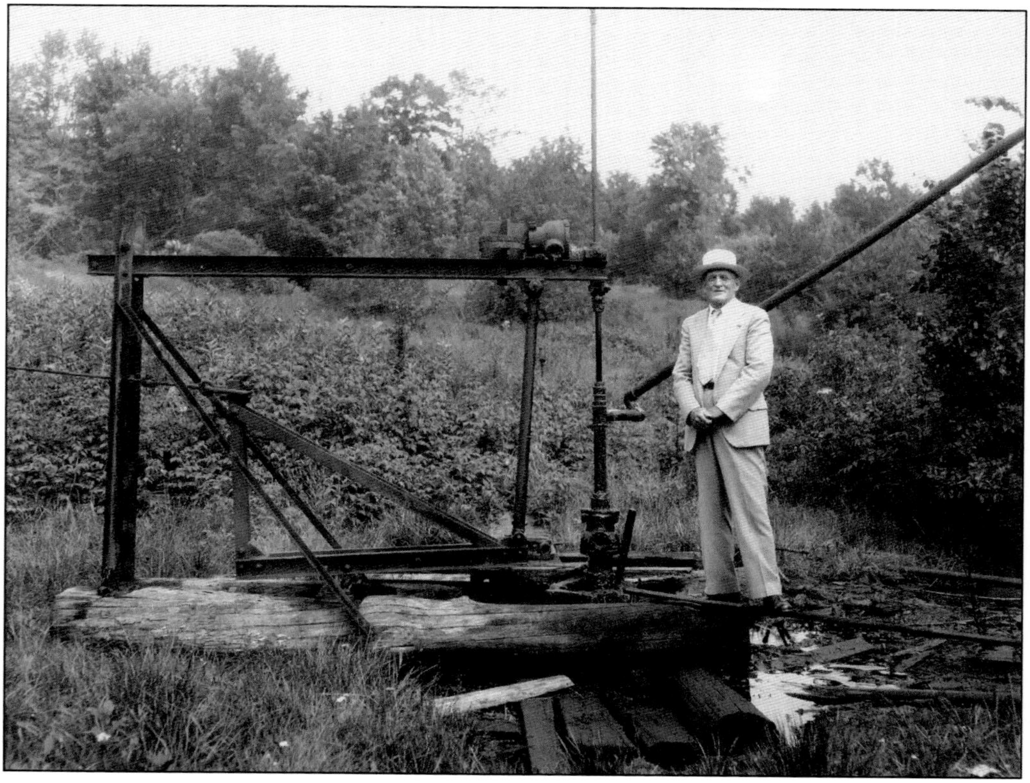

Two

1880 TO 1900

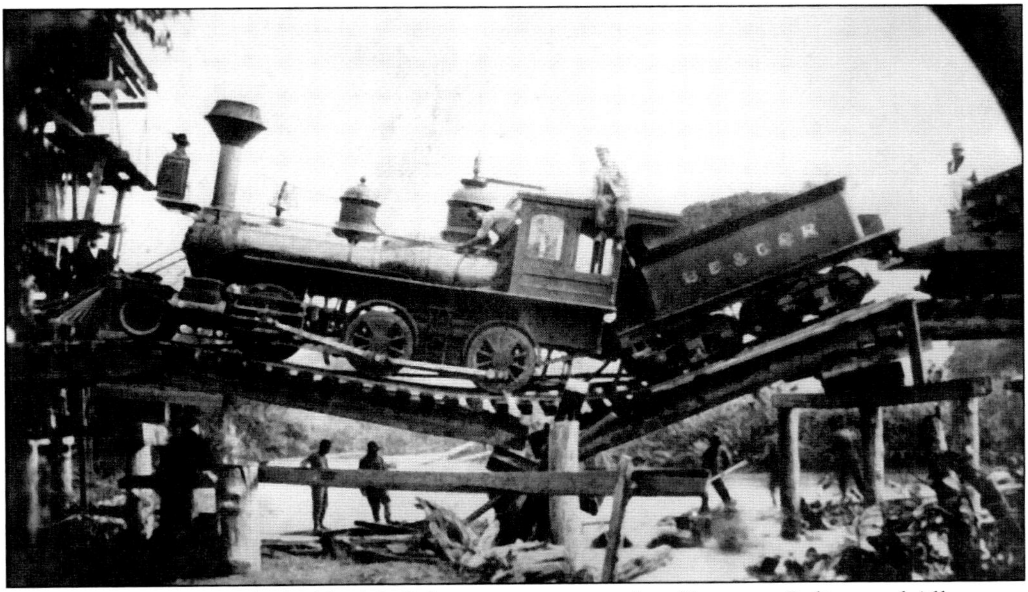

The tracks for the Bradford, Eldred & Cuba narrow-gauge railroad between Bolivar and Allentown were being laid in September 1881 when an unlucky engineer found himself in a sinking position. High water had caused the pilings of a new trestle over the Genesee to shift (near the present Bolivar Road), and the engine and tender dropped about four feet on the broken trestle. This was the only engine on the line at this time. The job of raising the train from its perilous position took two days using the power of a steam engine. The train was returned to work immediately, having suffered no damage. (Donald Baldwin.)

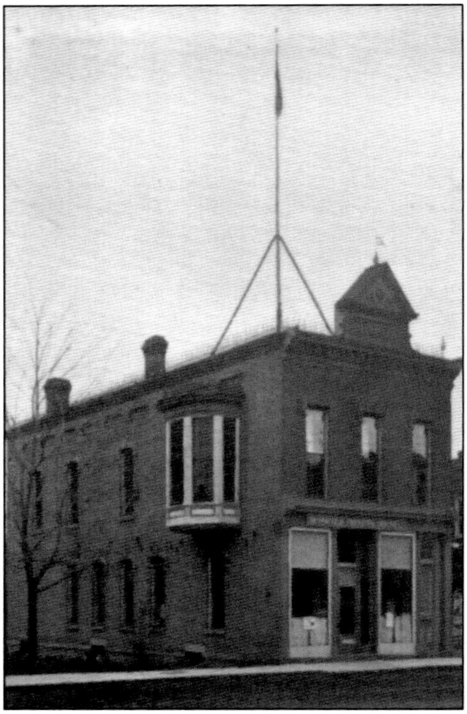

The *Wellsville Daily Reporter* was established in 1880 and is the longest-running business on Wellsville's North Main Street. For the first two years, the newspaper was published from an office in the Plum Block (now the Creative Arts Center). This building was constructed and occupied in 1882. The *Wellsville Daily Reporter* was considered a Republican voice because of the political affiliation of its owner, Enos Barnes, and his support of local business dealings. (*Wellsville Illustrated, 1898.*)

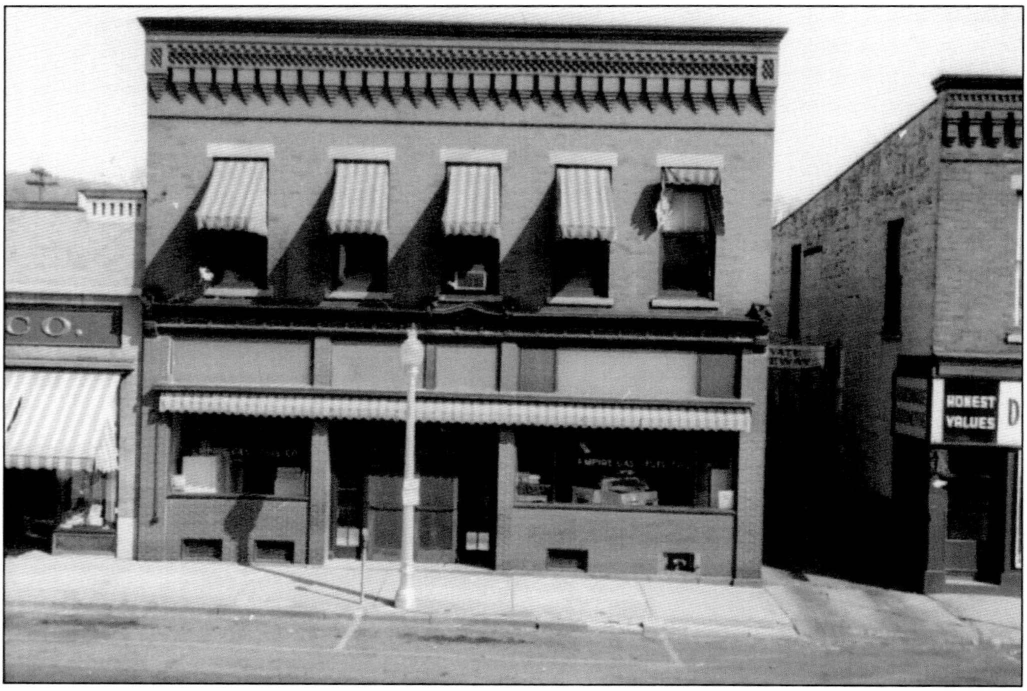

Edwin C. Bradley's Empire Gas Company brought natural gas to Wellsville from wells in Allentown and illuminated the village for the first time on the night of April 13, 1882. The first streets with gaslights were Main, East Pearl, State, and Loder Streets. This photograph shows the Empire Gas Building on North Main Street in Wellsville (with an electric light in front of it) in the 1930s. The building is now the home of Richardson & Stout Insurance. (Kristen Kruger.)

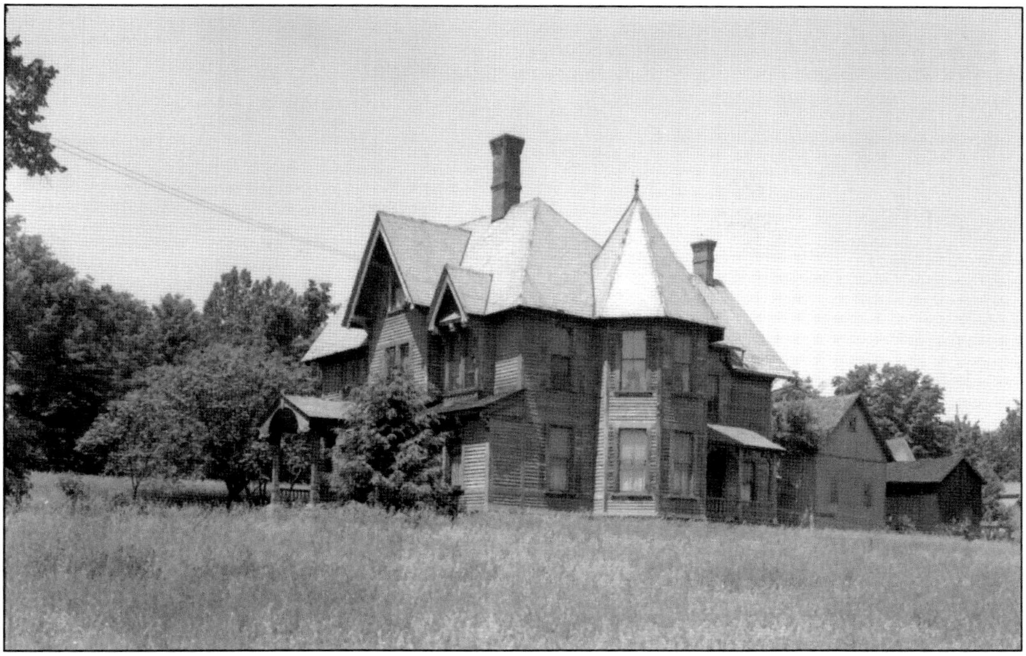

Insurance man Samuel F. Hanks built his large residence at the corner of West State Street and Highland Avenue in 1882. It was owned continually by members of the Hanks family until its demolition in the early 1950s. Dr. Irwin Felsen erected his family home on this property using parts of a house he moved here from White Hill in Bolivar. (Christina Wightman.)

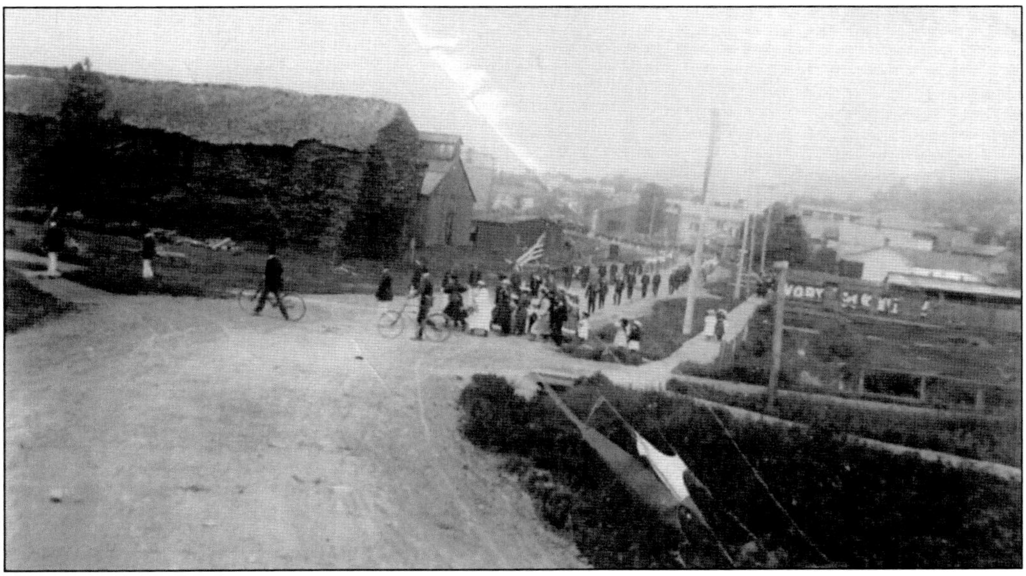

The 1883 Decoration Day parade in Wellsville was an impressive sight. The procession headed south to Farnum (now Woodlawn) Cemetery to honor fallen soldiers and mark their graves with flowers. Proceeding to Sacred Heart Cemetery, then northward to the Johnson Cemetery to repeat the honors, the parade marched to Lewis Grove (near the river at the north end of the village) for speeches and a picnic. This photograph was taken near the Allegany Tannery at the entrance to Woodlawn Cemetery and depicts the piles of tanbark that gave Wellsville the nickname Tanbark City.

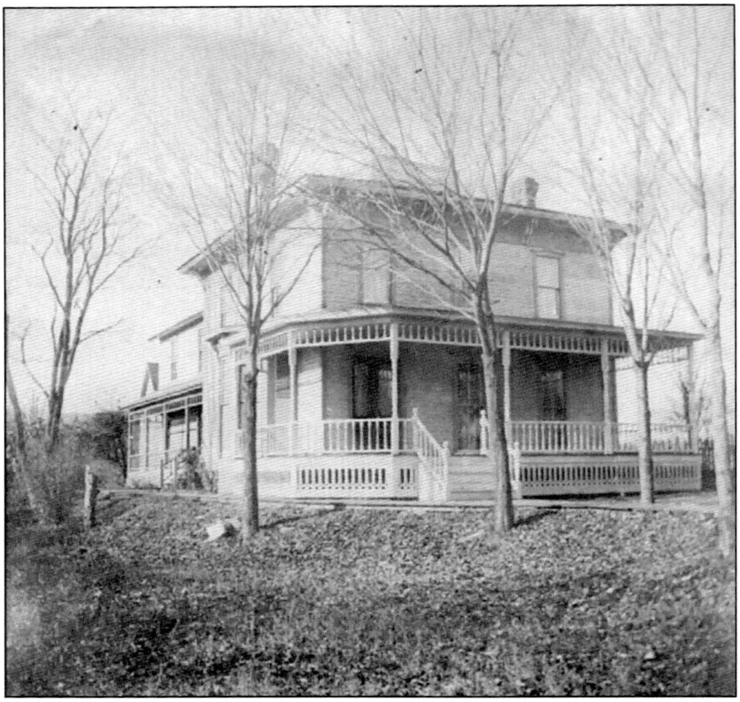

Oliver and Julia Rice Mather purchased their family home on North Main Street in 1883 from George and Margretta Russell. Oliver, an agent for the Erie Railroad as well as an oil producer and storeowner, saw his family grow and prosper here. Three generations of the Mather family called this house their home. (Mather Homestead.)

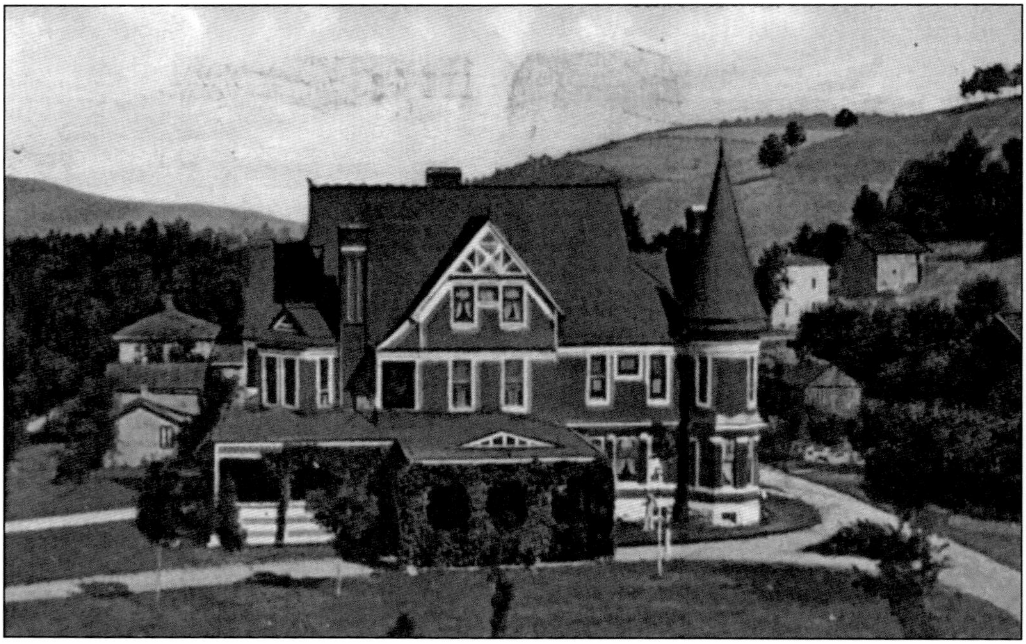

Lawyer Rufus Scott moved his family to Wellsville from Belmont in 1883 to be closer to his many oil interests. By 1889, he built and occupied this palatial abode on Third Street. Scott was a decorated Civil War veteran and lawyer, who had served as district attorney of Allegany County for two terms. The Scott family inhabited the home until the 1930s. Realtor Albert Howe demolished the house in the 1940s to make way for a development called Howe Terrace. In 1900, a house numbering system was instituted in the village, at that time, Third Street was renamed Scott Avenue.

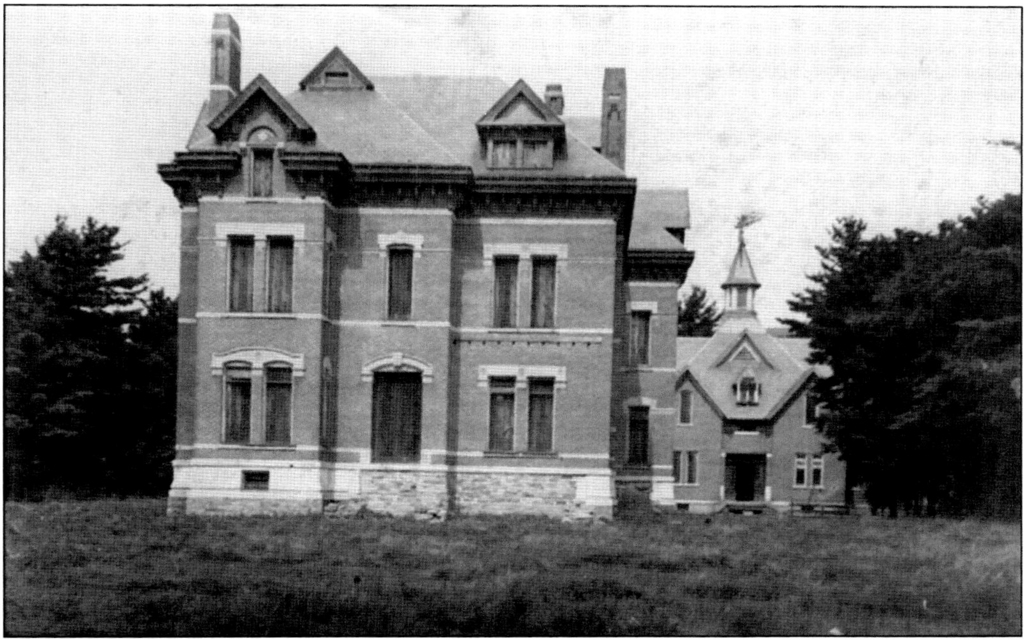

Aaron R. Hill began building his private residence on North Main Street in the early 1880s. Hill, manager of the Healy Tannery, fought illness for the last several years of his life and passed away in 1885 prior to the completion of the home. In 1904, Dr. Virgil Kinney of Cuba, New York, purchased the house from the village to use as a sanitarium. The Wellsville Sanitarium offered a place to receive the latest medical treatments, recover, rest, and visit. Treatment often consisted of modern electrical or magnetic devices. The building was enlarged at least twice in the years Kinney owned it. After Kinney's death, his family converted the building to the Wellsville Hotel, which operated until the early 1970s. Trinity Evangelical Lutheran Church is now located on this site. (Above, Christina Wightman; below, James Dello.)

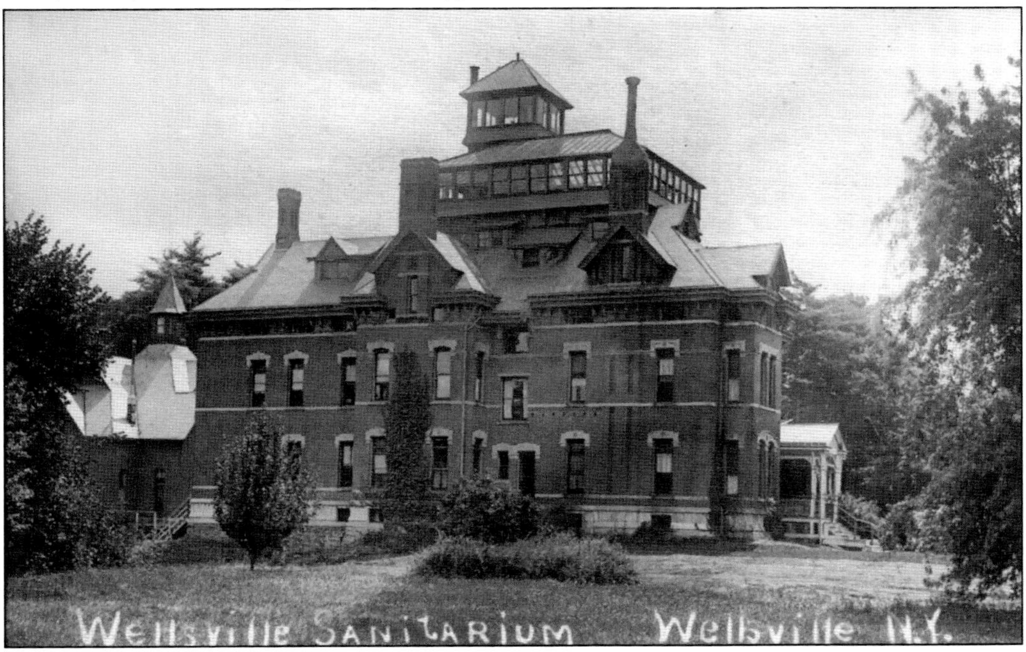

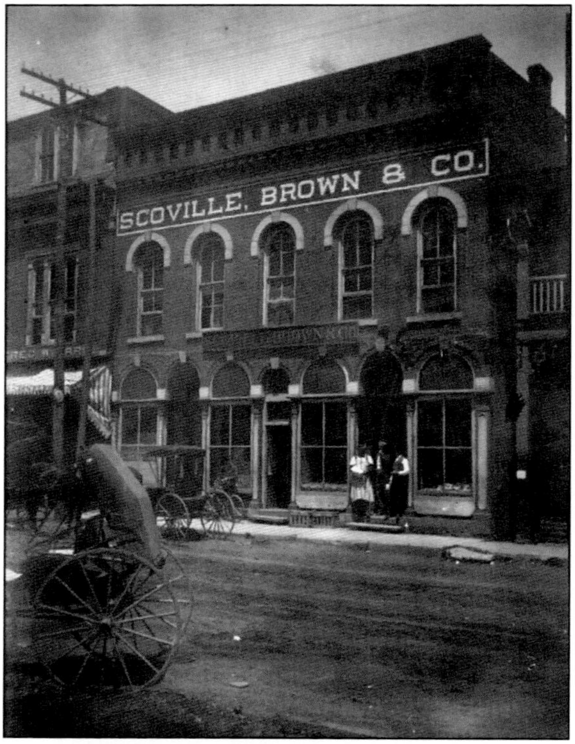

Luman H. Scoville was the owner of the Scoville Wholesale Grocery, located next to the Howell House on North Main Street. Taking on partners in 1883, the company was reorganized in 1886, with one partner being bought out, and the store Scoville, Brown & Company was formed. Scoville remained a silent partner while John H. Brown ran the business. The store offered retail and wholesale groceries, and was the first company to offer only groceries in the town. It offered personal service and home delivery as well. Scoville & Brown's Heart's Delight brand of canned goods was introduced in 1897 and quickly won favor with customers for its high quality and reasonable prices.

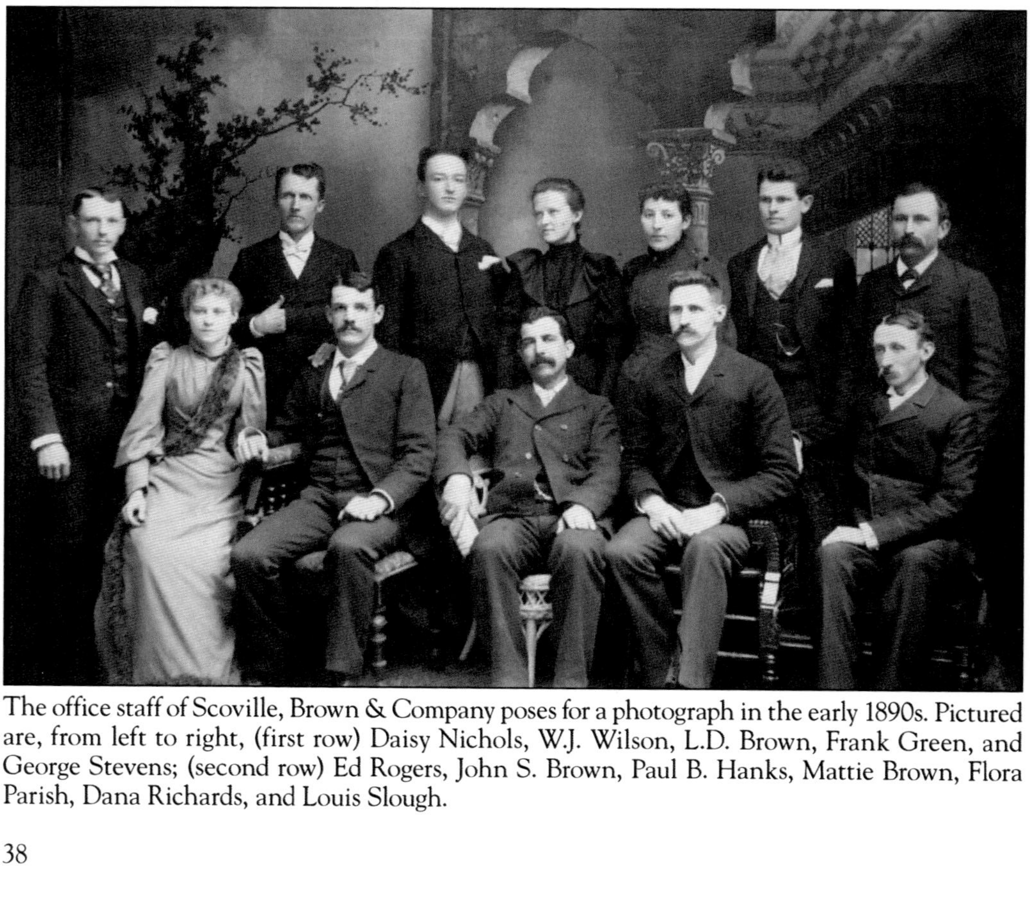

The office staff of Scoville, Brown & Company poses for a photograph in the early 1890s. Pictured are, from left to right, (first row) Daisy Nichols, W.J. Wilson, L.D. Brown, Frank Green, and George Stevens; (second row) Ed Rogers, John S. Brown, Paul B. Hanks, Mattie Brown, Flora Parish, Dana Richards, and Louis Slough.

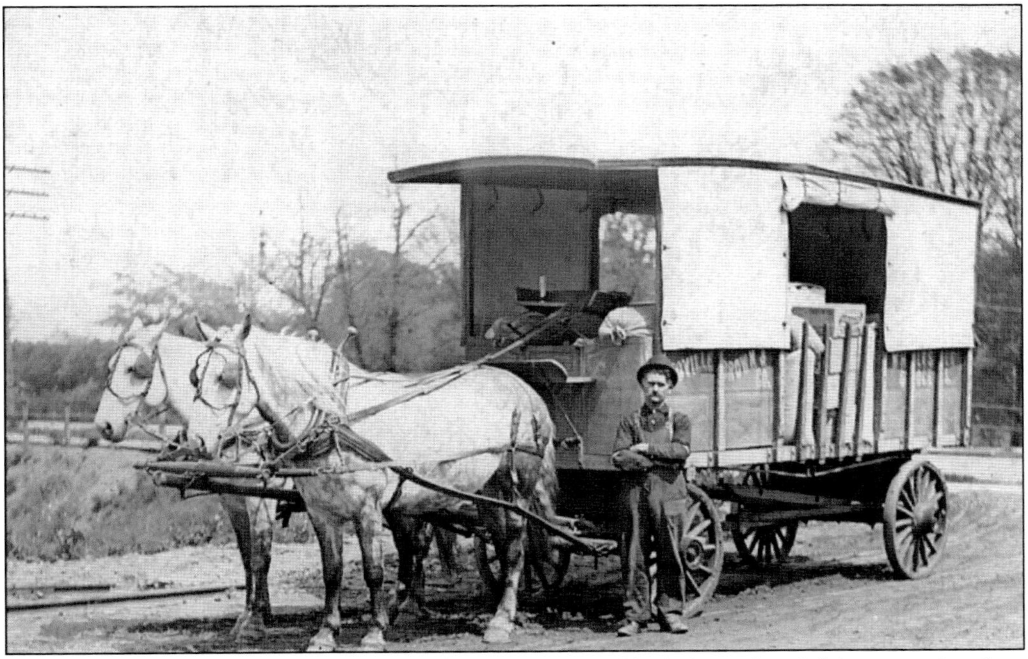

Scoville, Brown & Company employed drayman Cicero Black for its local delivery and pickup needs. Black was a former tannery worker who began working for Scoville Brown in 1894 as a drayman or deliveryman. By 1915, Black was working sales within the store. This photograph was taken around 1895.

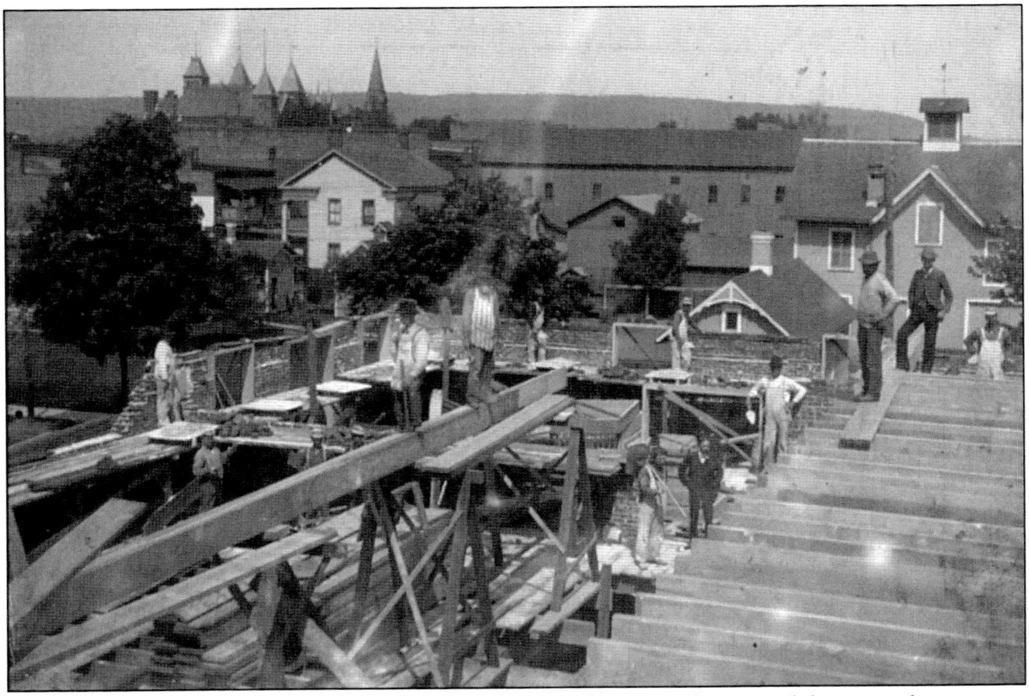

Scoville, Brown & Company built its cold storage warehouse at the rear of the store, fronting on Fassett Street and the Erie tracks in 1903. The company received and shipped merchandise by rail. The warehouse opened to a siding on the Erie tracks.

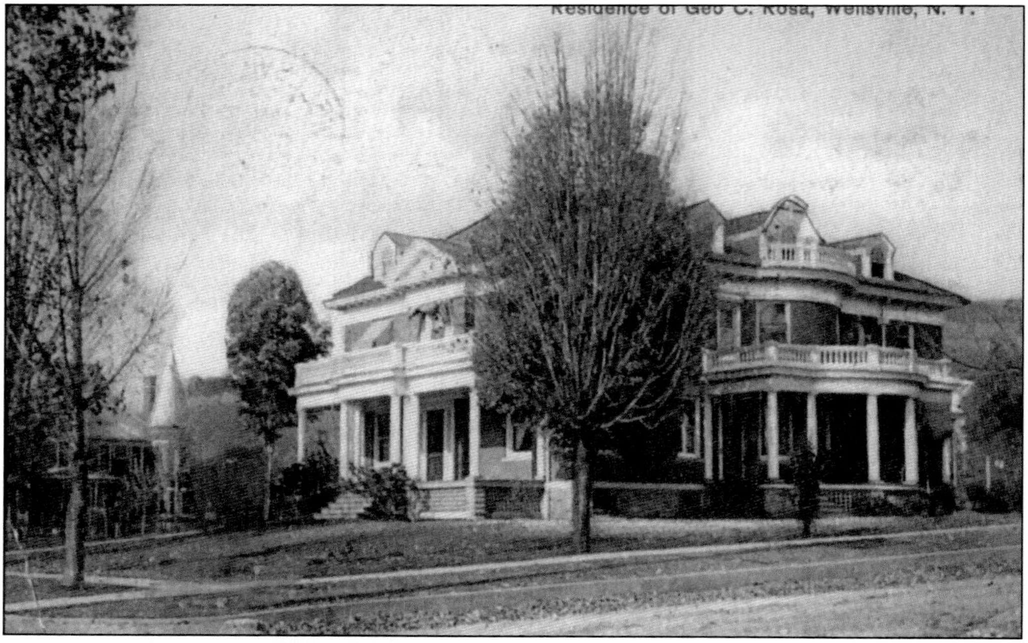

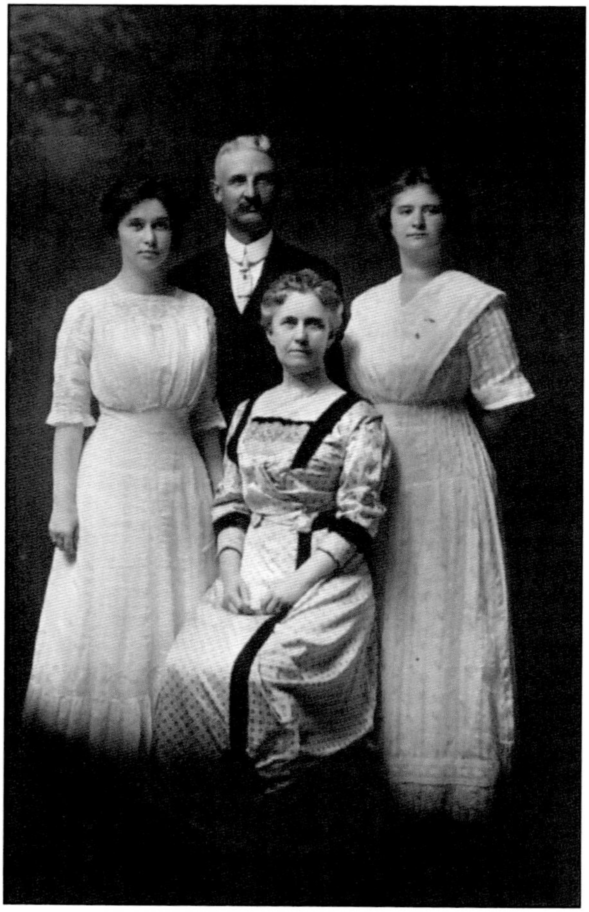

George and Laura Brown Rosa began building this beautiful residence in 1898. George was a partner in Scoville, Brown & Company, and became president of the company in 1906. George's easygoing manner endeared him to his employees and friends. Daughter Mary Rosa remained involved with the firm after her father's death until the store closed in 1969. At left, the George Rosa family poses for a photograph. Pictured are daughter Mary (left), George, Laura, and daughter Helen (right).

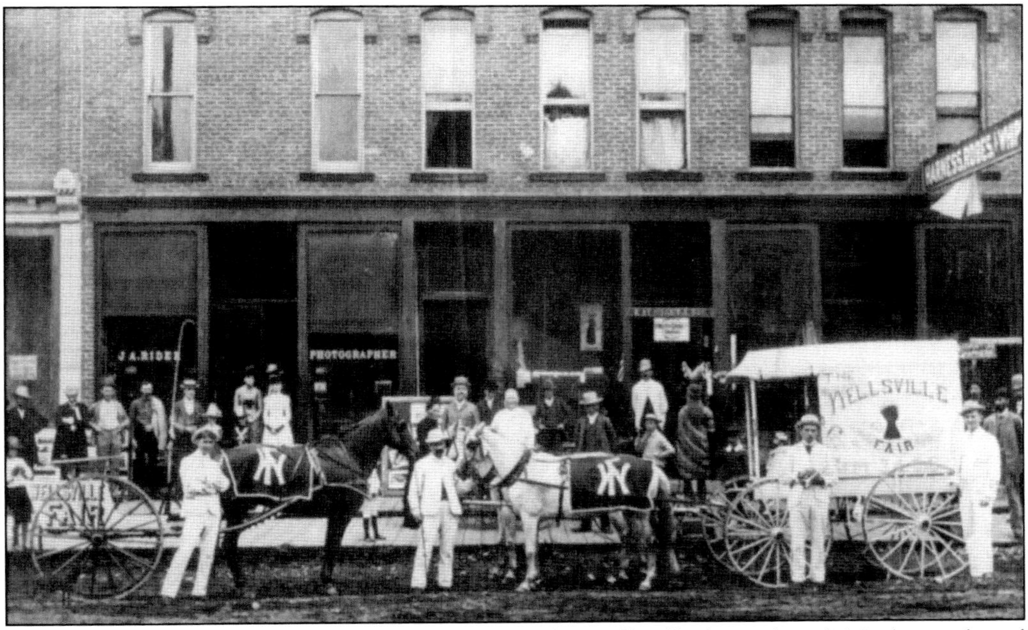

In preparation for its first fair in September 1888, the Wellsville Agricultural, Mechanical, and Breeders Association sent out advertising wagons. The wagons traveled to towns and villages in western New York and Pennsylvania, promoting the fair, hanging posters, and handing out advertising material. Traveling with the larger white wagon was Lewis, the bugler of the Belmont Cornet Band. (DAHPL.)

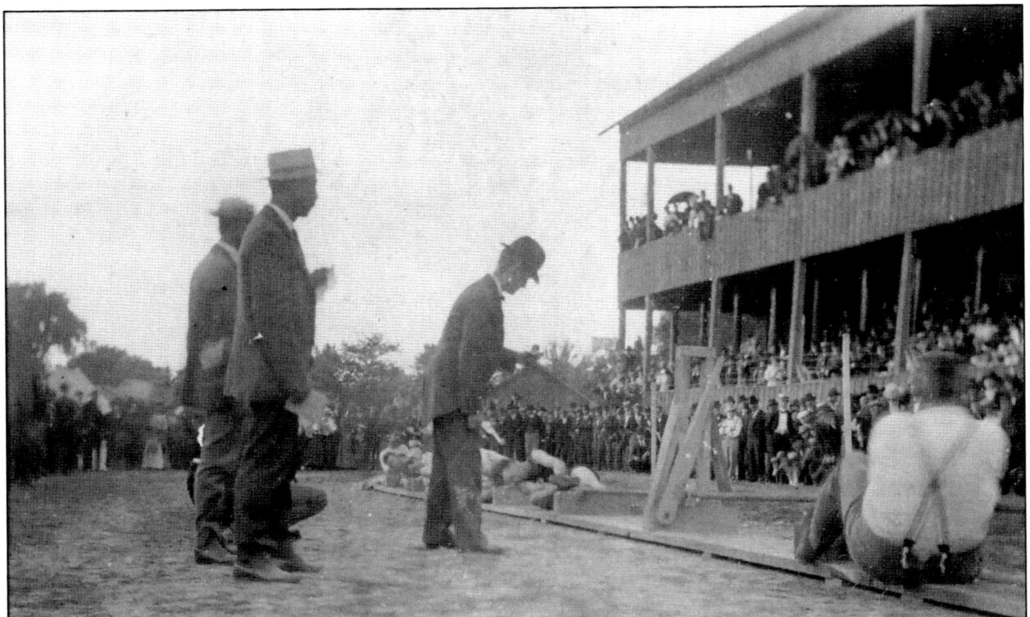

The first fairgrounds were built behind Woodlawn cemetery on the flats near the Genesee River. A half-mile track was laid out, stables were built, and a two-story grandstand was erected. Flooding forced repairs of the grounds and buildings too often over the years, and the fairgrounds were removed to farmland near Dyke Street in 1905. This undated photograph shows a tug-of-war taking place at the old fairgrounds. (Raymond McClure.)

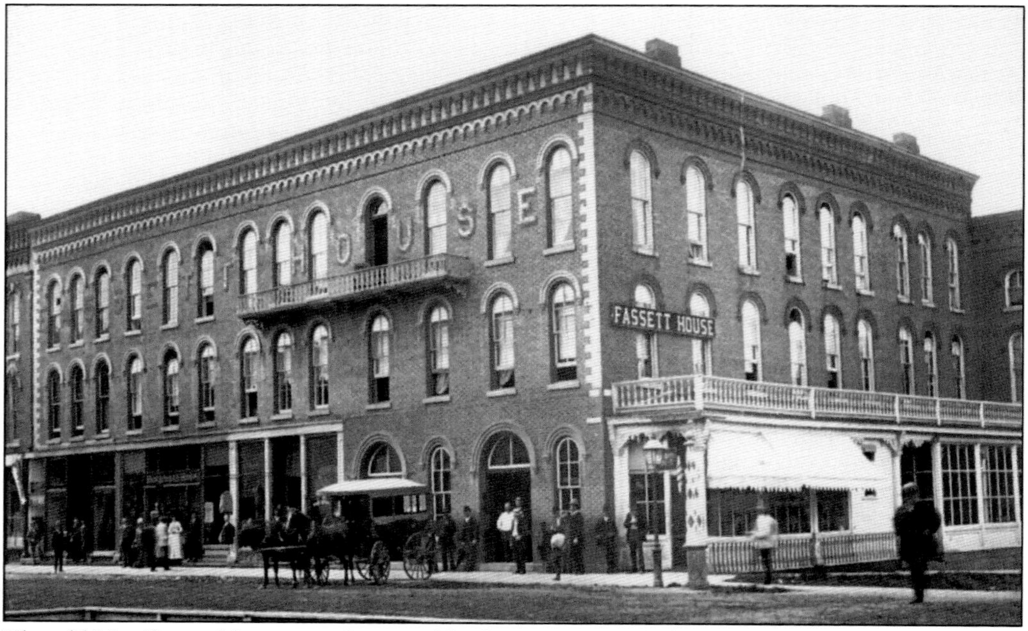

The old Van Buren House was destroyed by fire in 1867, and the lot was purchased by Isaac W. Fassett. Fassett hired Elijah T. Woodcock to design and build a hotel. Construction began in the summer of 1870, and the hotel opened in August 1871. It contained 62 sleeping rooms, 10 parlors, and 2 business stores, as well as a restaurant and bar. The Fassett Hotel was a Main Street favorite for over 100 years, closing its doors as a hotel in 1974.

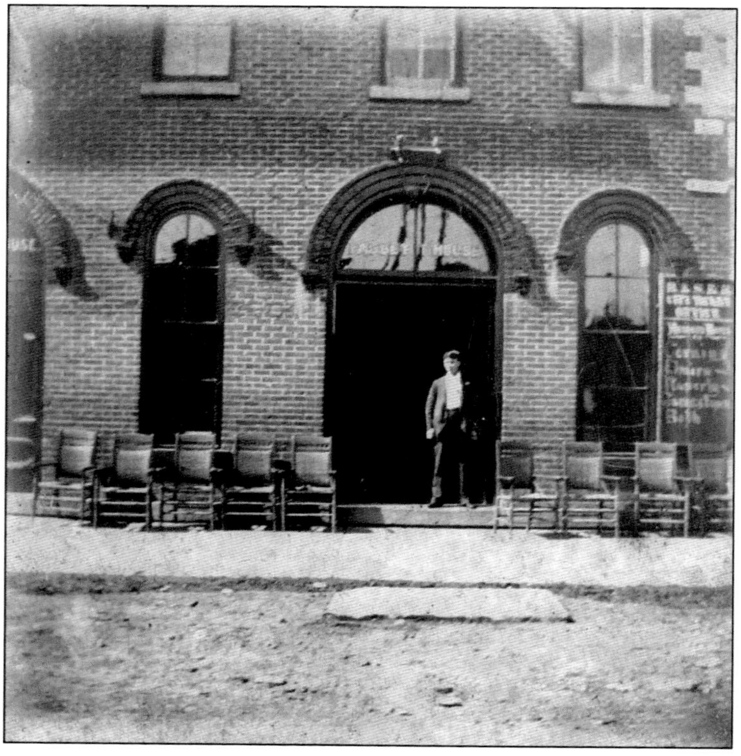

The travelers' waiting room at the Fassett Hotel was on the Main Street side of the hotel. It was a popular waiting area as travelers could avail themselves of the hotel restaurant while waiting for their transportation. At the onset of the oil boom, a stage left daily for Allentown and Petrolia. Joshua Corbin, of the stage line Corbin & Prince, would pick folks up at the Fassett Hotel waiting room and take them on a tour of the oil fields. (Mather Homestead.)

Alfred S. Brown and his wife, Louise Farnum Brown, built their home on Main Street next to the old Congregational church in 1890. Alfred passed away in 1908, and Louise remained here until she passed away in 1934. The house sat empty for a few years, and was last used as Republican Party headquarters during the Wendell Willkie 1940 presidential campaign. It was demolished in 1941 to make way for a modern building that housed Loblaw's Grocery Store. It is now a medical arts building.

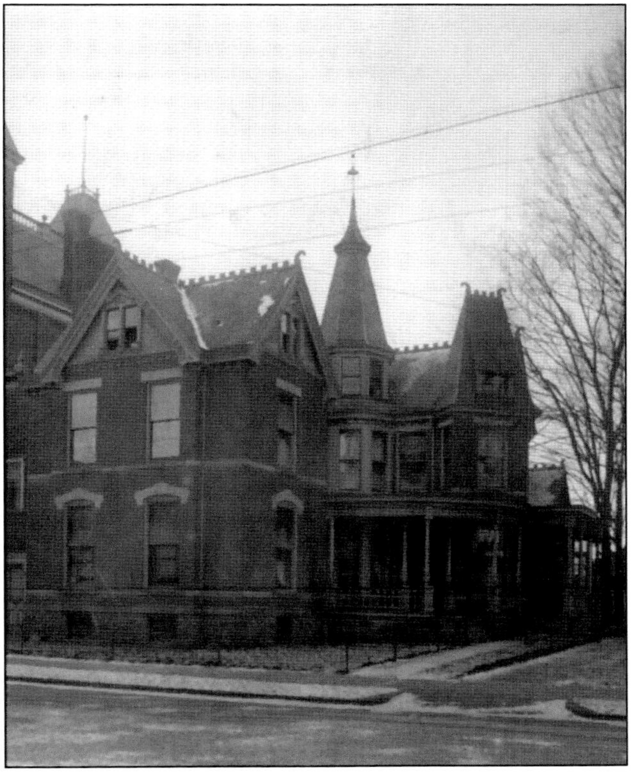

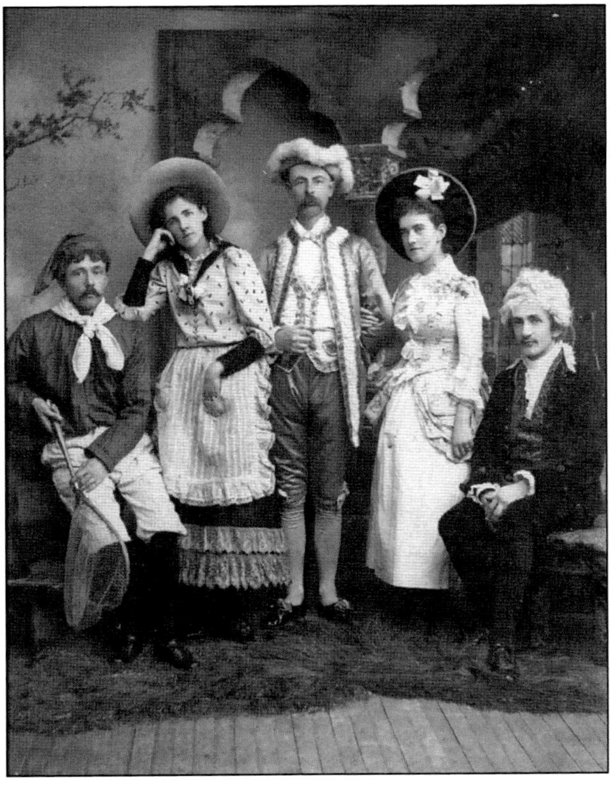

The Mozart Society was formed in 1887 for the purpose of "self-improvement through song." Its members, all well known for their beautiful voices, performed a comic opera called *The Chimes of Normandy* in the spring of 1889. Featuring costumes rented from New York City, their first show opened to rave reviews. Shown here, from left to right, are society members Charles Scheffer, Jett Wilson, George Alger, Laura Rosa, and William Hoyt.

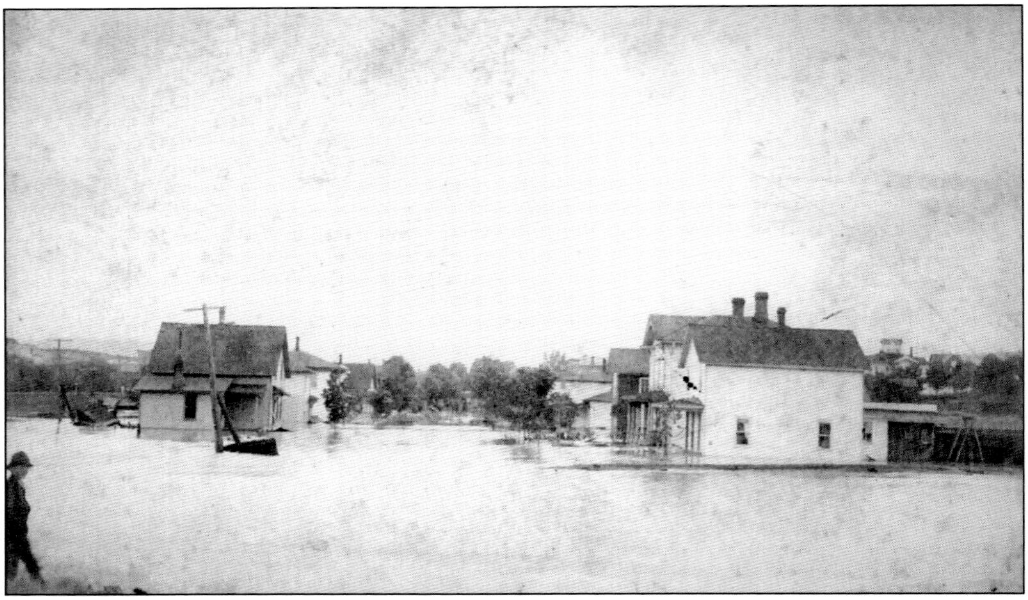

Heavy rains started on Thursday night, May 30, 1889, and continued until Friday night. By Saturday, the Genesee River and Dykes Creek had flooded many streets in the village. Broad Street, South Main Street, and Miller Street residents were evacuated in a hurry. The tanneries received two to three feet of water. This is a northward view of South Broad Street. The cupola of the Immaculate Conception parish house is just visible to the right in the photograph. (James Dello.)

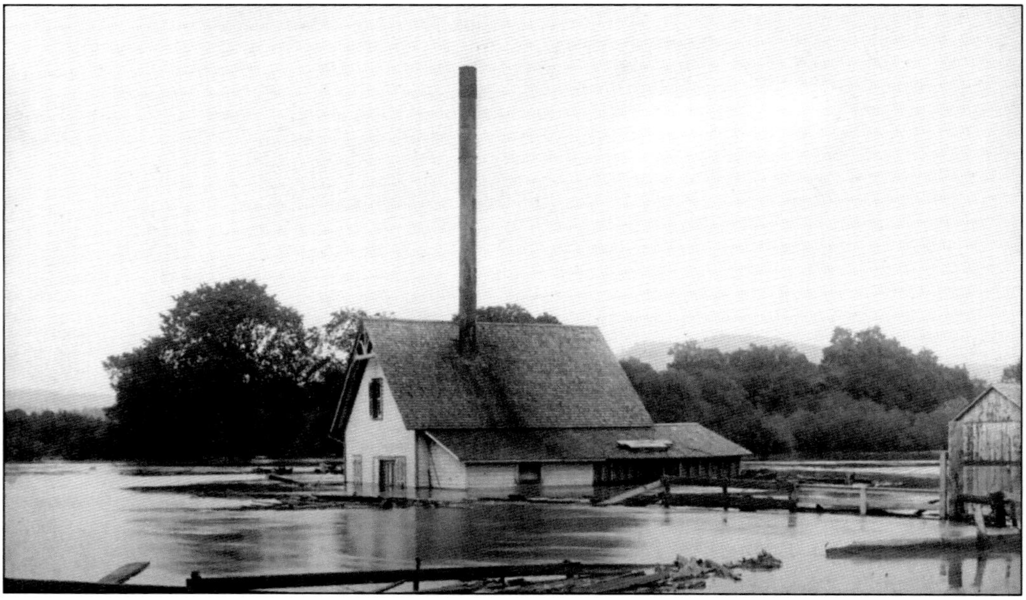

The volunteer firemen of Wellsville publically advocated for a reliable water supply to fight fires. A plan was adopted for a privately held company to construct a water-supply system. A reservoir was built above the village, which dammed Crowner Creek, and pipe was laid from the reservoir down West State Street to a waterworks building by Island Park. The first pumping station was a small structure on the riverbank at West State Street. This photograph, taken during the June 1889 flood, shows the original waterworks building. (James Dello.)

Welcome H. Coats was an early settler and businessman in Wellsville. By the late 1830s, he had built a cabinet shop, and his sons Hiram and Waters joined him in business. The sons purchased the business from their father in 1866 and operated as Coats Brothers. A fire in 1894 destroyed the factory, and 28 men were temporarily out of a job. Waters Coats organized a stock company and rebuilt the plant in the same year. (DAHPL.)

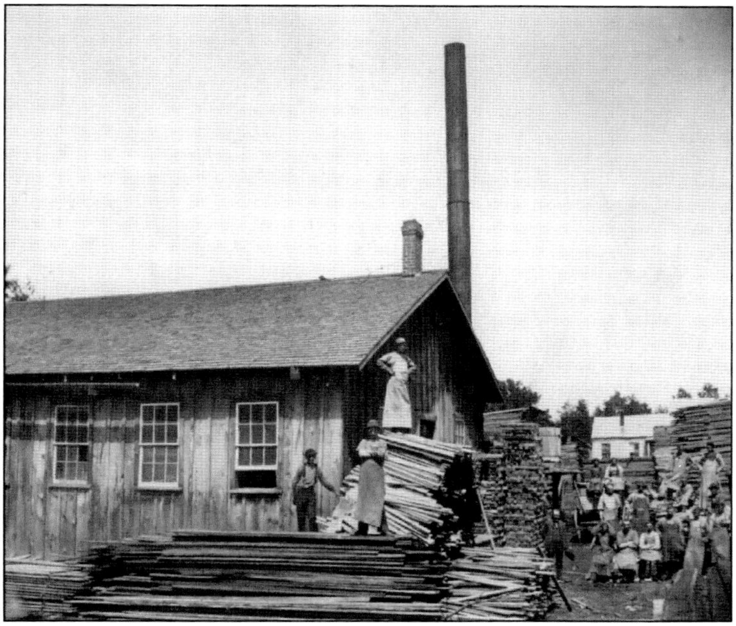

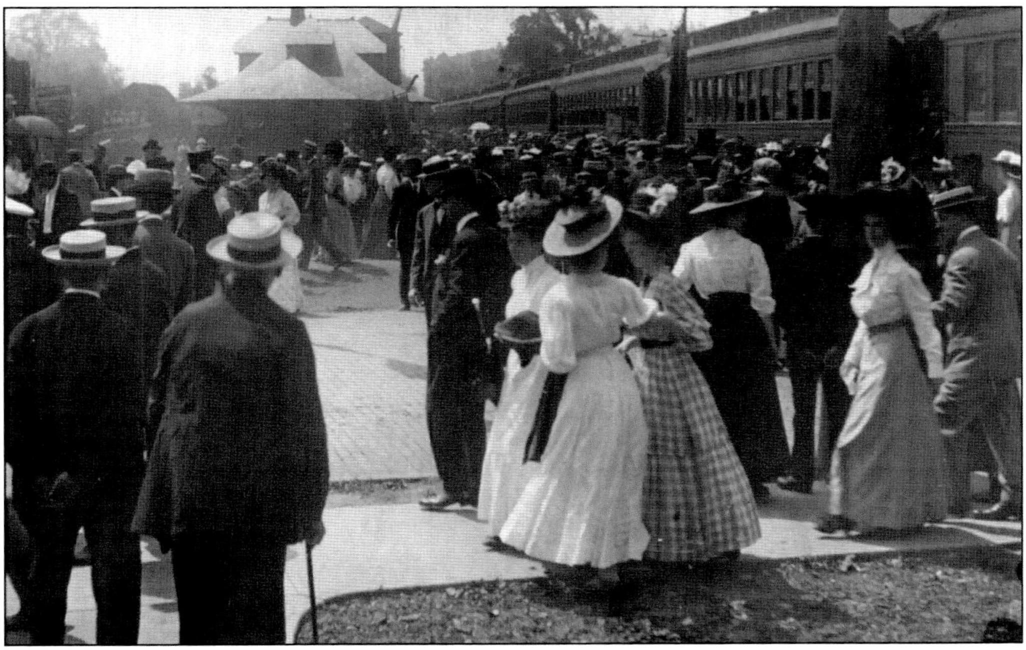

In 1895, the Buffalo & Susquehanna Railroad built a depot on its track on West State Street. This photograph shows a very busy Buffalo & Susquehanna platform as passengers arrive for the Great Wellsville Fair. After years of neglect, the depot was demolished in 1988 to clear room for a new village water-treatment plant. (Craig Braack.)

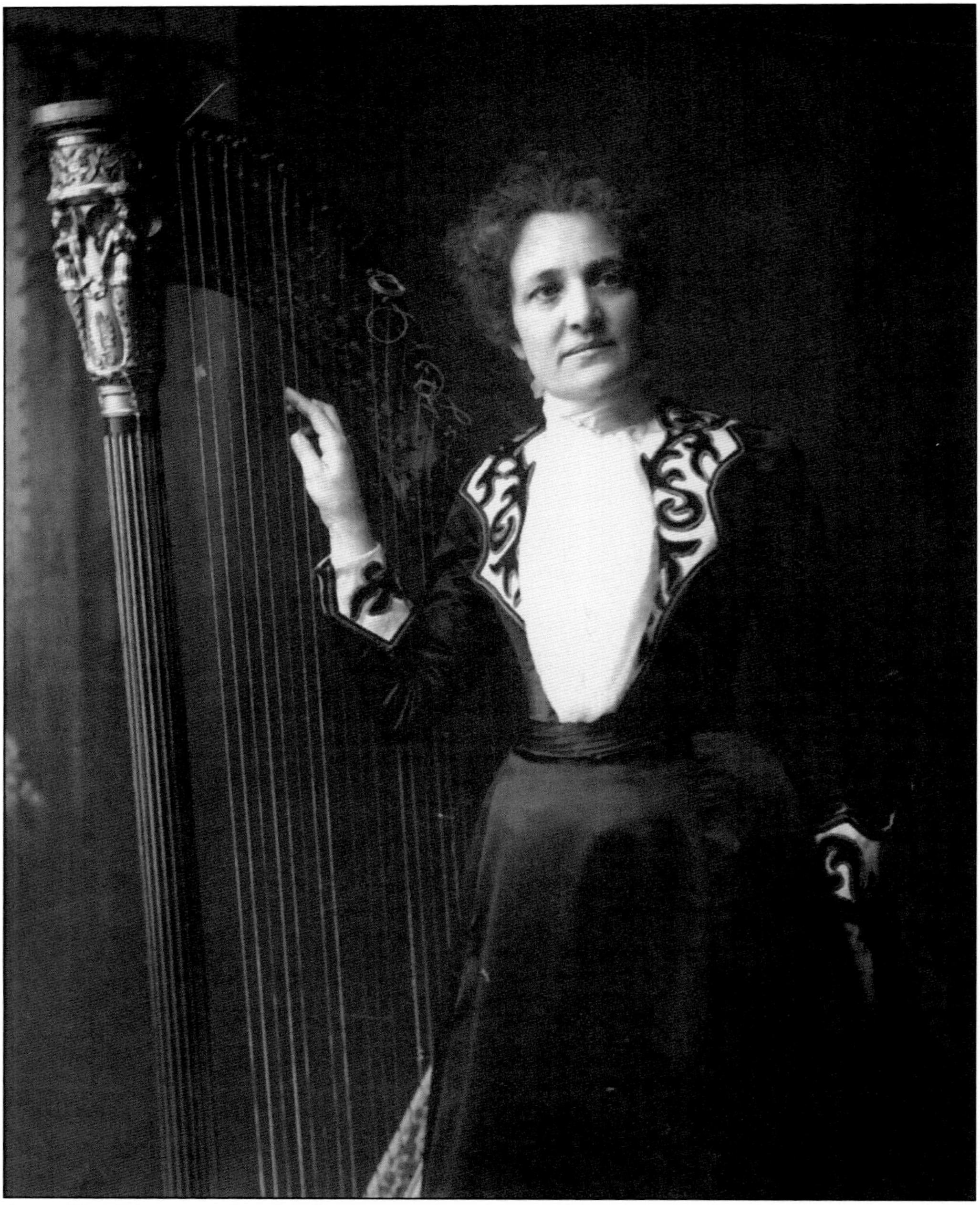

Anna Beechlin, raised in Madison, Wisconsin, attended the University of Wisconsin and the Chicago College of Music. She married Alexander Robertson in Madison, and they moved to Wellsville in 1883. The Robertsons purchased a large, unfinished home in the Riverside area. A downturn in Alexander's business in the 1890s motivated Anna to open the Wellsville Conservatory of Music. Instruction was held in classrooms above 126 North Main Street, and recitals were often held in the ballroom of the Roberstons' house. Anna Robertson and her faculty taught music to innumerable Wellsville children. (Esther Vossler Childs and Sharley Vossler Johnson.)

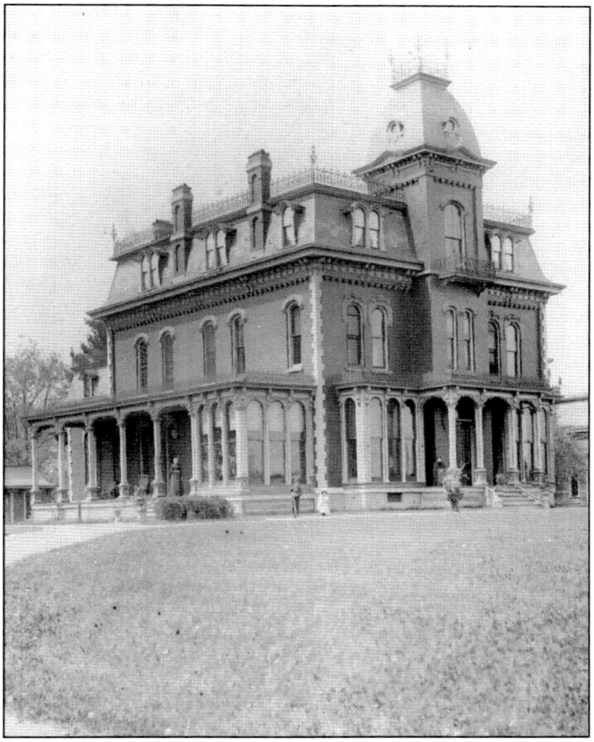

The home of Alexander and Anna B. Robertson in Riverside was commissioned by Charles Simmons in 1872. Simmons was promoting the Riverside area as a resort-type community with schools, a hotel, and a racetrack. He planned to make his home here. Unfortunately, Simmons passed away following an operation in 1875, leaving the Riverside house unfinished. The Robertson family came at the beginning of the oil boom and put the finishing touches on the place. After Anna Robertson's death in 1942, the house became a tearoom called the Evergreens, and in 1944, it was purchased by the American Legion for use as a clubhouse. The old home was destroyed by an intense fire in 1951, the cause of which was never discovered. (Right, DAHPL; below, photograph by Vic Neal, courtesy Allegany County Historical Society.)

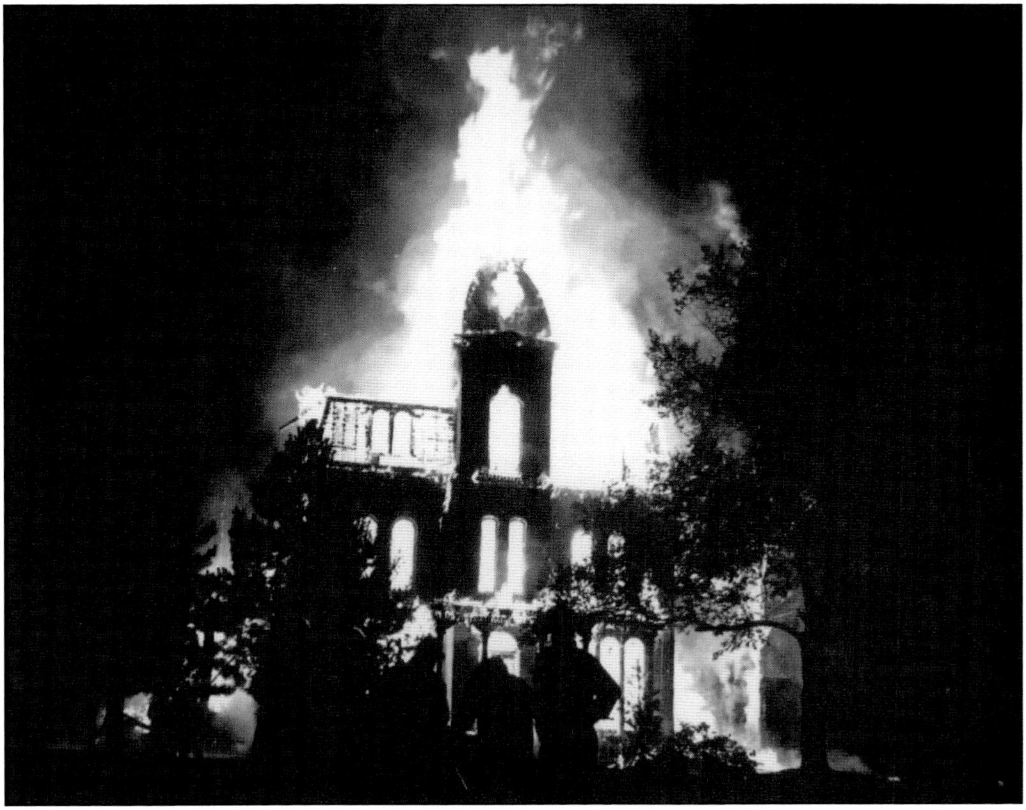

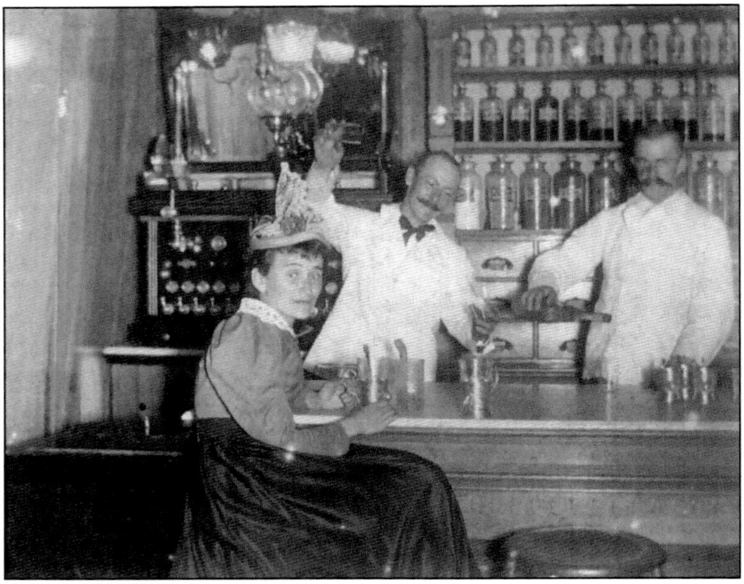

In 1892, Herbert Smith and Harry Teeple opened a drugstore in the Baldwin Block, in the heart of the business district. They named the store the Central Drug Store for its central location. This photograph shows Smith (left) and Teeple promoting their new soda fountain to an unidentified patron in 1895. (DAHPL.)

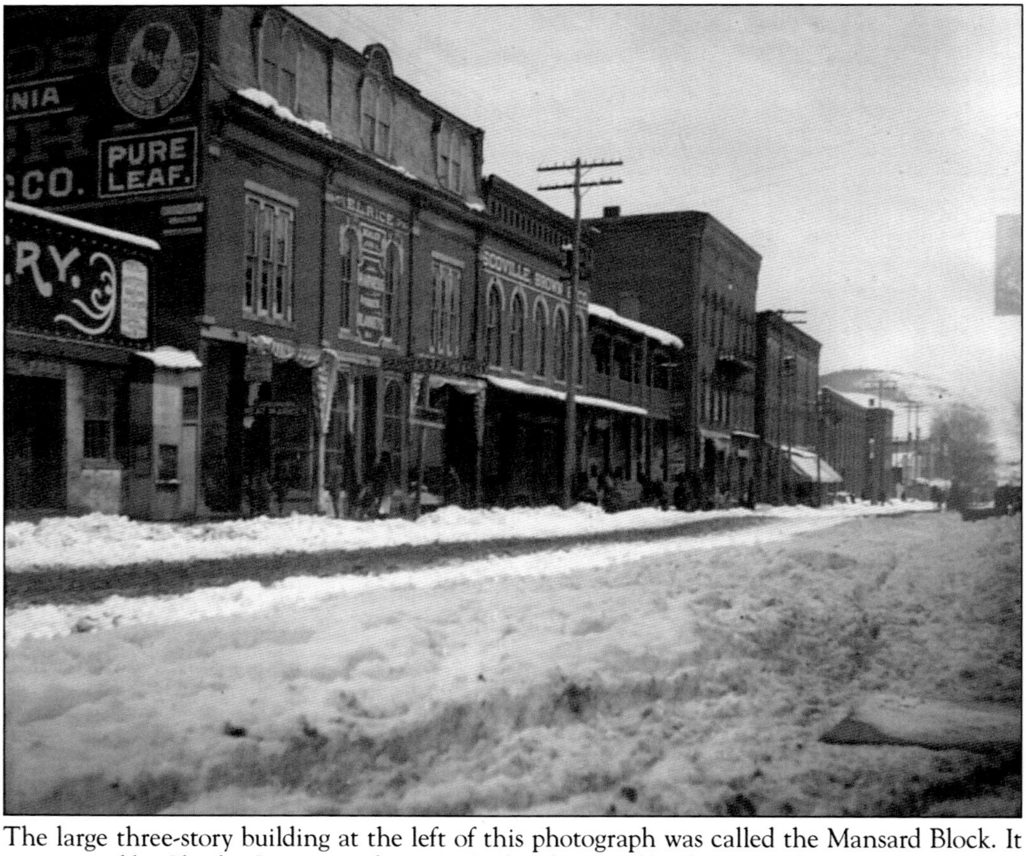

The large three-story building at the left of this photograph was called the Mansard Block. It was erected by Charles Simmons after an 1871 fire destroyed his home on the site. The design of the building was new to this area, and many people were very vocal about the new, disagreeable style the owner was imposing on the public. The Mansard Block was demolished in 2004, and a seasonal ice-cream shop is now located on that site.

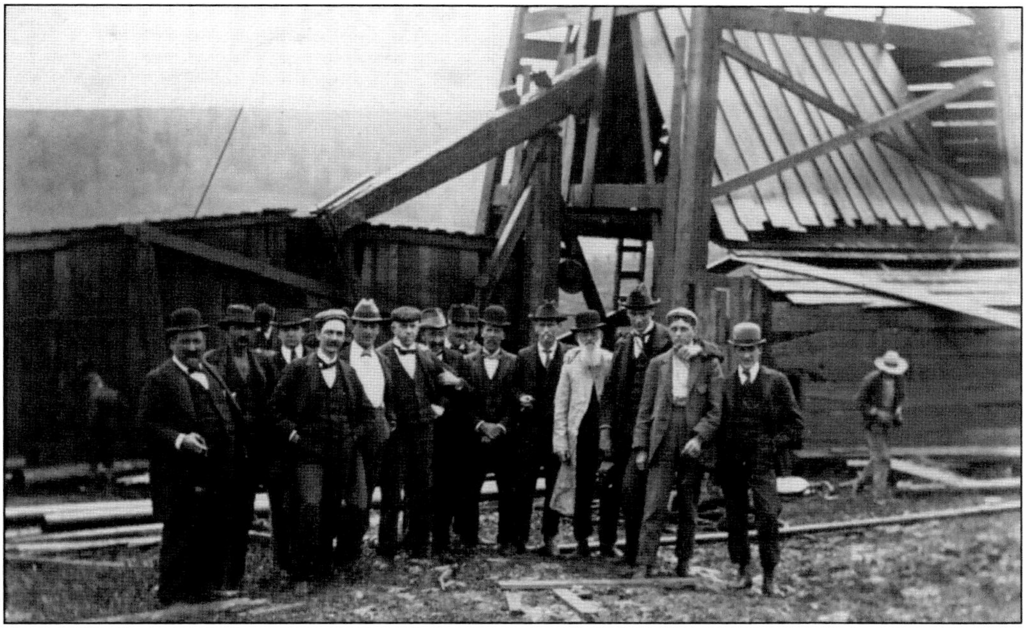

A group of investors in the Dugway Oil Company of Wellsville poses by its well on South Fords Brook in 1897. The men are, from left to right, John Sweeney, Frank Fanton, Harry Sackett, Lewis Thornton, Rufus Murray, Harry Teeple, Oscar Fuller, two unidentified, Fredrick Ward, unidentified, Hiram J. Torrey, Amory Stewart, Bob Whittaker, and Ernest Glauche. The well was not successful and was abandoned after weeks of drilling. (DAHPL.)

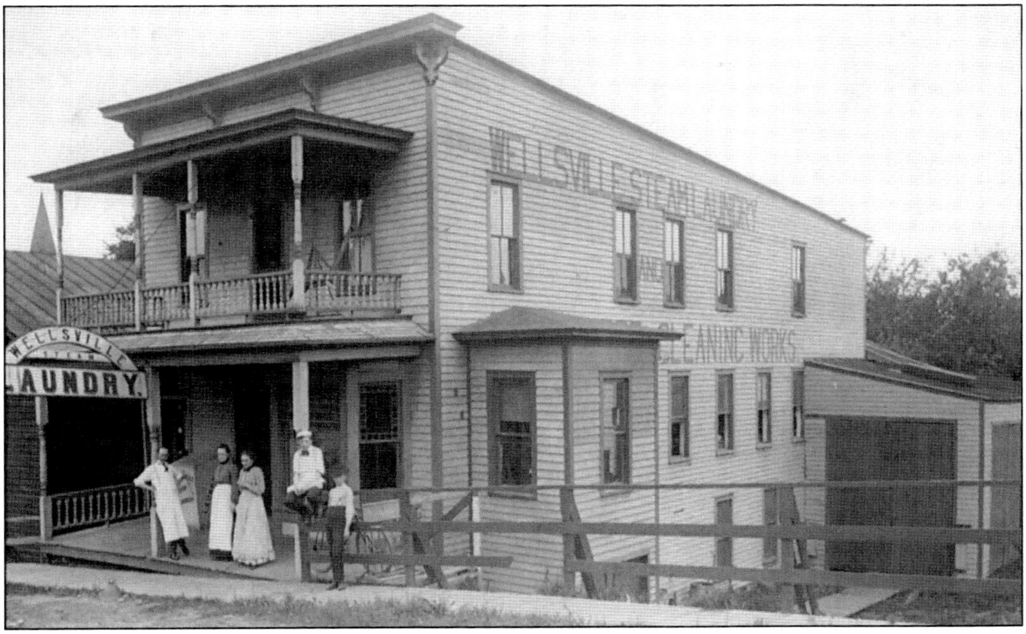

E. Mack Fulmer built his Wellsville Steam Laundry on Madison Street in 1896. In 1912, he took on partner E.E. Kellogg, and the name of the business was changed to the Banner Laundry Company. In 1913, the business was purchased by Ernest W. Glauche. The business suffered a fire in late 1915 from which it never recovered, and it was sold to entrepreneurs who had the building converted into apartments by 1919.

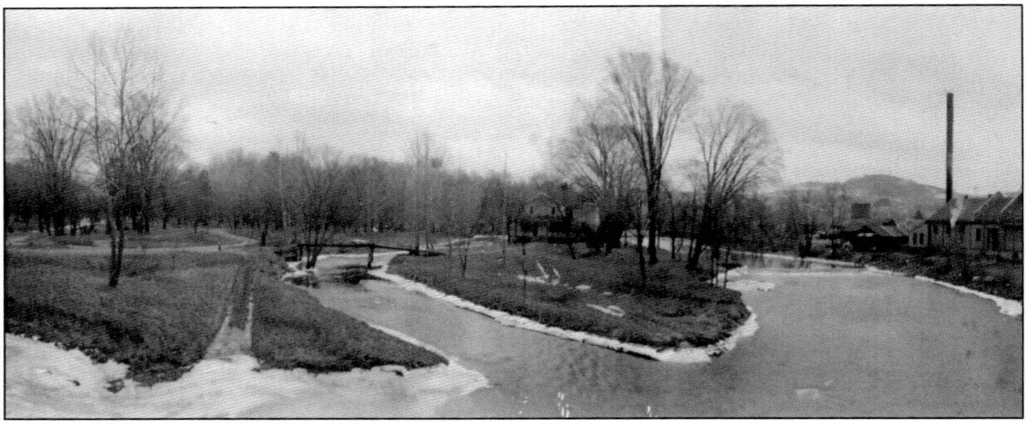

The men of the Grand Army of the Republic, Dexter Post, were given a little island near Island Park in 1898. With the help of many volunteers, the old soldiers used lumber from the dismantled John Clark store to build a meetinghouse there. It was dedicated on New Year's Day in 1900, and the GAR held meetings here and kept offices on the second floor. In the photograph below, the members of the Dexter Post pose for their photograph at their hall on GAR Island after Memorial Day services in 1909. In the early hours of May 31, 1912, after a Memorial Day celebration, the GAR hall went up in flames, never to be rebuilt. (Above, DAHPL.)

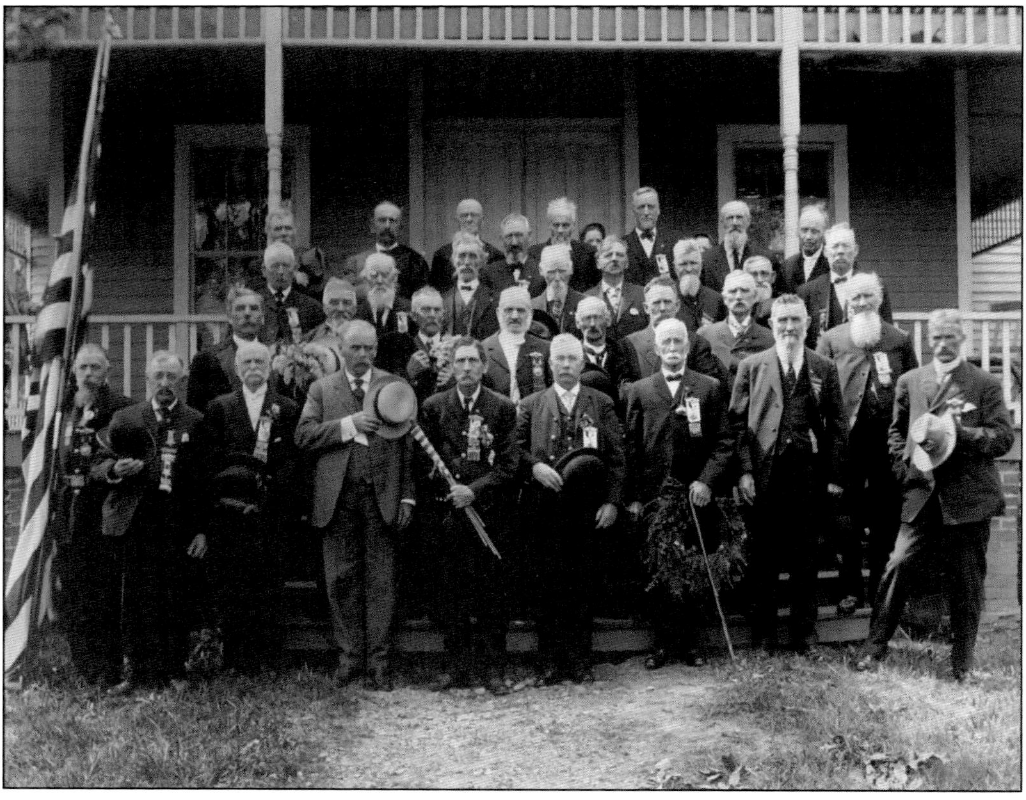

Three

1900 TO 1915

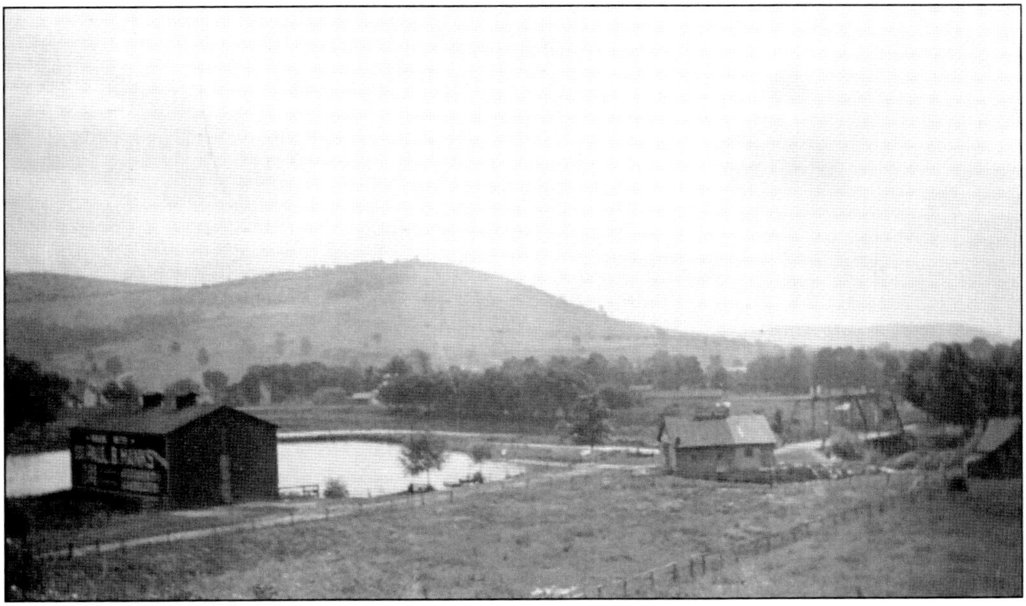

John Newman of the Wellsville Bottling Works purchased the rights to use the ice on this pond and every year waged war with young ice-skaters in an effort to keep the ice clean. The pond, located just off Miller Street, became known as Newman's Pond. This postcard shows Newman's old icehouse next to the pond. (Craig Braack.)

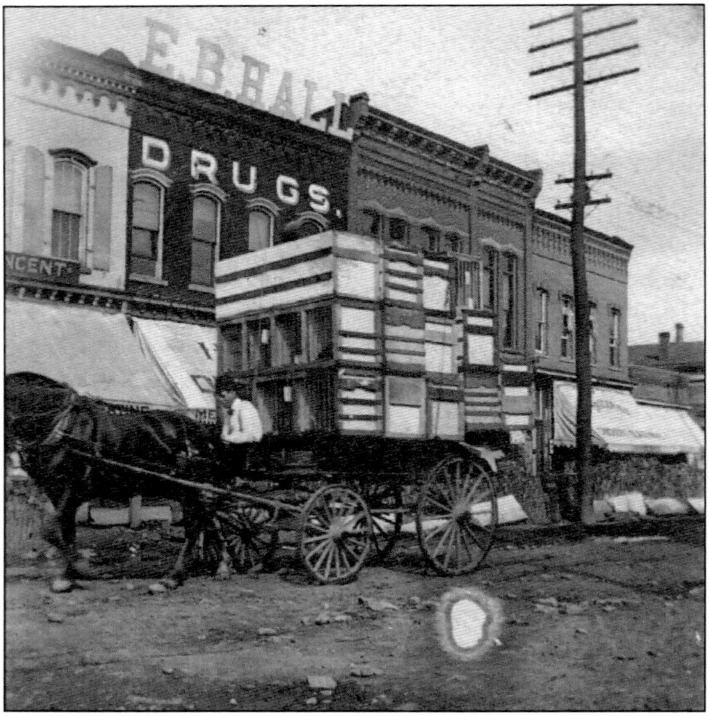

Joseph Kralinger, a longtime employee of Wells Fargo & Co., is shown here driving his team in front of Halls Drug Store on North Main Street in 1900, perhaps hauling poultry. The ground appears to have been roughly graded, and past his wagon, there are piles of brick on the side of the road in preparation for paving the street.

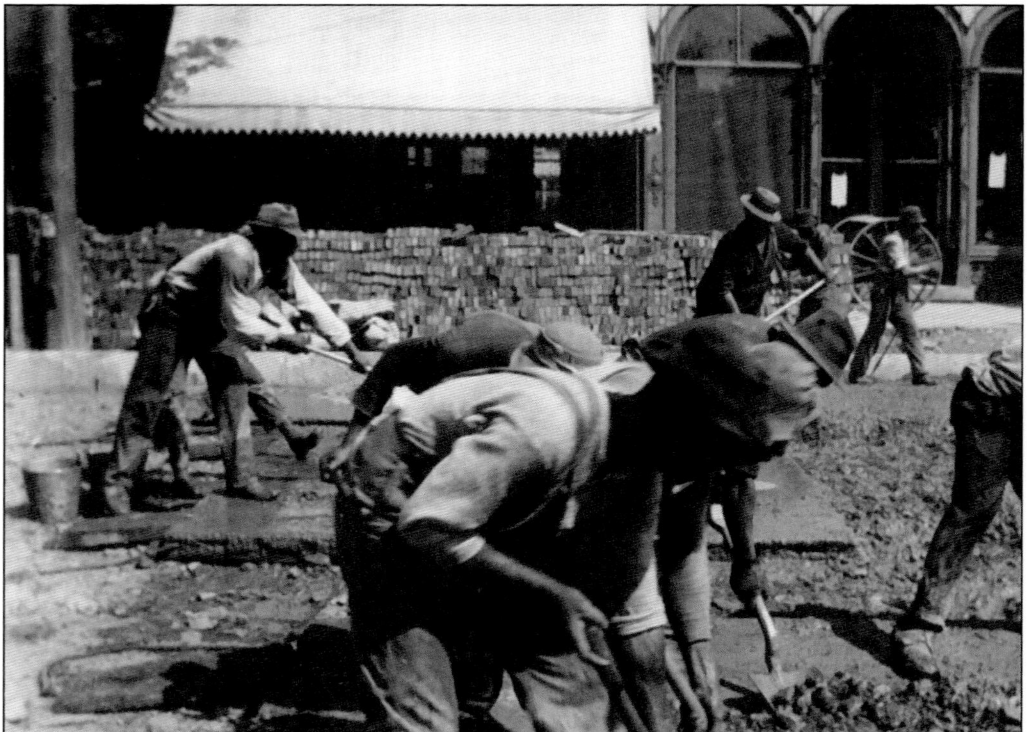

Workmen begin the backbreaking job of laying brick for the new pavement in 1900. The men are shown in front of the Lincoln Block at the corner of East Pearl and North Main Streets. (Raymond McClure.)

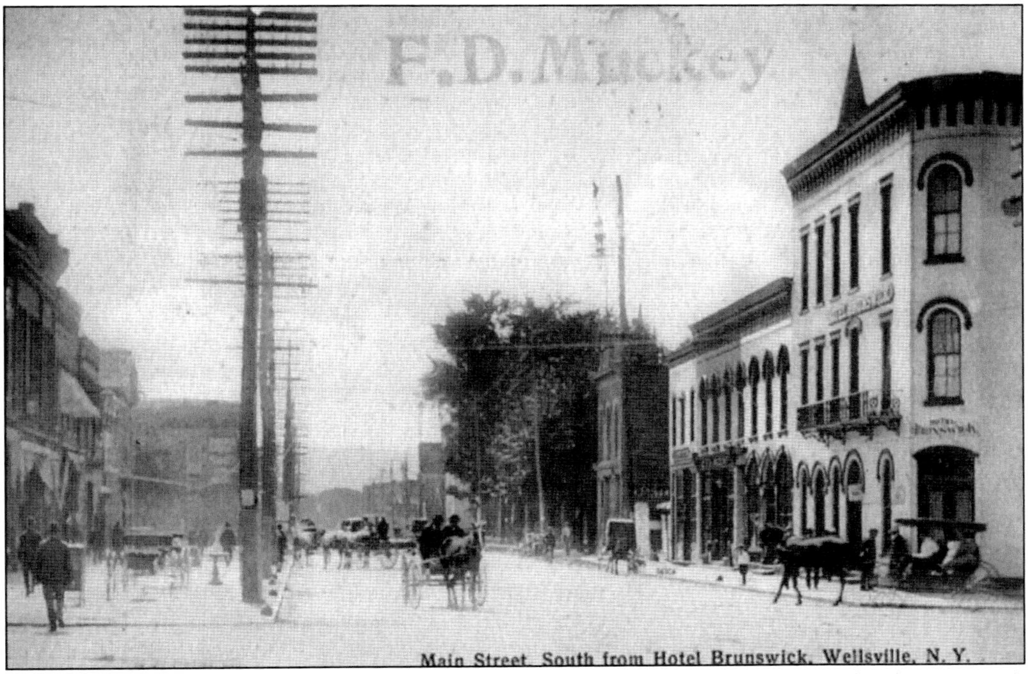

In Wellsville, there were at least two drinking fountains placed into operation by the Woman's Christian Temperance Union. This postcard shows one of the fountains in front of Hoyt's Hardware (near present-day Beef Haus on the left) at the northern end of the business district. The second fountain was in front of the Central Drug Store near the Baldwin Theatre in the center of the business district.

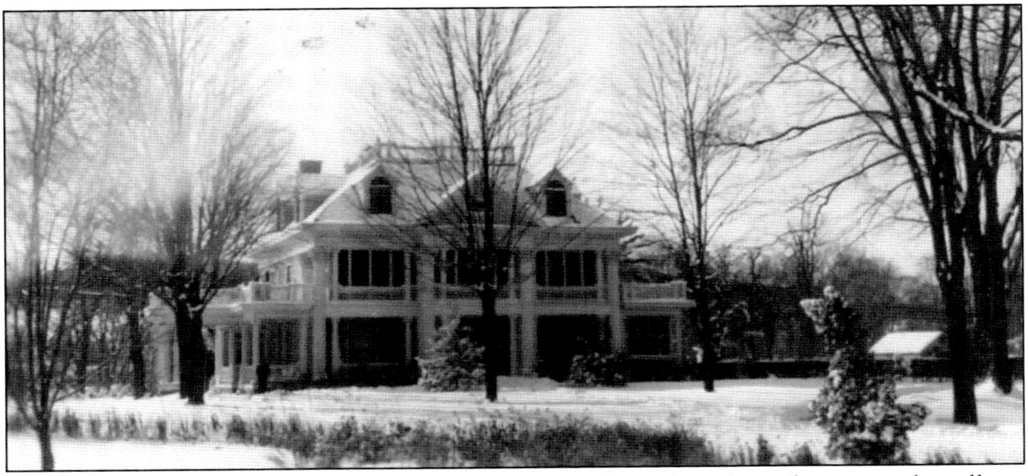

Ephraim and Janette d'Autremont Smith built one of the earliest frame houses in the village. Upon their deaths, Edwin C. Bradley purchased the home and the 15 acres surrounding it. Bradley began a massive rebuilding project in 1903, transforming the old house into the beautiful mansion shown here. Bradley descendants demolished the home in 1957 and erected the Bradley Producing Company headquarters. In 1989, the structure at 313 North Main Street became a medical arts building associated with the Jones Memorial Hospital. (John and Ellie Spicer.)

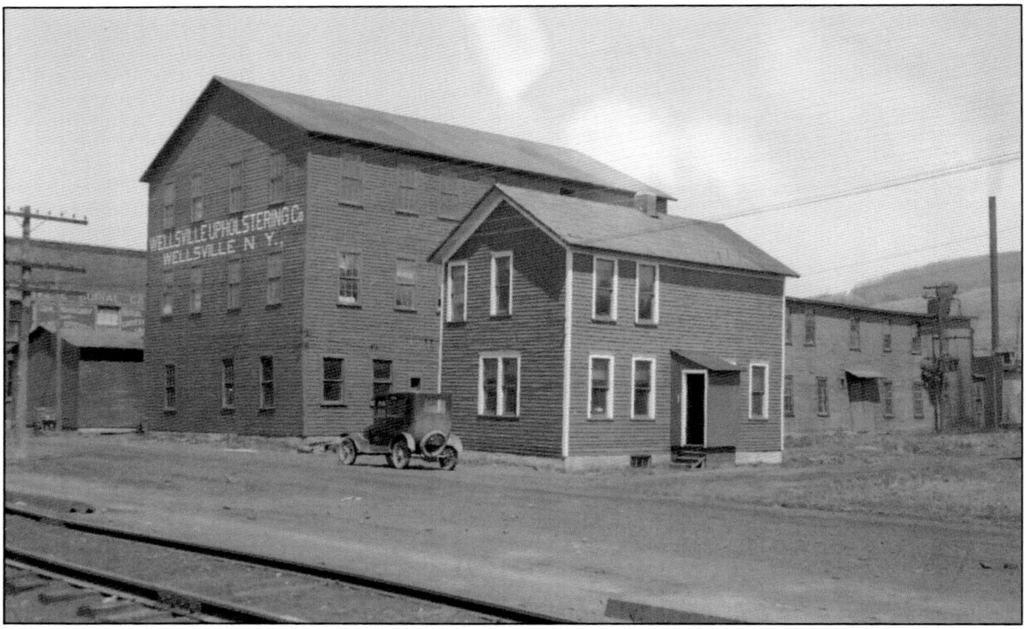

The two companies on this page were located next to each other on Railroad Avenue. The Wellsville Upholstering Company was formed in 1903 by Frank Gent and William Beckwith. In 1907, they purchased a large wooden building on Railroad Avenue that formerly held the Doty Carriage Factory. The business did well, employing 25 people, until 1932, when the old building was destroyed by fire, effectively ending the business. The Wellsville Burial Case Company (below) was formed by Fred C. Damon and John C. Darcy in 1907. The men purchased the assets of the bankrupt Wellsville Manufacturing Company and reopened that shop to build wooden caskets. In 1910, the company constructed this three-story addition to its existing wooden building on Railroad Avenue. The Burial Case Company remained in Wellsville until the early 1950s. (Above, Kristen Kruger; below, Donald Baldwin.)

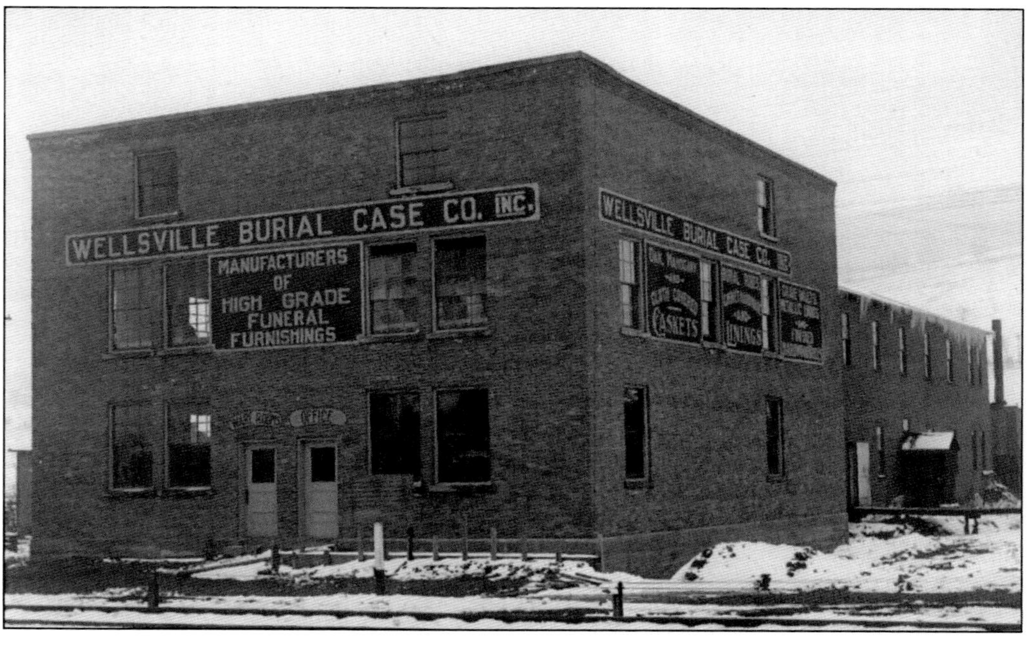

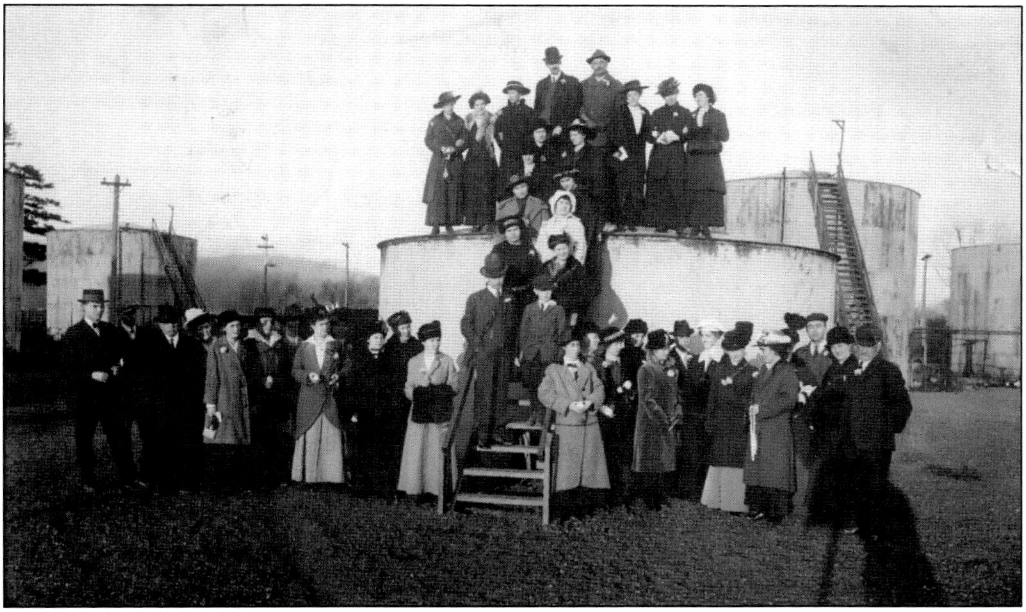

In December 1901, Wellsville businessmen announced the formation of a stock company to build and operate a refinery in Wellsville. Riley Allen, Henry Norton, James McEwen, Harry Breckenridge, Oak Duke, and A.R. Dougherty were the primary Wellsville investors. A grand opening was held in September 1902, with 400 invited guests touring the new facility. Here, some of the guests pose for this commemorative photograph on the new tanks located on the grounds south of the village. (Walter Gardner.)

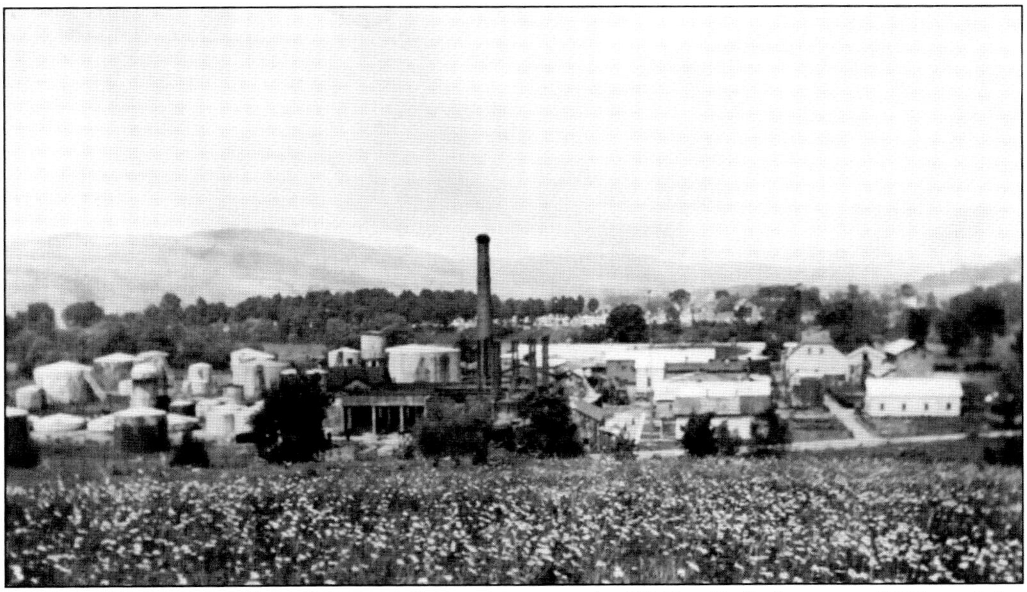

Union Petroleum purchased a controlling interest in the Wellsville Refinery in 1905, and the refinery was reorganized. New directors included John C. Herrick, E.M. Lyons, W.J. Richardson, J.H. McEwen, and W.H. Norton, as well as several directors from Union Petroleum. Sinclair Oil purchased the Union Petroleum Company in 1919. It is the Sinclair Refinery that is remembered when people speak of an oil refinery in Wellsville. (Alexandrina Vigh.)

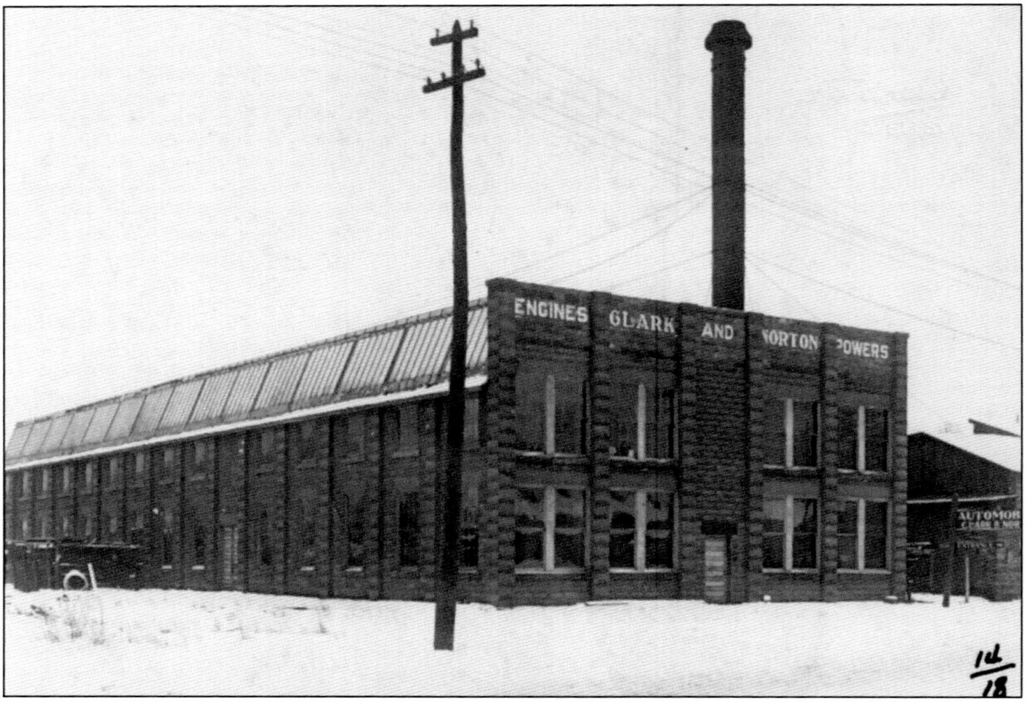

Charles Clark of Belmont and William H. Norton of Wellsville began operations in 1903 on the old tannery site on South Main Street. The new Clark and Norton foundry and machine shop offered machining of any type, specializing in oil well equipment. This was the only location in town that was served by two railroads, the Buffalo & Susquehanna and the Erie Railroad. This is now the location of Arvos Inc., Ljungstrom Division. (Donald Baldwin.)

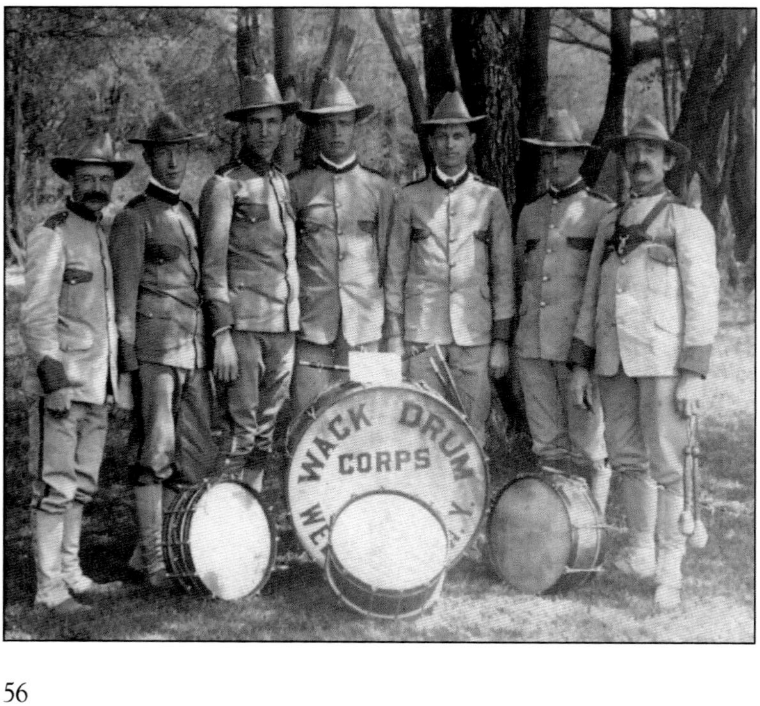

The Wack Drum Corps was formed in 1903 by manager William Wack, shown at the left of this photograph. The men played their drums and piccolos in many parades and conventions and in 1908 reorganized into the Sons of Veterans Drum Corps. Their ranks swelled to 12 members upon reorganization. The Sons of Veterans Drum Corps disbanded in 1912. (Donald Baldwin.)

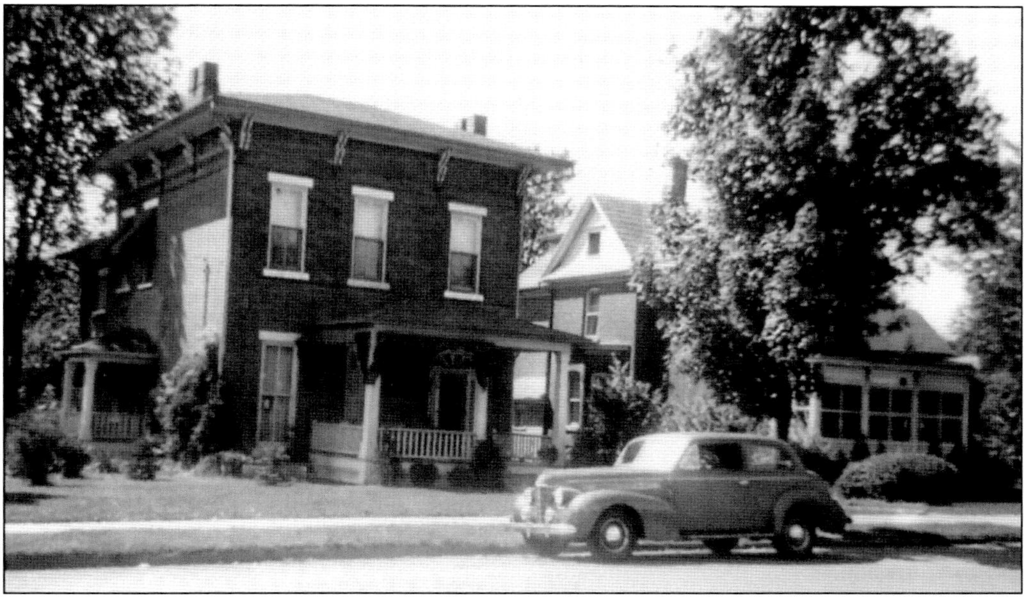

The brick home at 10 South Main Street, seen at left in this photograph, was built by merchant John B. Clark. Clark's dry goods store was located on the corner next to his residence. At Clark's death, the house was deeded to his daughter Betty Potter, who owned it until she passed away in 1941. It became the home of Timothy and Jennie Shine shortly after that time. (David and Teresa Shine.)

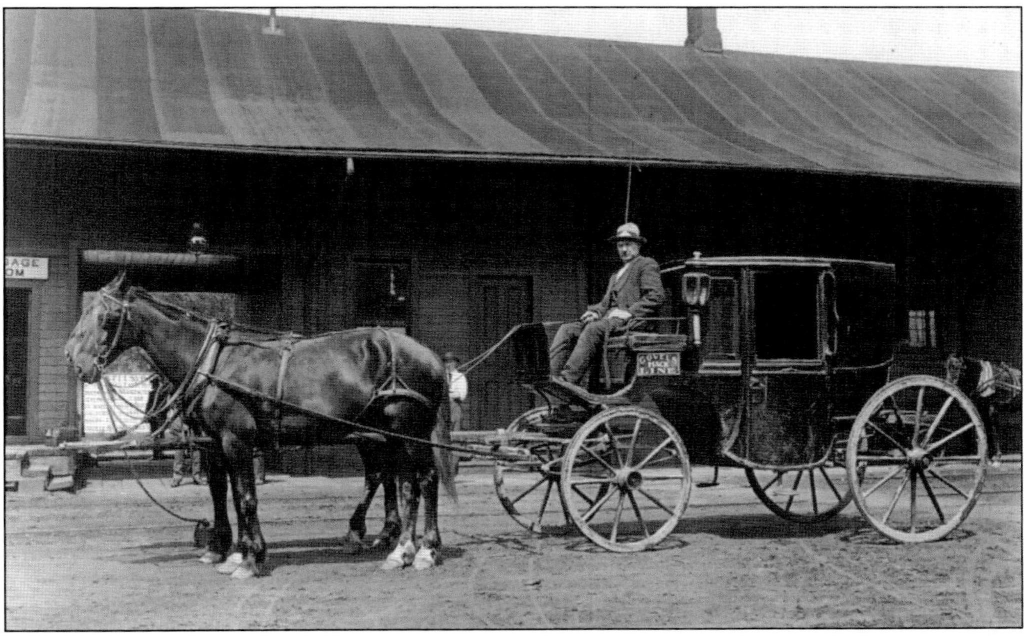

Fred Covel was an expert horseman and conducted a hack service for many years, moving travelers and their luggage from the train station to their hotel or their homes. In later years, he advertised his Rubber Tired Hack Line and Baggage Transfer, which was sure to give a passenger a smooth ride on brick-paved streets. Fred was deeply involved with Dyke Street Hose Company, and he owned a horse that was said to be as eager to get to a fire as any of the members of the company. (Donald Baldwin.)

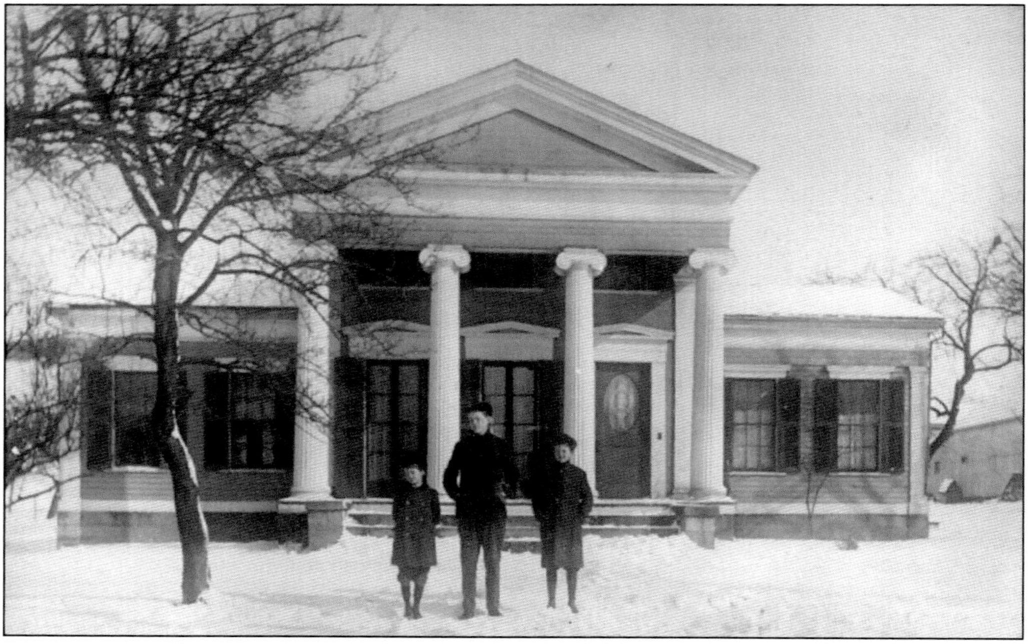

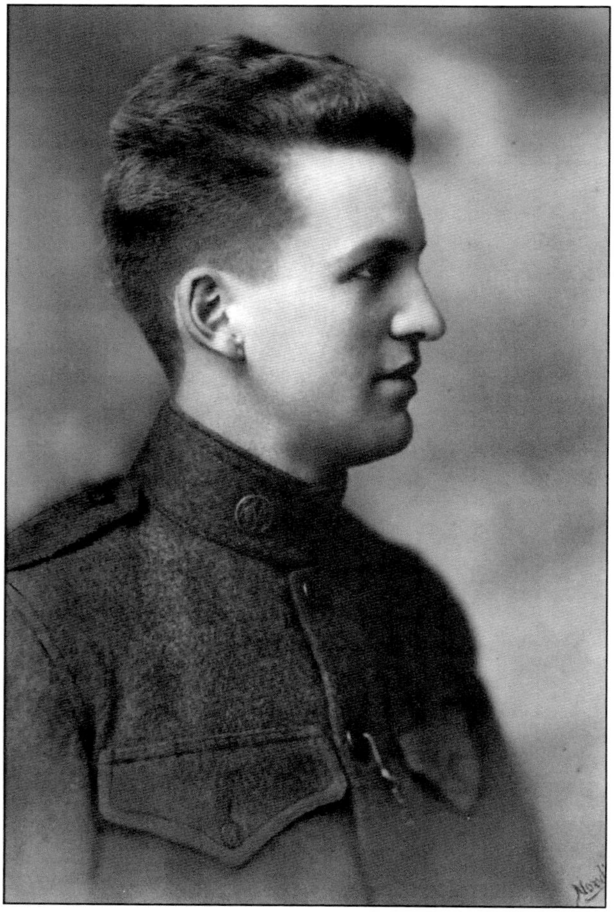

Nathaniel Johnson built this dwelling on Maple Avenue shortly after his arrival in Wellsville in the 1850s. It remained the Johnson homestead until his wife, Sally, passed away in 1892. It was purchased by Frederick Church in 1898, and he and his wife, Nellie Moore Church, raised their children here. Standing in front of their home in 1905 are the Church children—Frederick (left), Warren (center), and Frank.

The members of Frank B. Church Veterans of Foreign Wars Post 2530 purchased the old Nathaniel Johnson house in 1945 for use as a clubhouse. The building is the old home that Frank B. Church grew up in. Church had enlisted at the start of World War I and returned to civilian life in 1919. He passed away in 1920 at the young age of 24, the result of his war injuries.

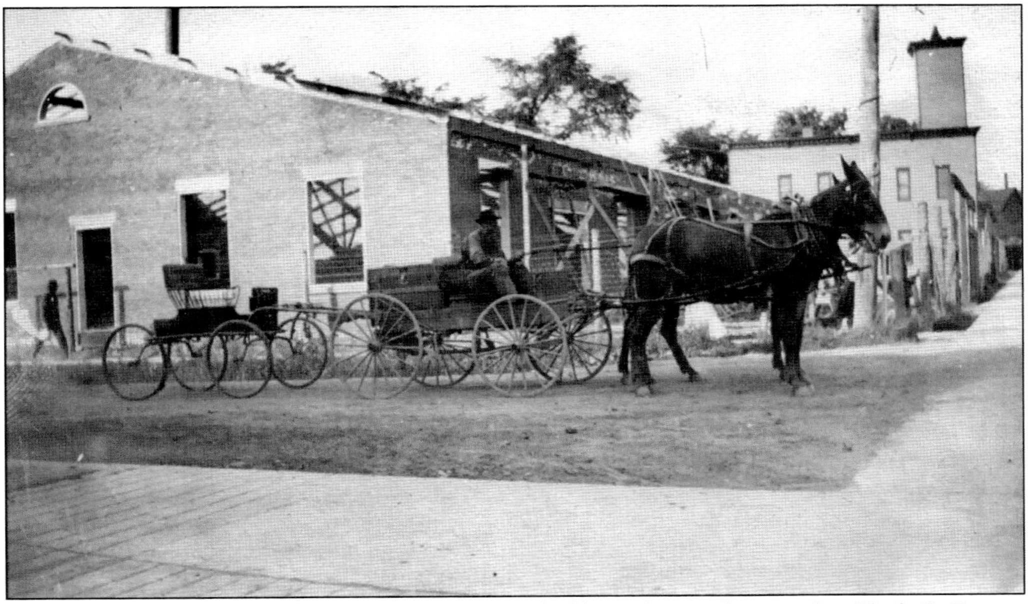

The Oak Duke Lumber Company expanded its holdings by purchasing the Clark & Easton Mill on the west side of the river in the 1890s. A fire in December 1908 destroyed the old mill. The Oak Duke Lumber Company reorganized shortly after the fire, and William Duke and his son William Jr. built their fireproof mill, which still stands on the corner of Stevens Street and Brooklyn Avenue.

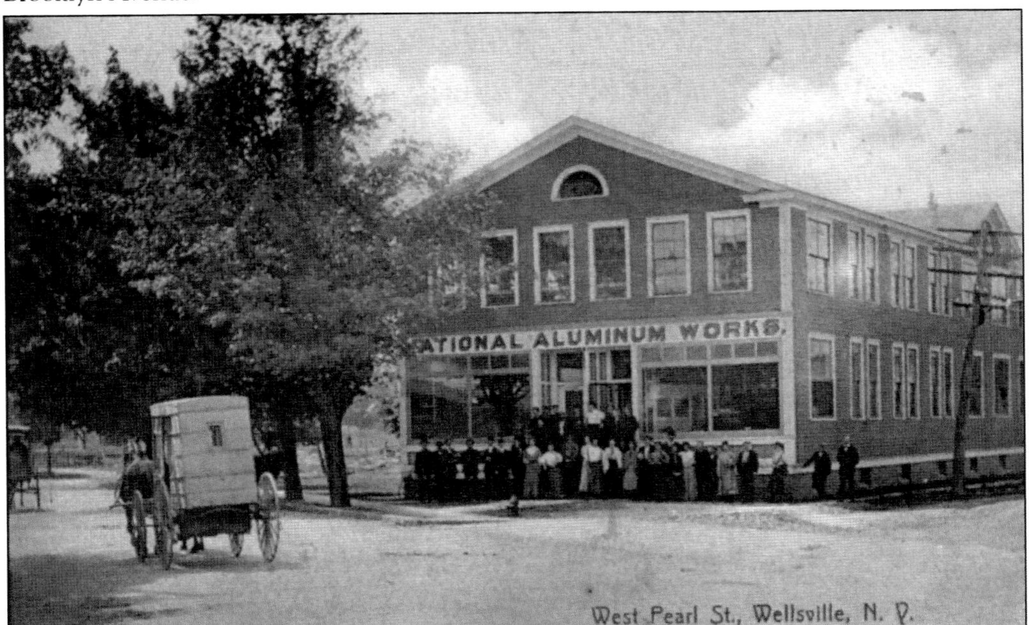

John E. Potter of Pennsylvania purchased the Strootman Shoe factory in 1906. Potter enlarged the building at West Pearl Street and Stevens Street and moved the contents of the Buffalo Aluminum Company into it. He called his new company National Aluminum and provided employment for many men and women for several years. A costly fire gutted National Aluminum in 1914, and the merchants of Wellsville were dismayed to learn that Potter chose to remove his plant to Elmira instead of rebuilding here.

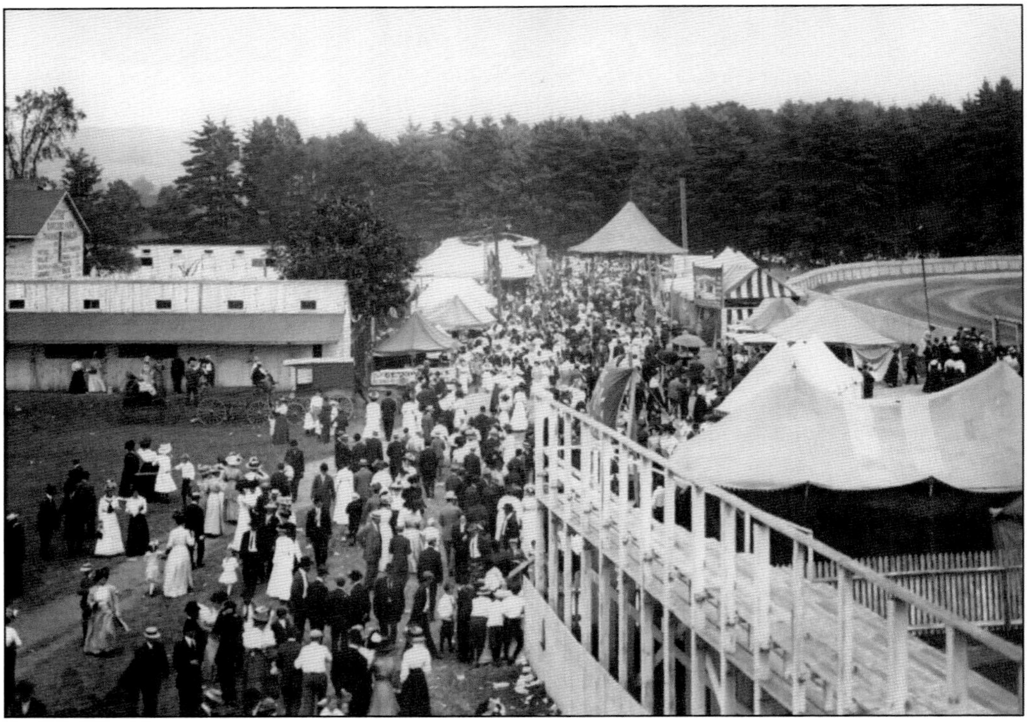

The William Miller farm near Dyke Street was purchased by a group of investors in 1904 with the intent to develop the property into a new site for the Wellsville Fair. The property contained more than 100 acres of land, including a stand of maple trees called Millers Grove, a picnic destination spot for many people in the village. The first fair at this new location was held in 1905. A half-mile track for horse racing was a feature of the new fairgrounds. (Both, DAHPL.)

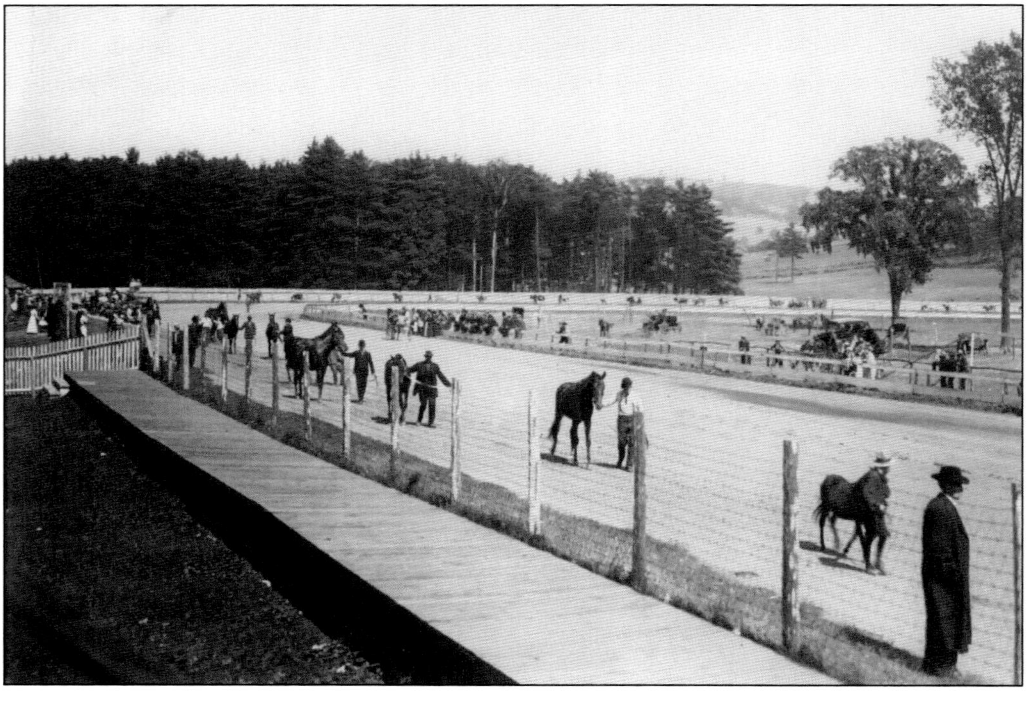

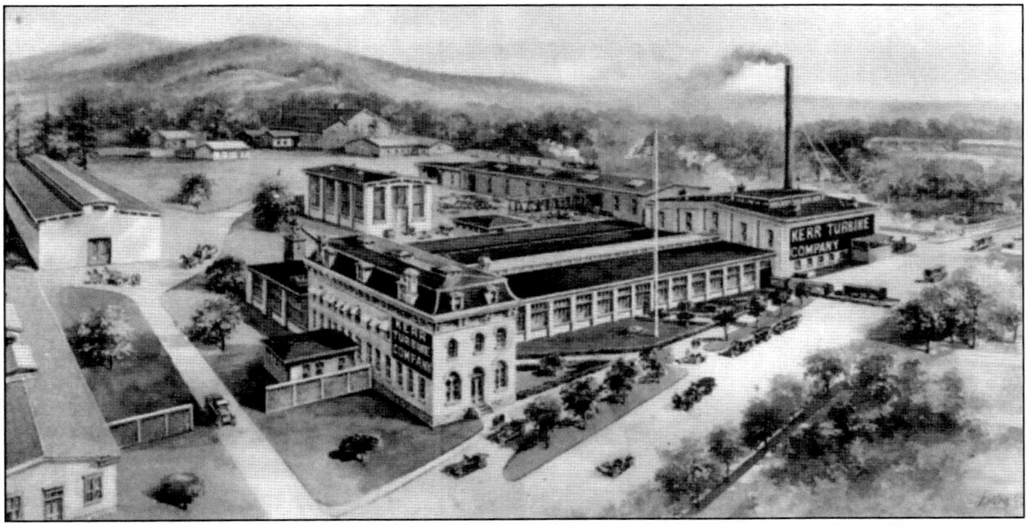

Wellsville was the home of two steam turbine companies. Charles Kerr started the Kerr Turbine Company around 1906 (above) but sold the company to a group of investors shortly after that time. The company was again sold in 1923 to the Elliot Company, who moved the shop to Jeanette, Pennsylvania, in 1928. James L. Moore was an employee of Kerr Turbine but struck out on his own in 1916 to form the Moore Steam Turbine Company (below). Originally working out of an office at the McEwen shops, Moore purchased land from the newly formed Wellsville Country Club and built his factory on the east side of the Erie tracks. Moore Steam Turbine has operated under the names of Moore, Worthington, Turbodyne, and Dresser Rand.

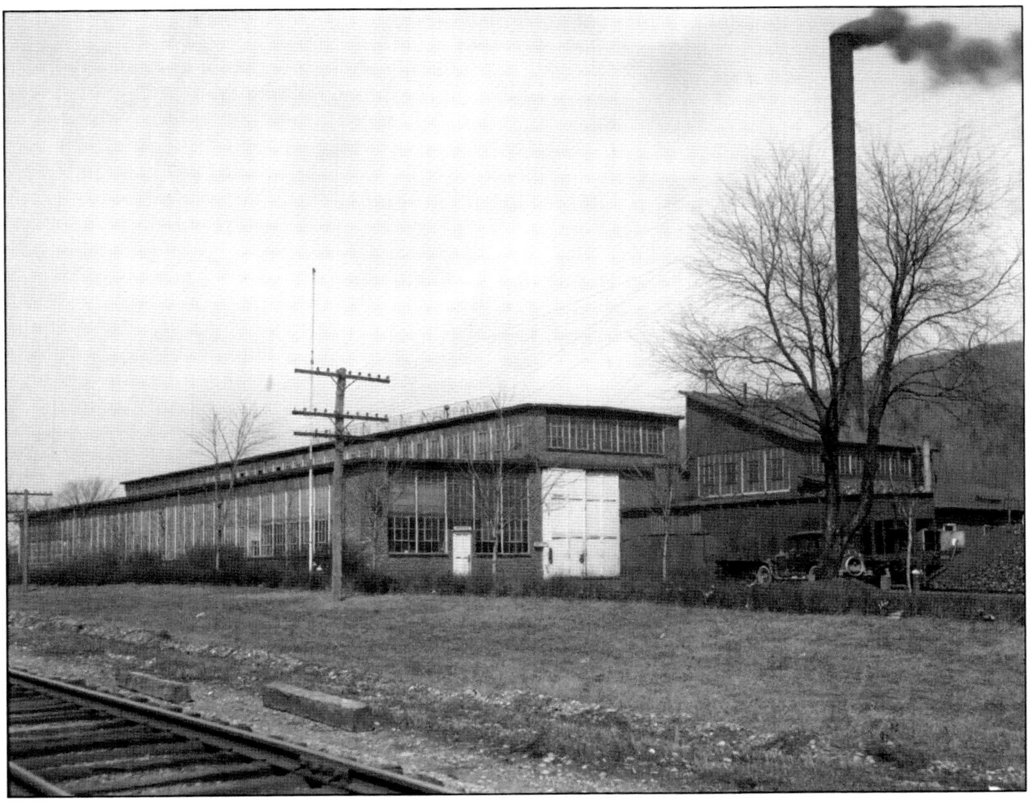

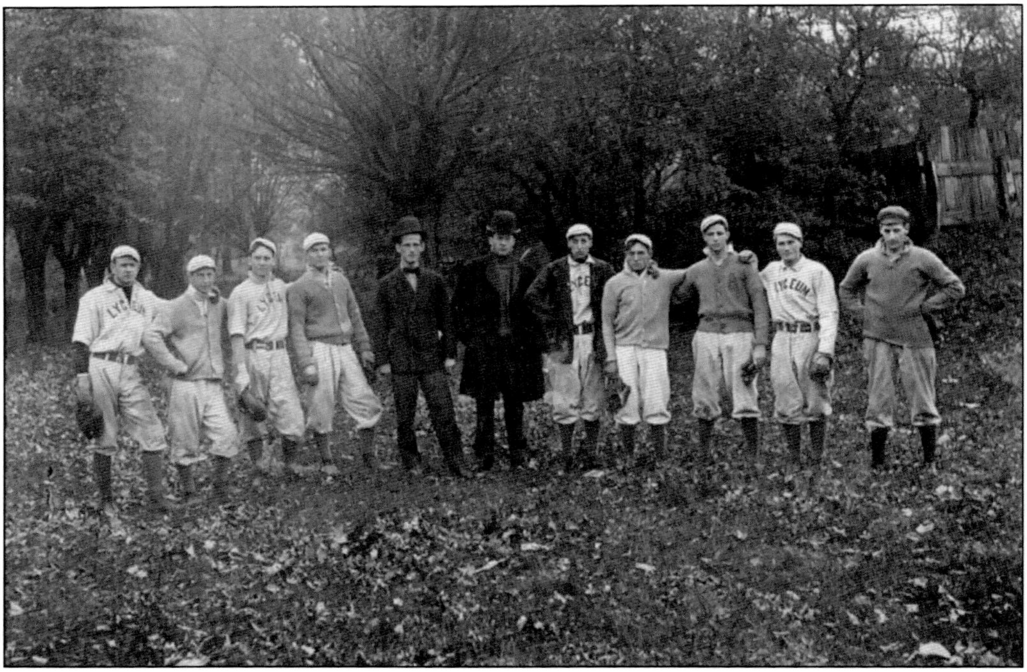

The young men of the Immaculate Conception Lyceum formed a baseball team in May 1908. Composed mostly of men who had played ball in high school, the group earned a reputation as a hard-hitting, fast-playing team. By October, the team was pronounced the "Undisputed County Champions" by a local newspaper. Pictured, from left to right, are Slip Rooth, Lou Harrington, Jay Rogers, Edward Searle, James Renwick, Frank Wall, Tom Dean, Jerome Dean, Pink Ryan, George DeBarbieri, and Otto Reesher. (Nancy Shine Monroe.)

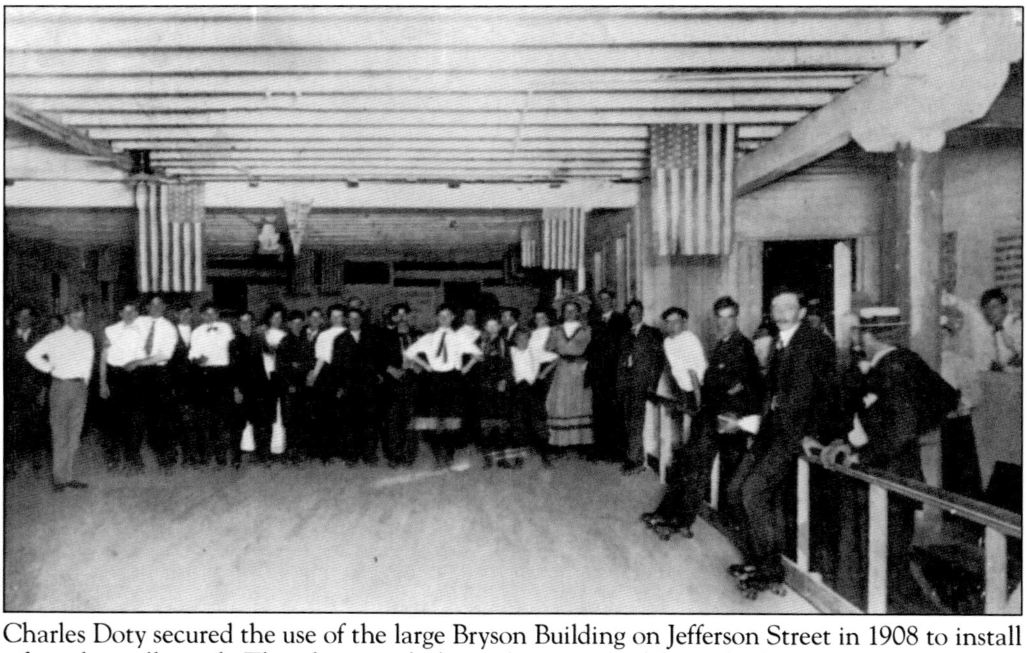

Charles Doty secured the use of the large Bryson Building on Jefferson Street in 1908 to install a first-class roller rink. This photograph shows the interior of the rink where the skaters rolled to music from a brand-new steam organ. (Donald Baldwin.)

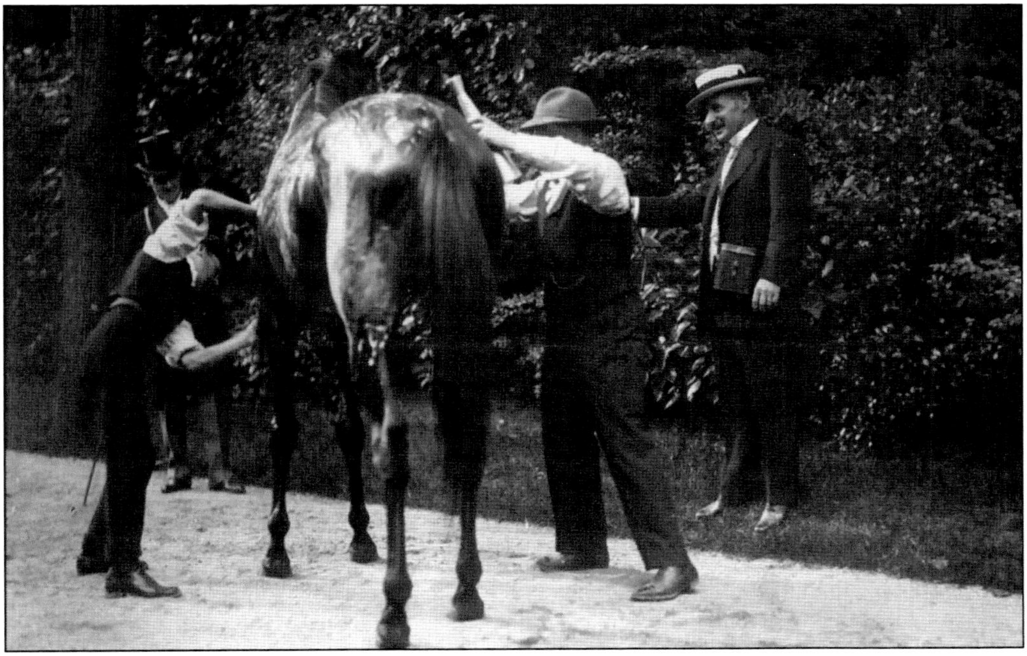

William Duke of Wellsville spent most of his career training racehorses in Europe. In the photograph above, Duke (far right) is shown with the winner of the 1908 Grand Prix de Paris, a horse he trained for William Vanderbilt. By 1925, Duke was in the United States, training for Gifford Cochran. During that year, horses he trained won the Preakness Stakes at Pimlico, the Kentucky Derby, and the Travers Stakes at Saratoga. Duke was inducted into the National Museum of Racing and Hall of Fame in 1956. At right is a family portrait with Duke's son-in-law Mark Hyslip standing (left), Mark's father Charles Hyslip holding Mark Hyslip Jr., and Duke on the right. (Above, George Duke; right, David Brown.)

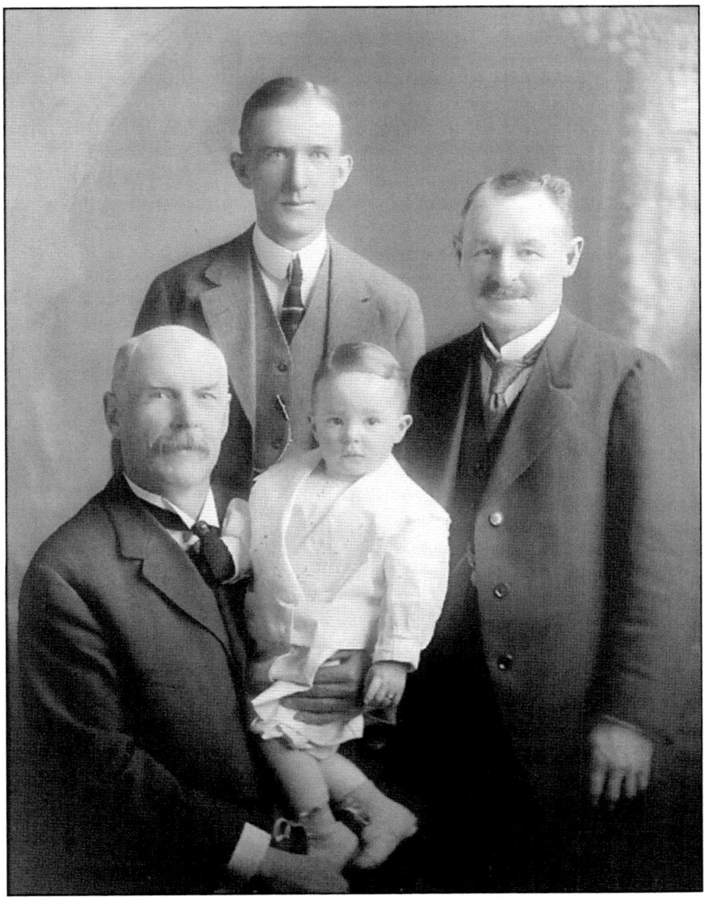

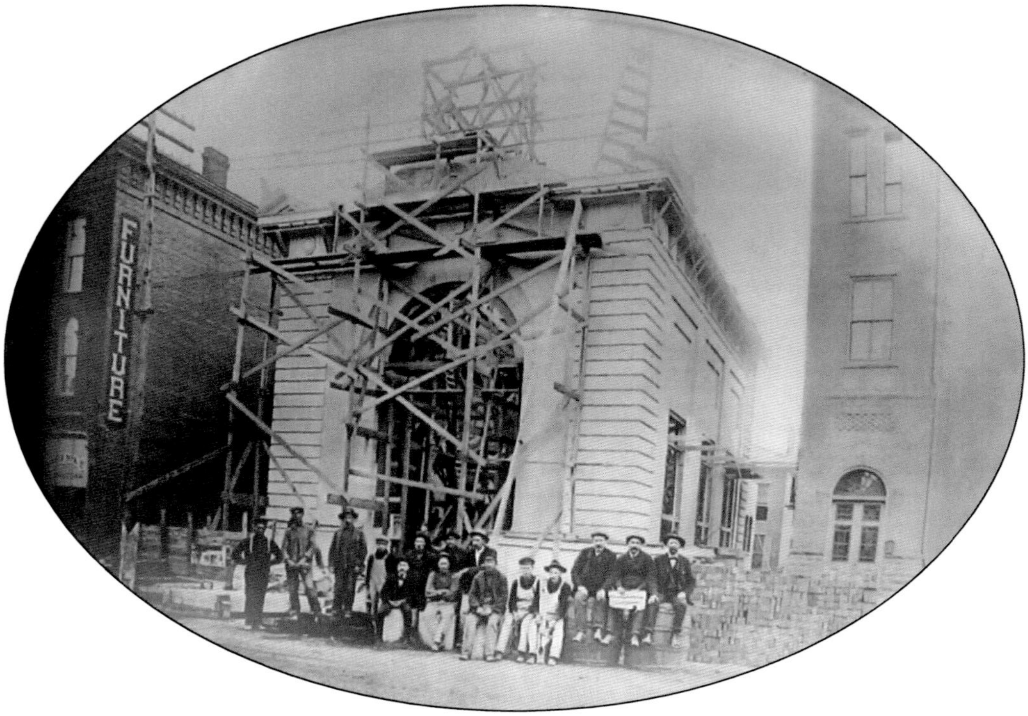

The First National Bank of Wellsville at 115 North Main Street was built in 1906 from plans developed by Edward P. York of York & Sawyer, an architectural firm in New York City. York was a Wellsville native, the son of Hiram and Harriet York. In preparation for building the bank, contractor Lorenzo D. Hurd was hired to move an existing brick home 95 feet back from the street. The bank was occupied in August 1906, and it has been a banking institution since that time.

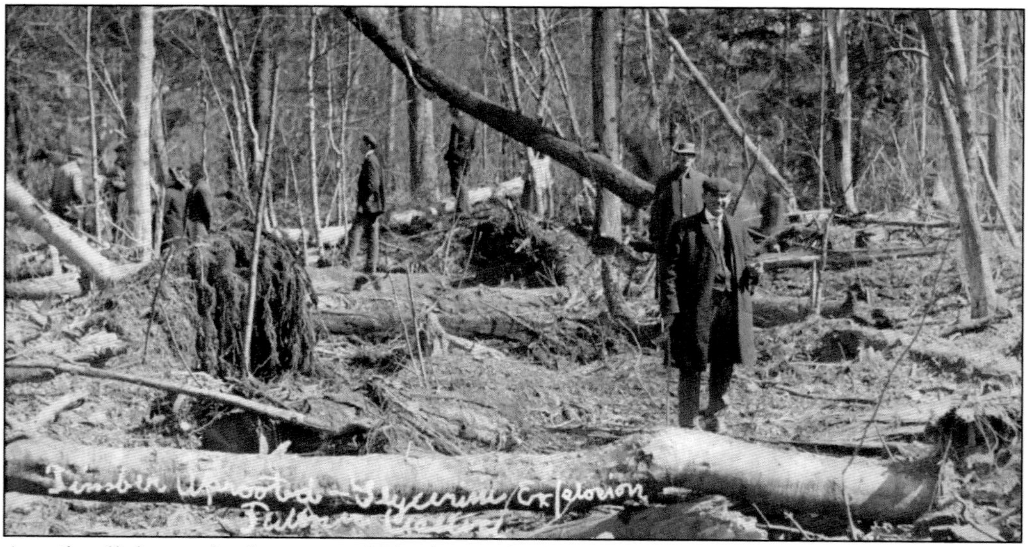

An oil well shooter by the name of Charles Key had driven his horse and wagon to a magazine in Fulmer Valley when the nitroglycerin in the magazine suddenly detonated. No reason other than the unstable nature of the material could be given for the explosion. Windows were shattered for miles around, and little could be found of Key. This postcard reads, "Timber Uprooted, Glycerin Explosion, Fulmer Valley April, 1910."

Four unidentified boys pose for a photograph used in the local newspapers in opposition to a liquor-licensing proposal. The town of Wellsville voted "no license" for saloons, wholesale stores, drugstores, and hotels in November 1911. (David Brown.)

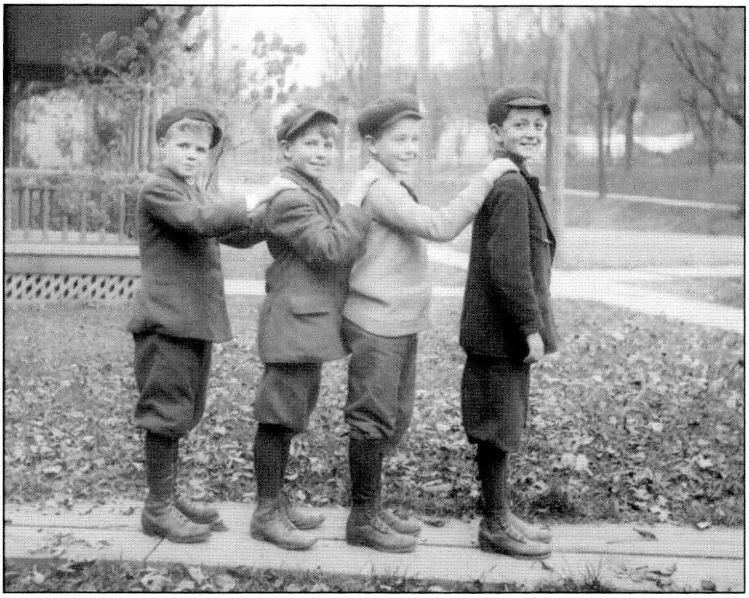

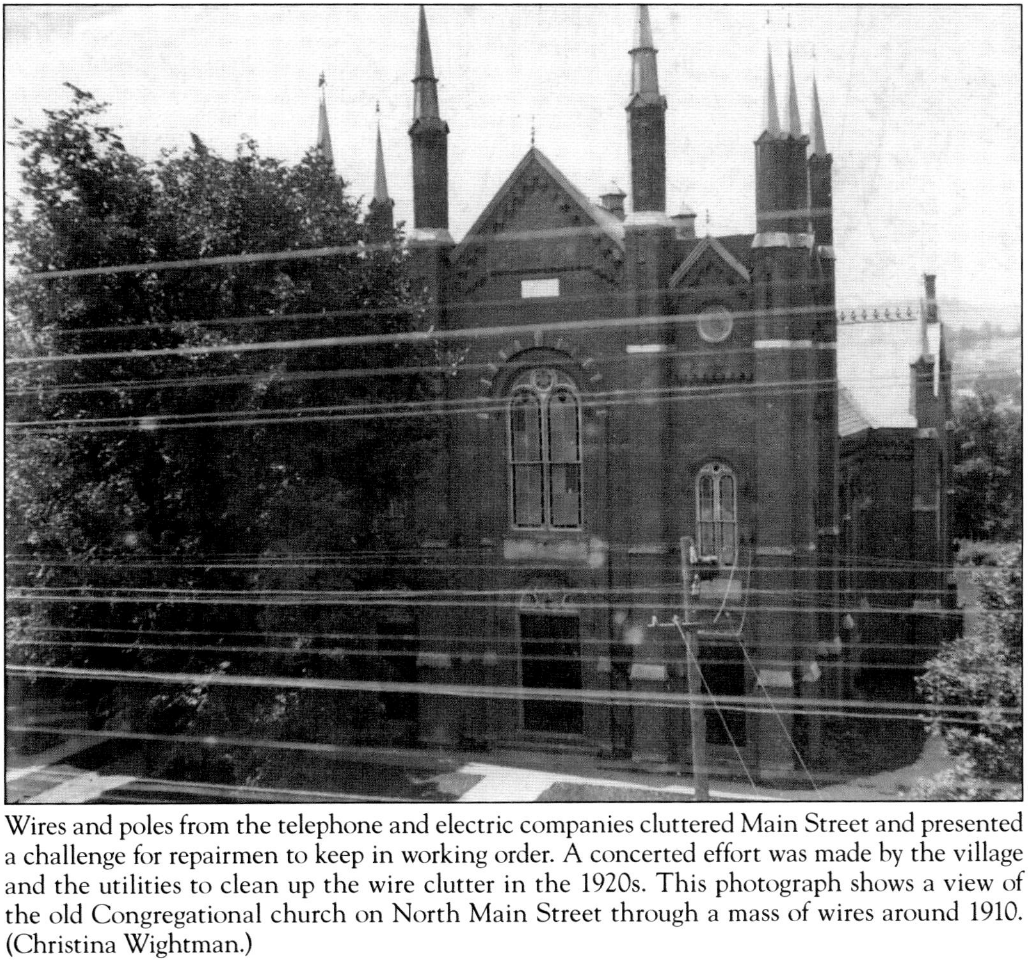

Wires and poles from the telephone and electric companies cluttered Main Street and presented a challenge for repairmen to keep in working order. A concerted effort was made by the village and the utilities to clean up the wire clutter in the 1920s. This photograph shows a view of the old Congregational church on North Main Street through a mass of wires around 1910. (Christina Wightman.)

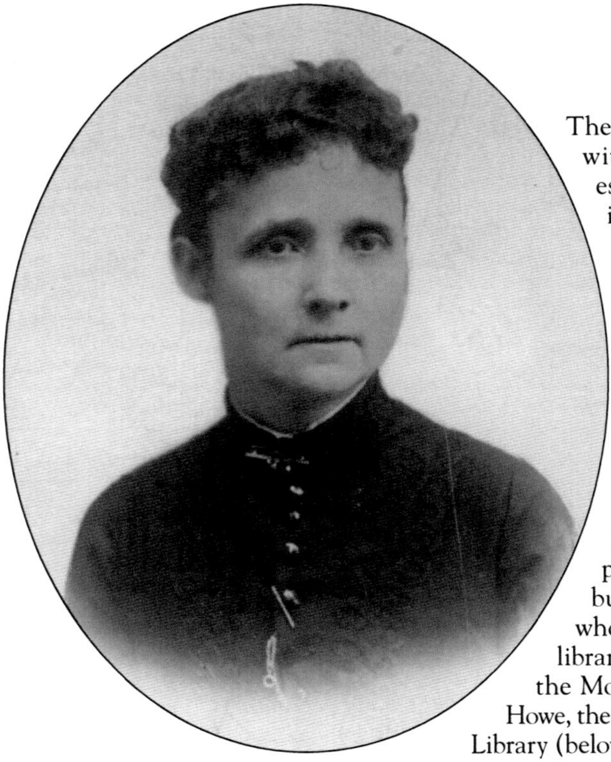

The Monday Club was organized in 1891 with the purpose of raising funds to establish and maintain a public library in Wellsville. The ladies of the club sponsored lectures, teas, and concerts in their efforts to raise the necessary funds for a library. In 1896, Louise Farnum Brown became president, a position she held for 38 years. While searching for funding for the library, she sought her nephew's advice in approaching philanthropist Andrew Cargenie. David A. Howe's response to her was, "Why not a David A. Howe Library?" Louise replied, "Nothing would please me more." Howe was a prosperous businessman from Allegany County who was living in Pennsylvania. With a library site provided through the efforts of the Monday Club, and funding provided by Howe, the community's first David A. Howe Public Library (below) was built in 1909. (Left, DAHPL.)

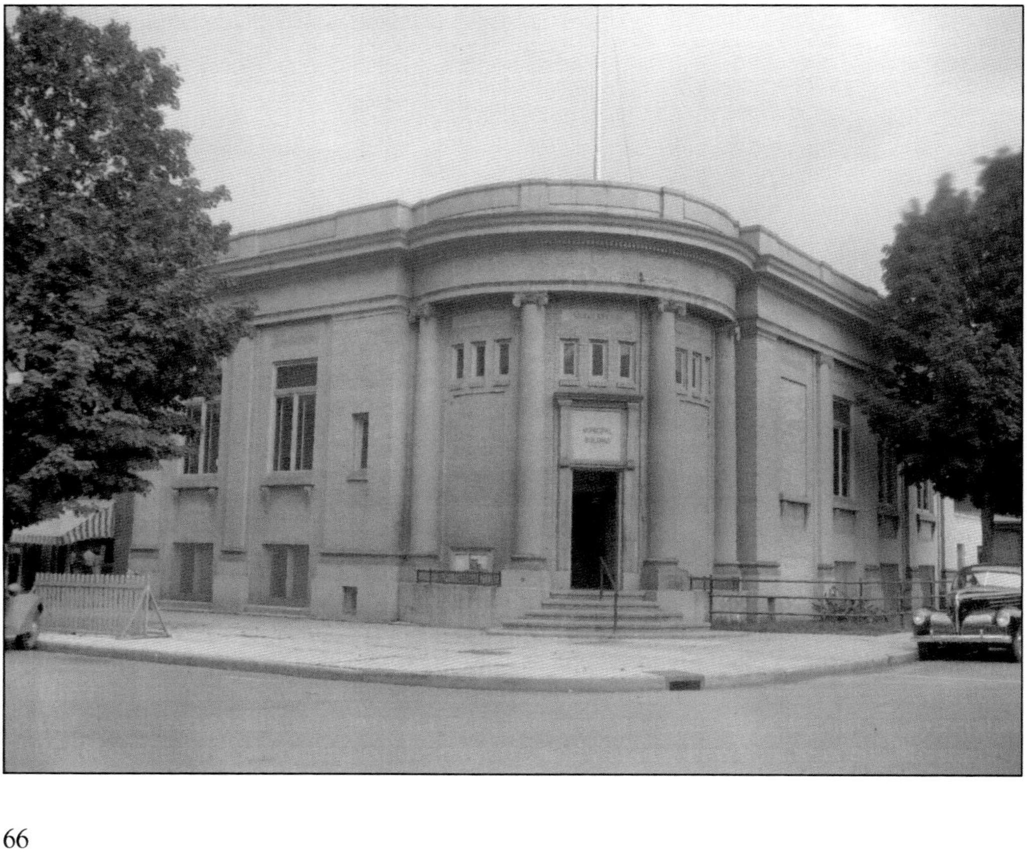

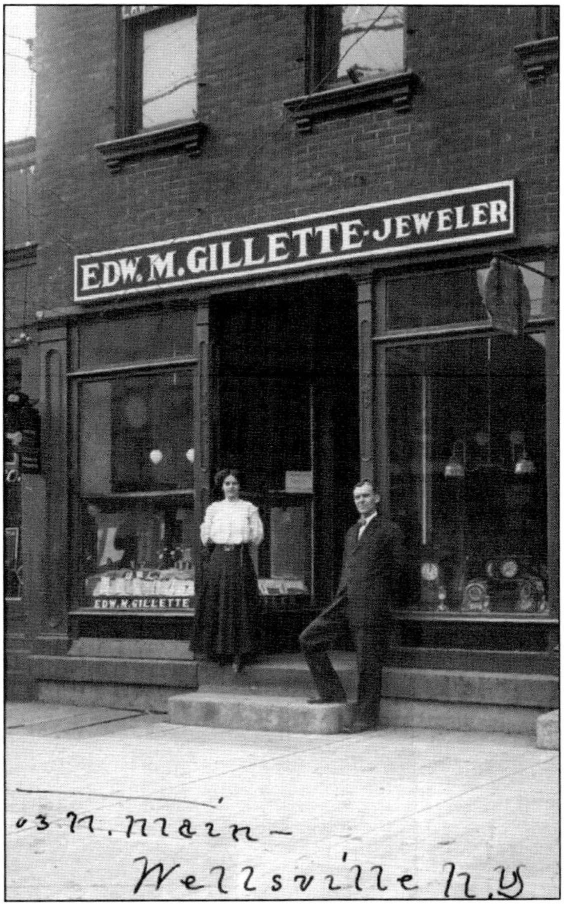

Edward M. Gillette purchased a jewelry store from Porter H. Torrey in 1909. He conducted the business for just a few years until his death in 1917. This store, at 103 North Main Street, was one of several cast-iron storefronts in the village that were manufactured by the McEwen Brothers shop in the early 1870s. Only two stores with cast-iron fronts now survive in the village; the second one is located across the street at 110 North Main Street. (Donald Baldwin.)

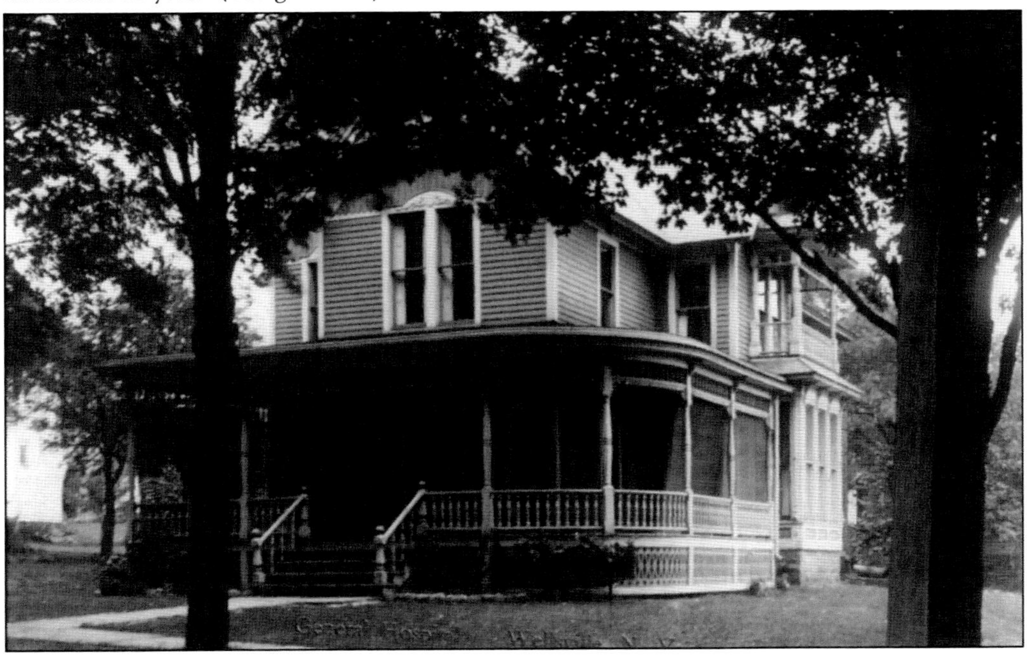

Wellsville's first hospital was opened in 1910 in a small house on Harder Place, but it quickly proved to be far too small. Within five months, patients were transferred to this house at 92 Jefferson Street. The Wellsville General Hospital was located here for at least 11 years. (Craig Braack.)

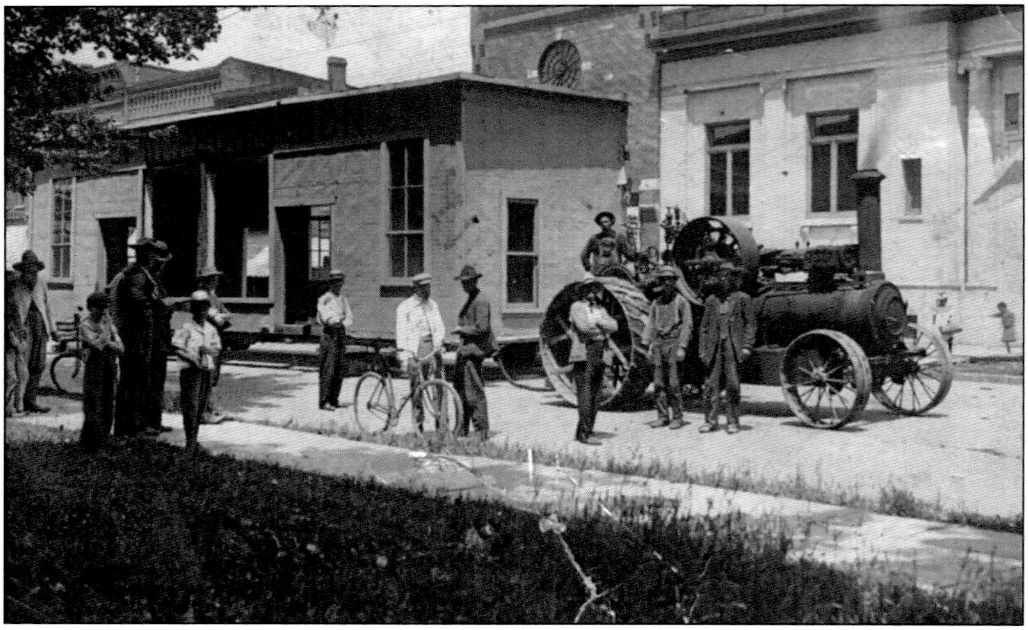

This photograph of the George Peck Monument Works building being moved down North Main Street has appeared in the newspaper and social media many times. In June 1910, the Erie Railroad required Peck's property for a new station. Peck purchased a new lot on the south side of the village and moved everything. Martin Moogan won the contract for the work, and Archie Knox drove his steam tractor. The photograph below shows the building after it was moved to the corner of South Main and Hanover Streets. (Above, Sandy Wright; below, Curt Crandall.)

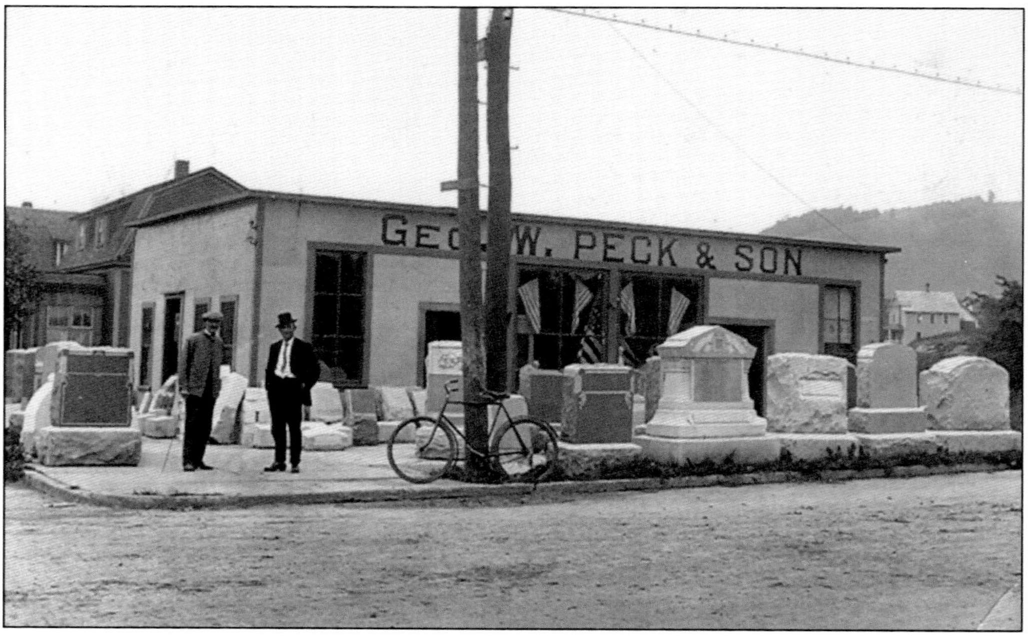

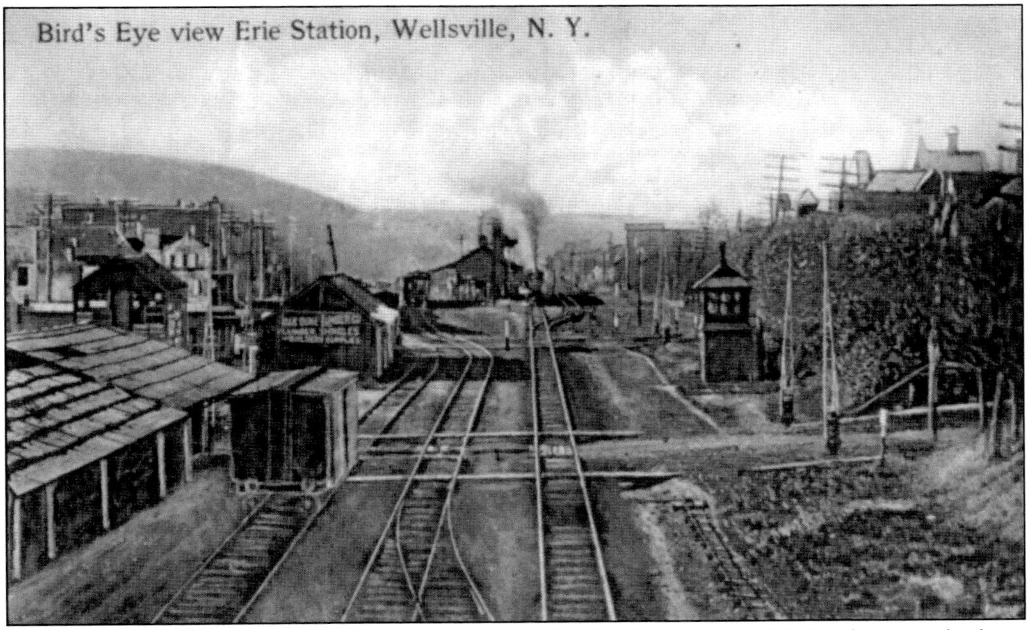

An old postcard shows the Erie Railroad tracks in Wellsville prior to 1910. In this view looking north from the Madison Street bridge, readers can see Jefferson Street crossing the tracks and a switch tower that controlled the gates for Jefferson Street and East Pearl Street. The Erie Station in this view was the old station at Central Place and Loder Street. (DAHPL.)

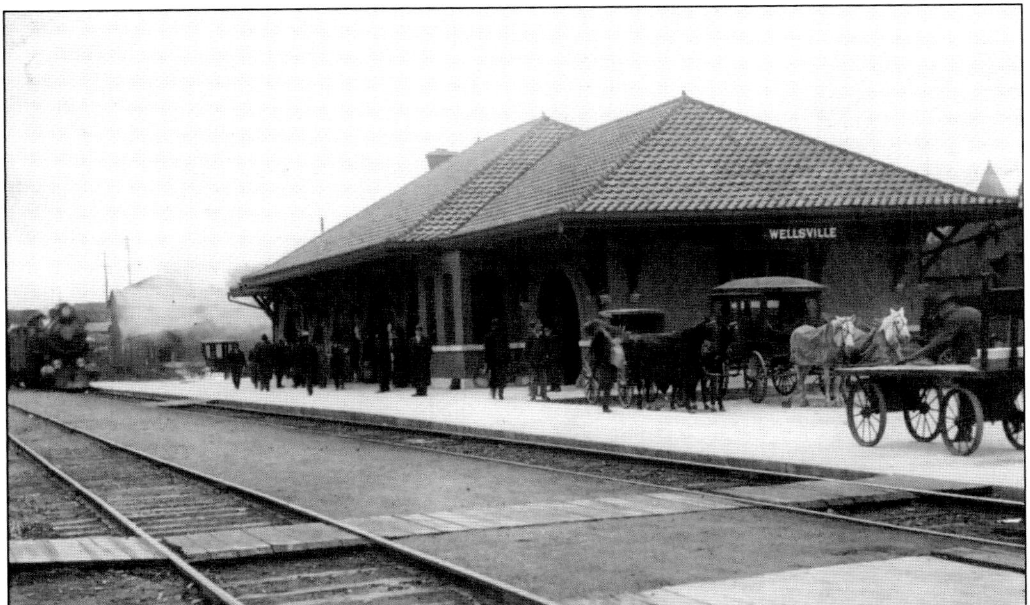

Businessmen of Wellsville lobbied the Erie Railroad for a new station for a number of years. The old station was just too outdated for a traveler's comfort, and it did not befit a busy village like Wellsville. The Erie would not place a station in this location unless the crossing for Jefferson Street was closed to all traffic, which the businessmen and the village legally did in February 1910. The Erie Railroad purchased the property, and the new Erie Station opened to traffic in September 1911. (James Dello.)

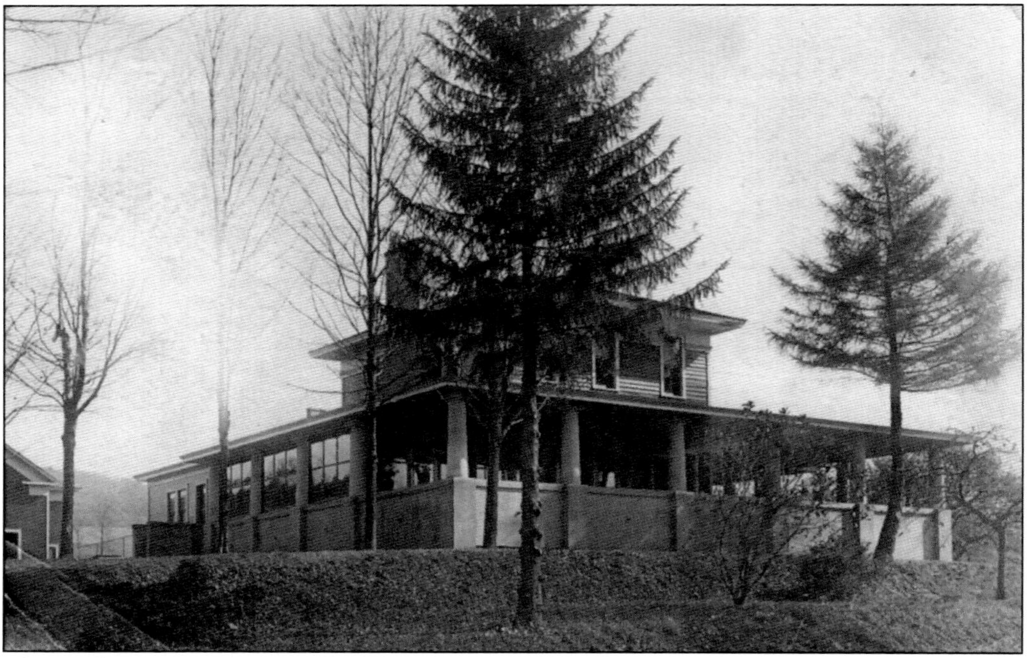

The Ambrose Coats house was purchased by the members of the new Wellsville Country Club in 1911. Club members added the large porches shown in this photograph almost immediately, and they quickly became a very popular place to hold a porch party or have a relaxing lunch. The porches were closed in by 1914, giving the members more room for dining and dancing. (James Dello.)

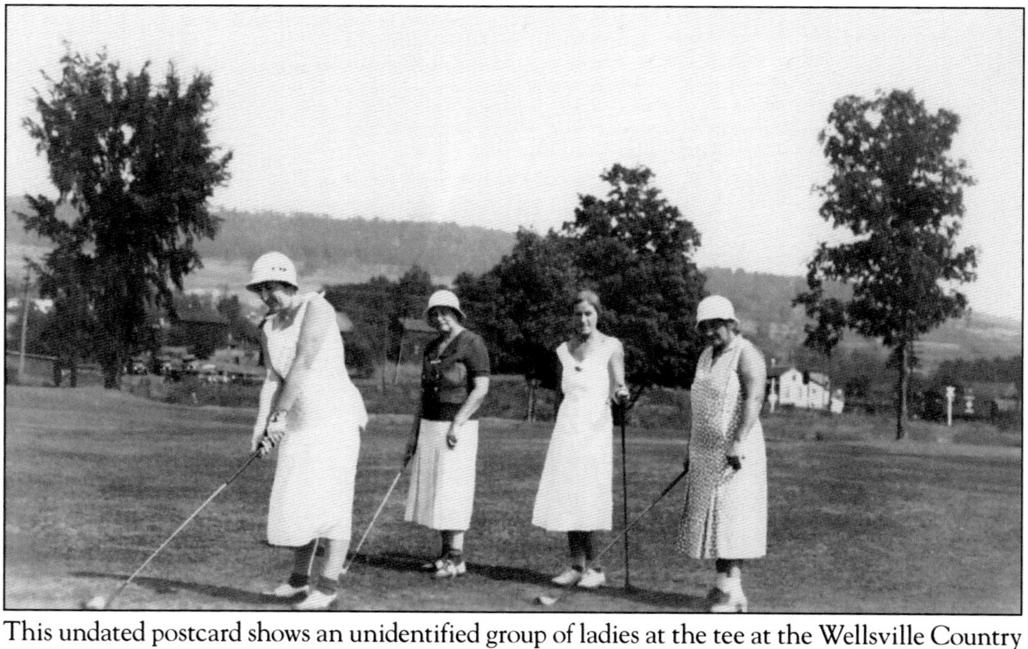

This undated postcard shows an unidentified group of ladies at the tee at the Wellsville Country Club. Behind them are the tracks of the Erie Railroad on Coats Street. (Ladies Golf Association of the Wellsville Country Club.)

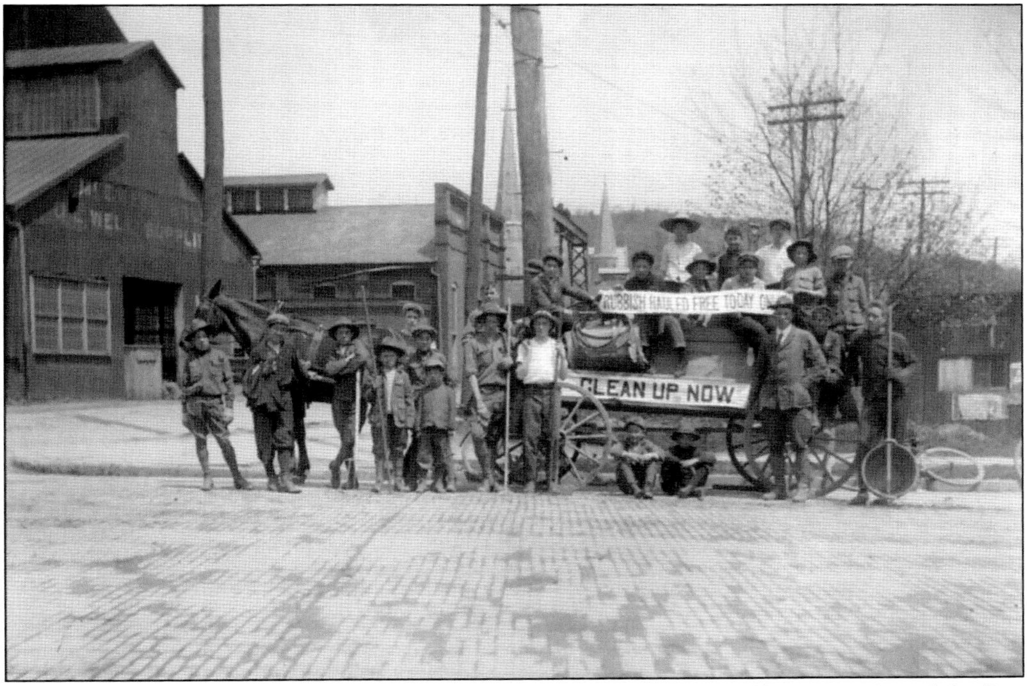

The Businessmen's Association started an annual cleanup day in the village in 1913, and the Boy Scouts played a major role. Under the direction of high school principal and Scoutmaster Ford R. Park, the boys were assigned specific streets to canvas to pick up rubbish that had been placed on the side of the road. The campaign was considered a huge success, thanks in large part to the hard work of Wellsville Boy Scout Troop No. 1. (David Brown.)

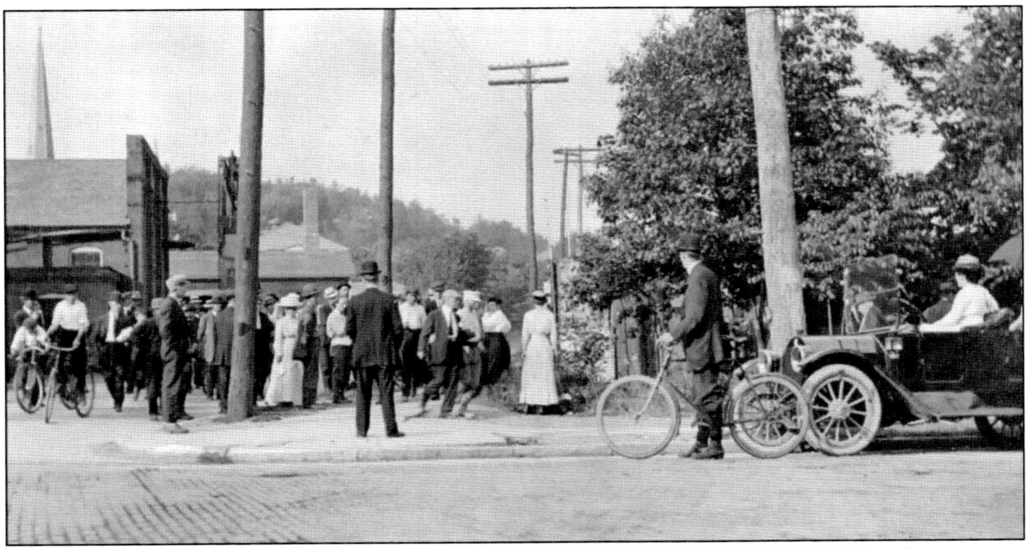

This photograph shows "Weston the Walker" as he enters Wellsville in June 1913 on his journey from New York to Minneapolis. Edward Payson Weston (shown here in a white kepi and light shirt) had been making long-distance walks since Lincoln's inaugural in 1861. This 1913 walk totaled 1,546 miles and was Weston's last national walk. Brought here by the Businessmen's Association, Weston entered Tullar field at the end of a baseball game, said a few quick words, and retired to his hotel room. (Craig Braack.)

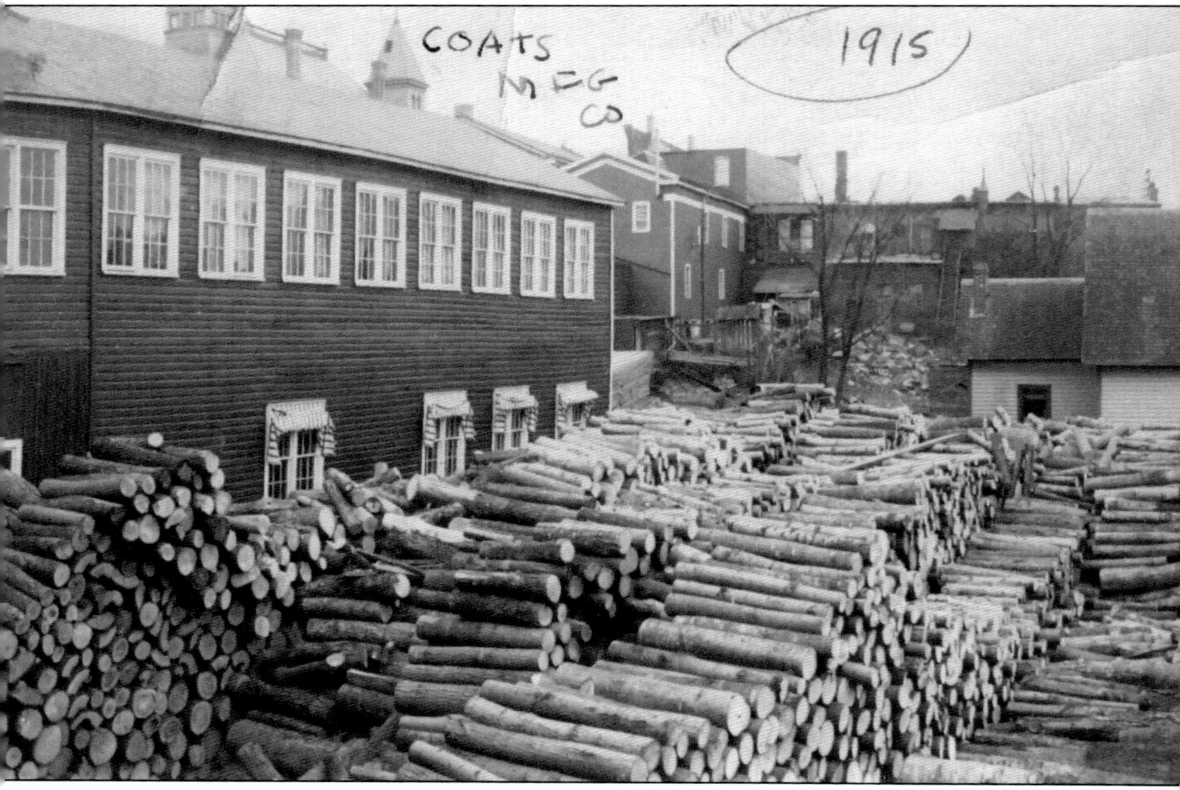

A group of investors purchased the Coats Cabinet Shop by 1915 and modernized the business. Furniture became mass-produced and was shipped out of the village by rail. At the top of this photograph, the towers of the old city hall building rise above the Coats Manufacturing plant. Lumber is stacked in the yard along River Street, which ran west from North Main Street to the Genesee River. The Louis G. Arnold Carriage and Blacksmith Shop, repaired after a fire in 1913,

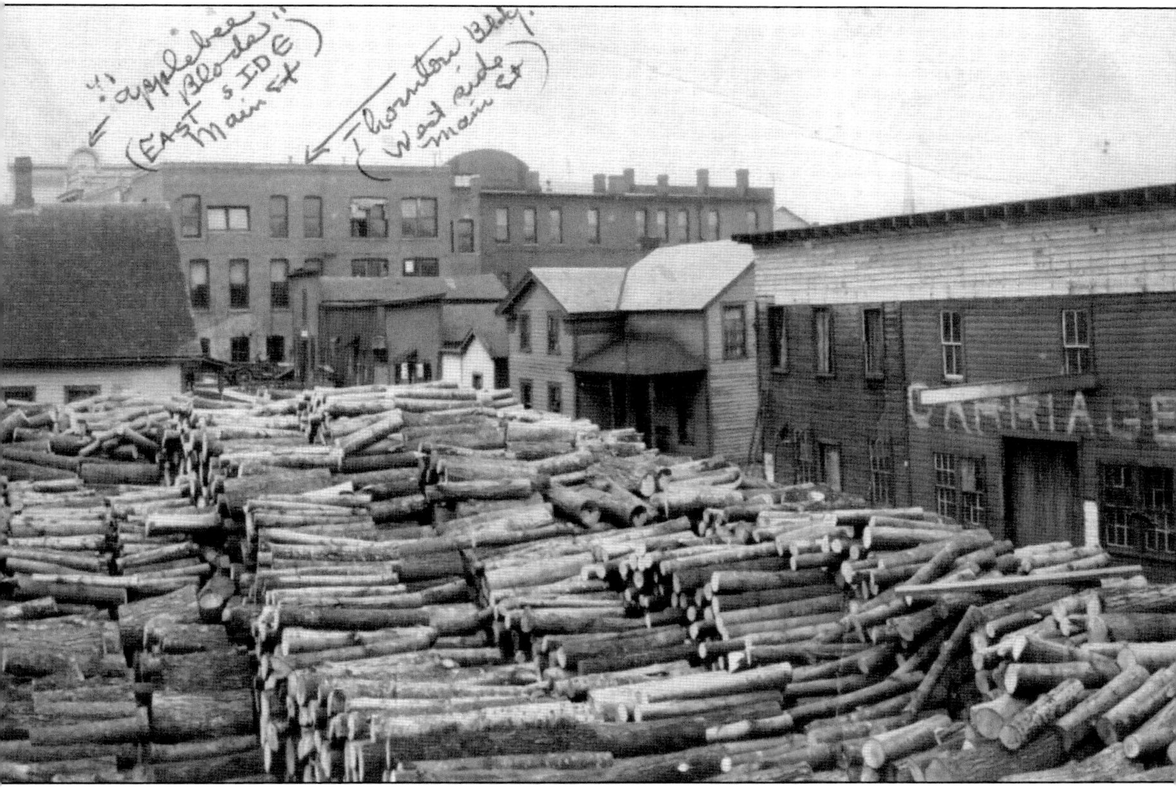

is shown on the bottom right of the photograph. A home that fronts on River Street appears to rise from the piles of lumber in the center of the photograph. Some smaller homes can be seen on the south side of River Street. The back of the Thornton Building on North Main Street appears at the top center of the photograph, much as it looks today. (Donald Baldwin.)

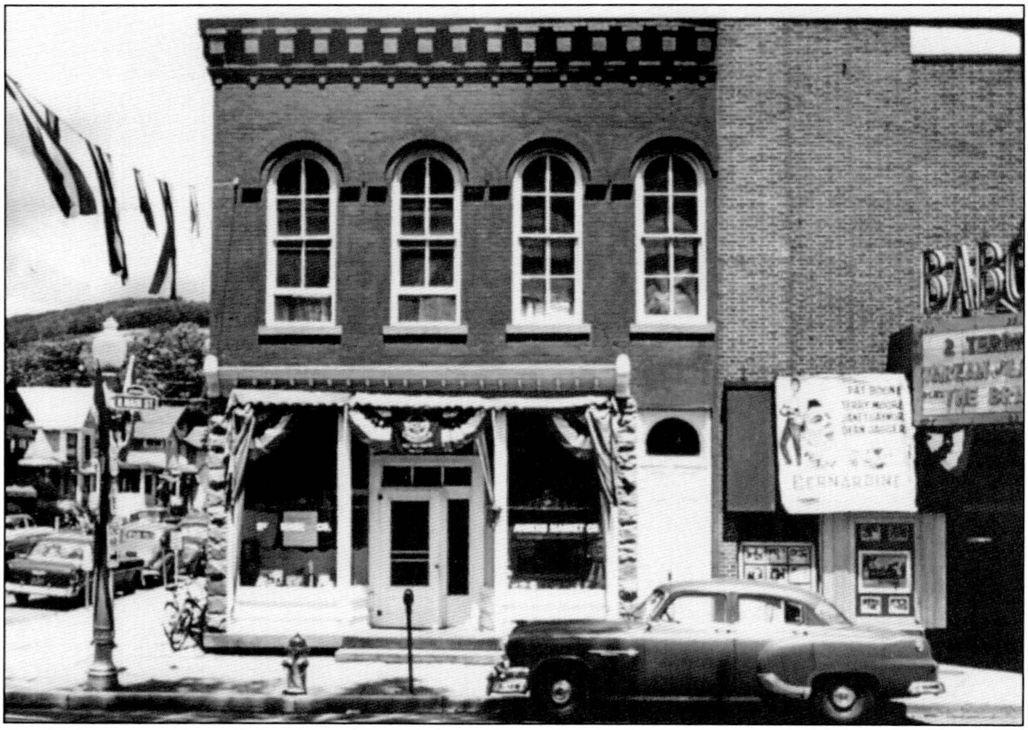

Fred Ahrens purchased the Beever Brothers Meat market at the corner of North Main and Jefferson Streets in 1911. About 1915, T. Morton Halladay began working at the market. Halladay served in World War I and, upon his return, married Grace Ahrens, Fred's daughter. Halladay ran the business at 148 North Main Street until he sold the building in 1959. (Clair Heysham.)

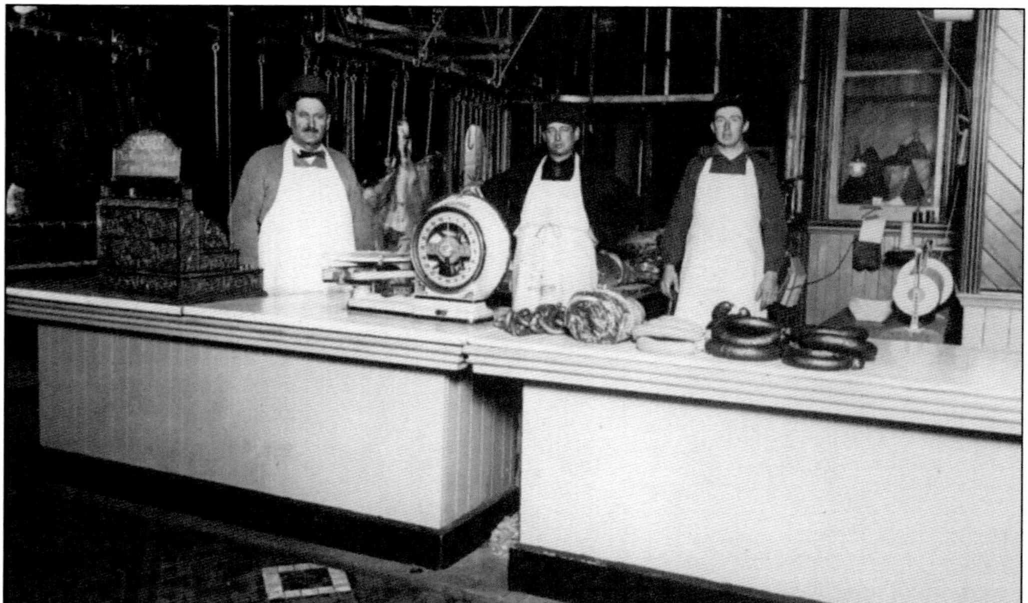

Fred Ahrens (left), T. Morton Halliday (center), and William Brennan stand behind the counter of Ahrens Meat Market store in 1915. (Clair Heysham.)

Four

1915 TO 1950

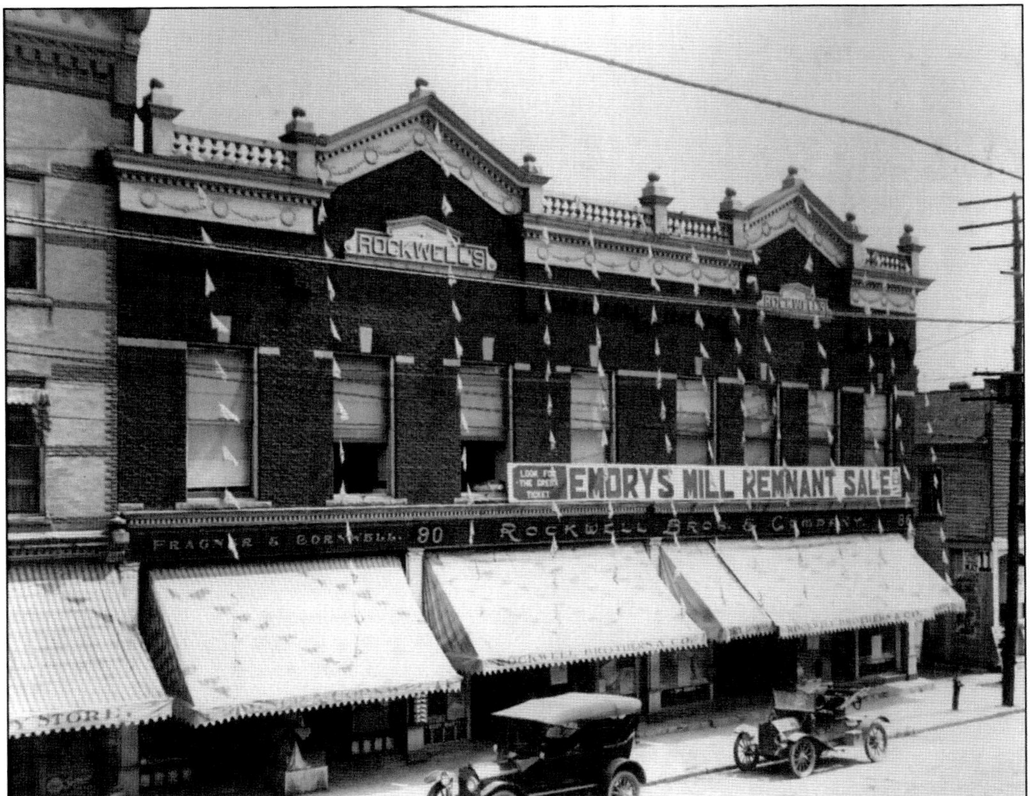

The Rockwell brothers were associated with the firm of M.A. Tuttle and Company when they first came to Wellsville in 1881. The name of the store was changed to Rockwell Brothers in 1885. Hobart and Lemuel Rockwell erected their own building in 1897 at 86–88 North Main Street, and expanded it in 1902. The brothers planned on renting part of the store to another business until they needed the space themselves. In this 1915 photograph, the Rockwell Brothers store shares the building with Fragner & Cornwell. (Robert Sweet.)

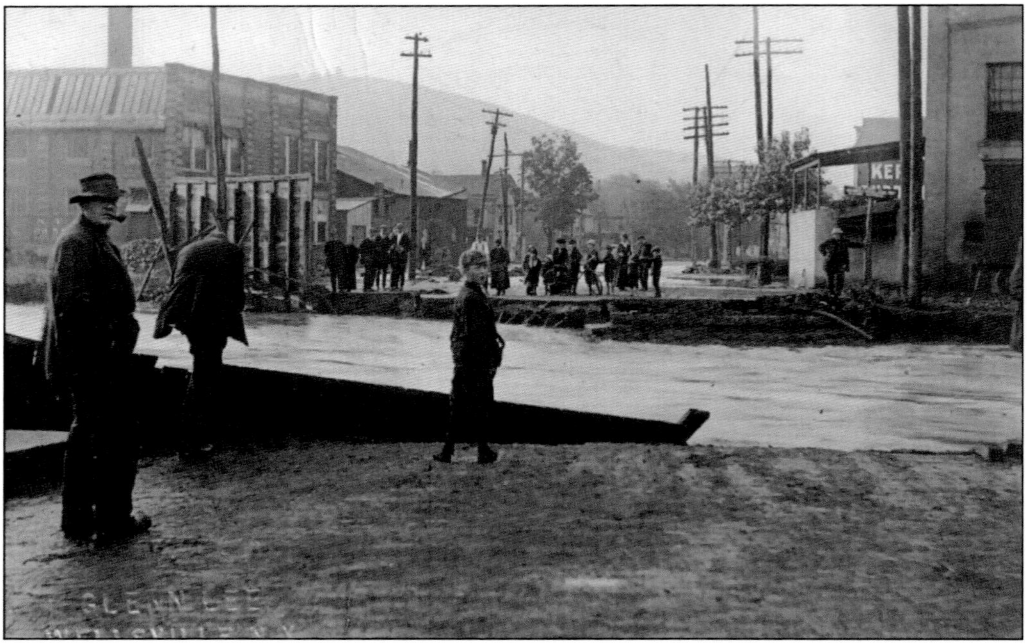

People in Wellsville were awakened in the early morning of June 17, 1916, by an alarm rung by the water and light department. The houses of the Ward Annex, as well as those on Chamberlain Street, West Dyke Street, and West State Street, were in danger of flooding. The bridge over Dyke's Creek at South Main Street was washed away. It was not until a year later that the village voted to replace it. (Craig Braack.)

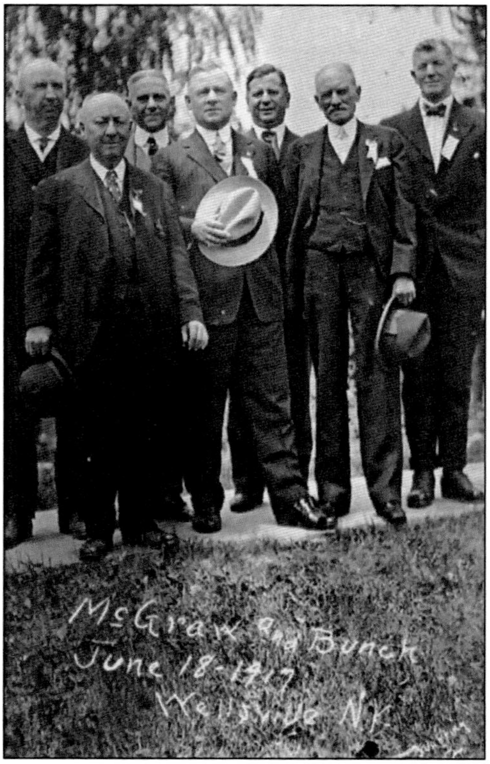

A very young John J. McGraw joined the Wellsville Tanbarks baseball team as player/manager in 1890. That year, the Tanbarks won the Western New York League pennant, thanks largely to McGraw's management. McGraw went on to national fame as the manager of the New York Giants. Wellsville baseball officials were successful in bringing McGraw and the New York Giants to Wellsville for an exhibition game on June 18, 1917. In this photograph, Tanbark teammates and Wellsville baseball officials pose at the Wellsville Country Club prior to the game. Pictured are, from left to right, former teammate George "Hoss" Carpenter, former manager Thomas O'Connor, Fred Bixbie, McGraw, Ed Rathbone, baseball fan James Macken, and former teammate Pat "Red" Moran. (Donald Baldwin.)

Citizens of Wellsville responded well to the call to buy bonds during World War I. This float was engineered by the War Committee of Wellsville to boost sales of Liberty bonds in 1918. Pulled through the streets by a Cleveland tractor loaned by the Duke Motor Company, the float shows a tank with guns protruding from the windows. The men are with the State Guard and are accompanied by Wellsville's cannon, the same one that resides in Memorial Park. (Christina Wightman.)

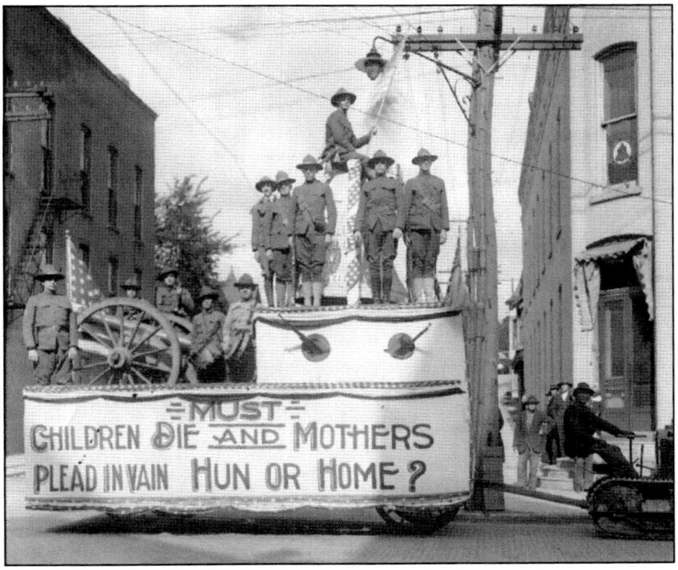

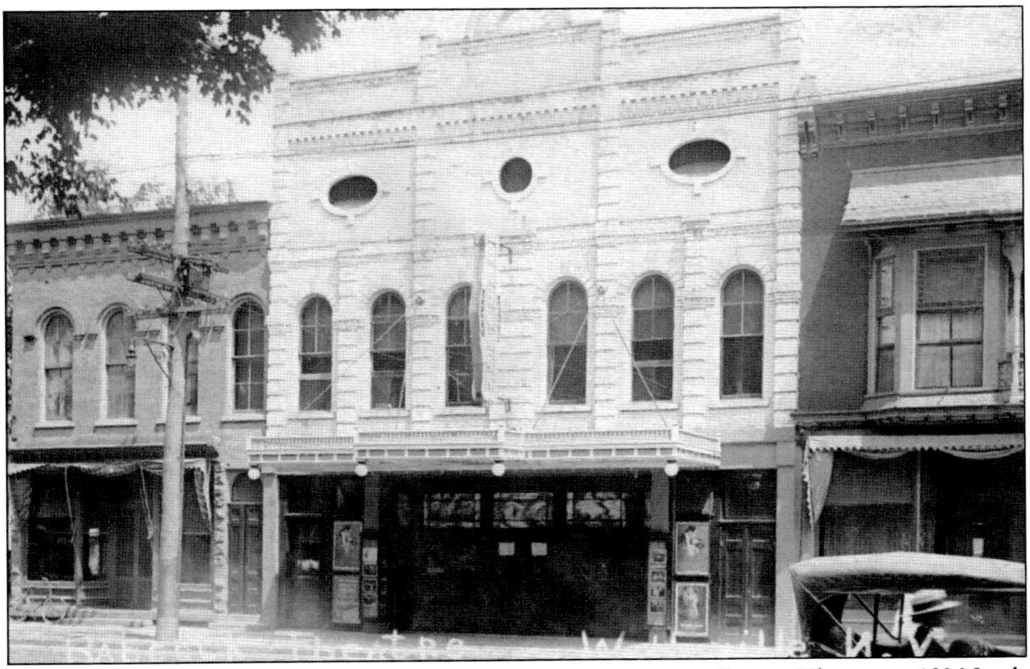

Charles Babcock came to Wellsville in 1914 as manager of the small Lyric Theatre at 132 North Main Street, but he soon developed plans for a theater on a grander scale. Babcock purchased two existing buildings just a few doors north of the Lyric and completely renovated them into a theater fit for the new age of talking pictures. The Babcock Theatre opened its doors on April 21, 1919.

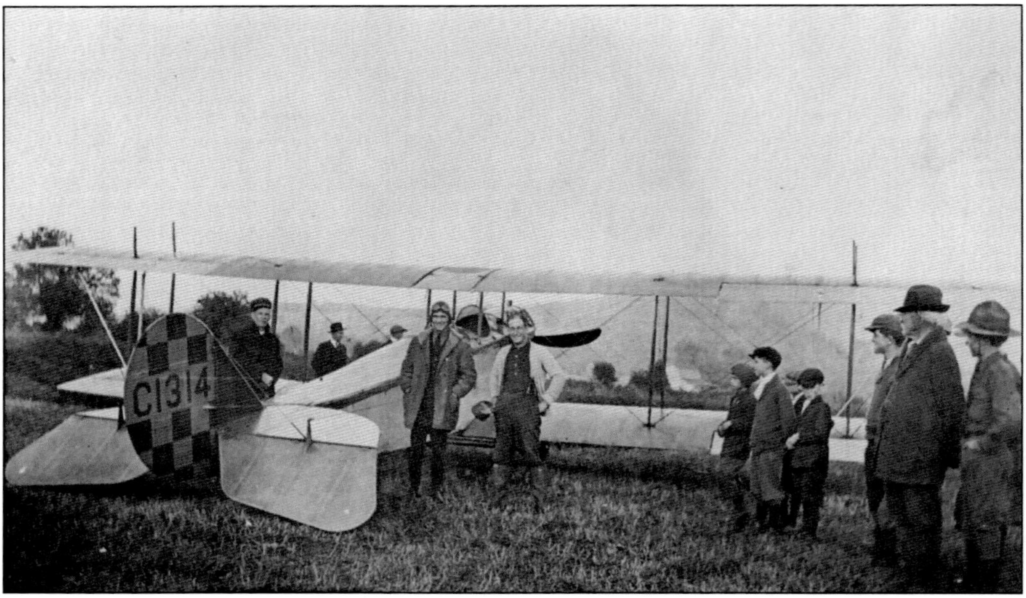

Randall P. Ellis set his Curtiss aircraft down on the George Bowlby farm in the Proctor District on Friday, September 12, 1919. Ellis was flying from Buffalo to Reading, Pennsylvania, but started out just a little too late in the day. He was following railroad tracks for navigation and needed to set the plane down as he was losing light. Before Ellis left the next day, he took several paying customers up for a whirlwind tour of Wellsville. Alva York, Edward Duke, and a Mr. Kemp all paid $25 for a ride.

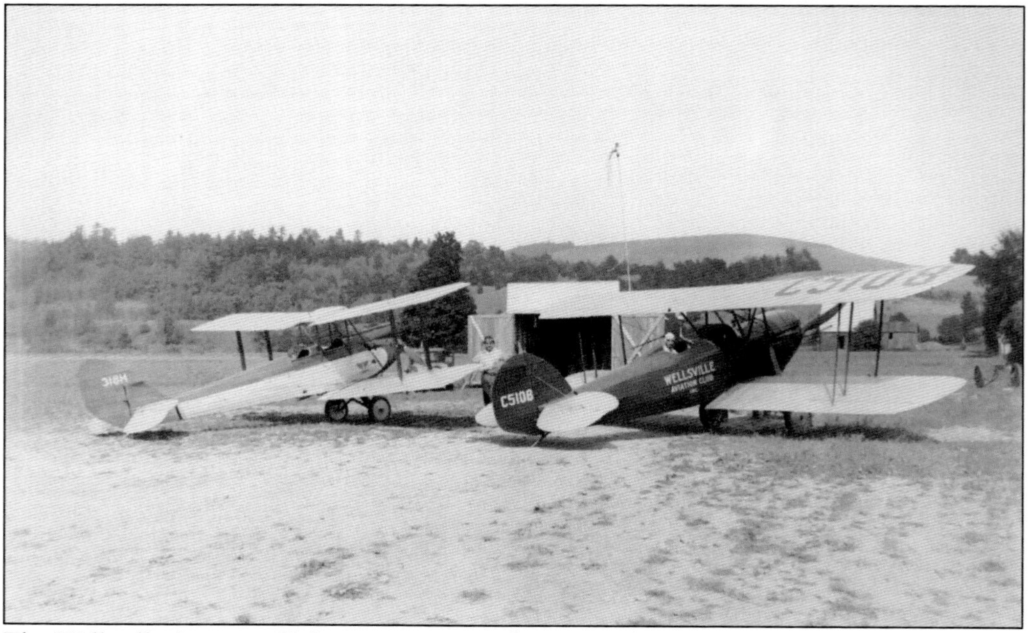

The Wellsville Aviation Club was incorporated in 1928, the year it purchased its first WACO airplane. Pilot John J. Grady (in the cockpit on the right) brought the plane to Wellsville from Troy, Ohio, landing on the Bierman farm, off Stannards Road south of the village. J. Farnum Brown, a member of the aviation club, is shown in the cockpit on the left. An unidentified aviator is in the center.

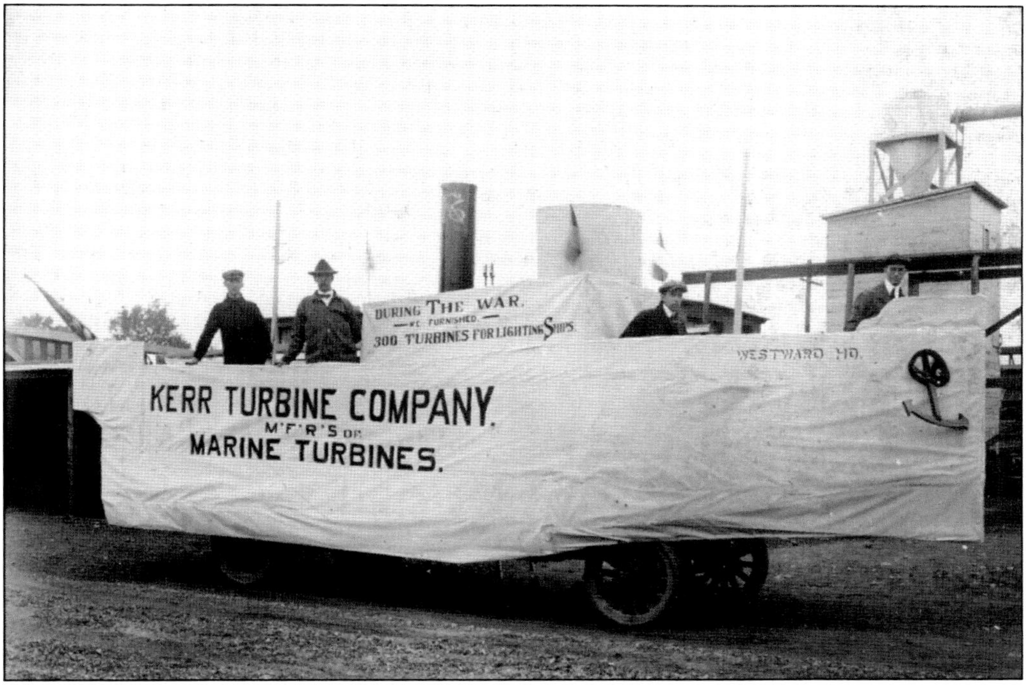

Kerr Turbine employees organized a float for an Armistice Day parade in Wellsville in 1920. This float, in the shape of a ship, heralds Kerr's wartime efforts in manufacturing 300 turbines used to power the electrical plants aboard Navy ships.

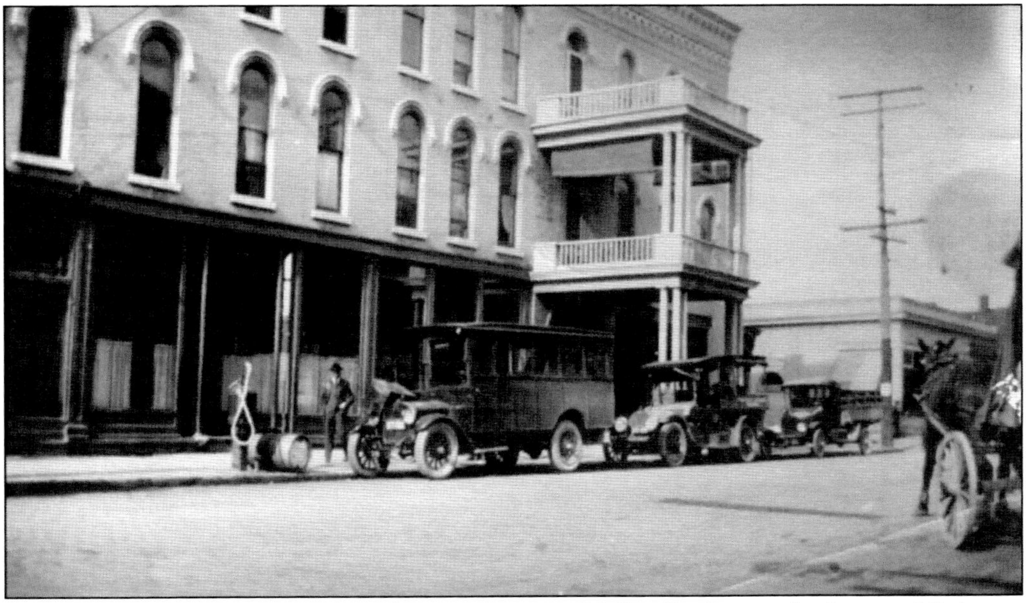
A motor bus company planned regular trips between Wellsville, Stannards, Scio, and Belmont in 1914, but the operators soon learned that they could not operate the bus on the muddy roads beyond Scio and amended their schedule to eliminate the Belmont stop. The Alfred Red Bus Line, shown in front of the Fassett Hotel around 1917, made the trip from Wellsville through Andover, Alfred, and on to Hornell every day except Sunday. In this photograph, the buses are awaiting passengers, as well as a full tank of gas.

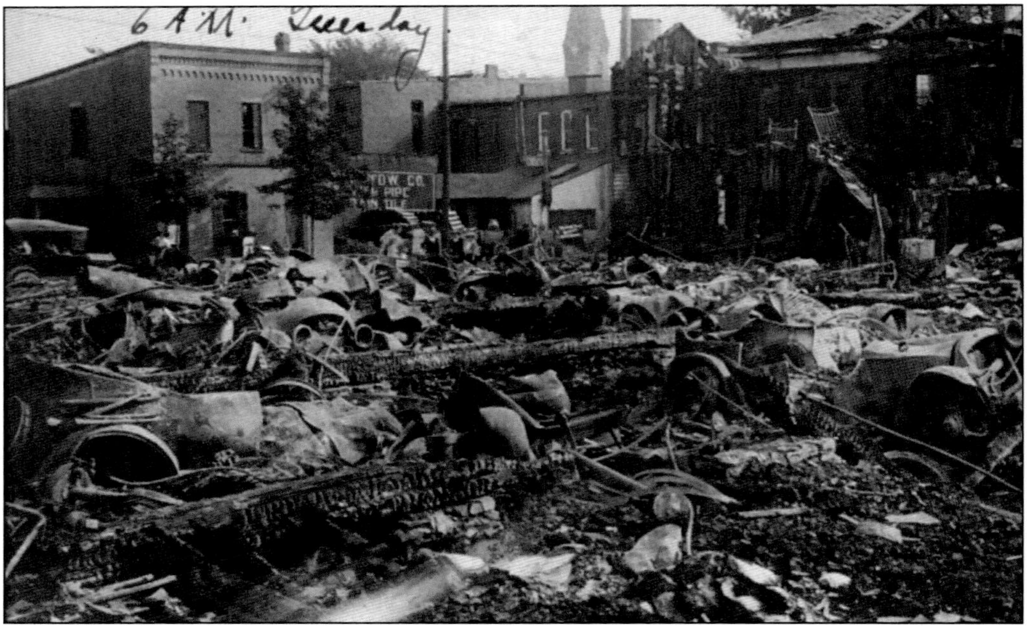

The Duke Motor Car Company was located on the corner of East Pearl and Loder Streets. In the early morning of August 24, 1921, an alarm was called in that the structure was in flames. Volunteers reached the building quickly, but the wood and gasoline of the garage served to fuel the fire. The blaze left 16 families homeless and destroyed 18 buildings before the flames were finally extinguished. (George Duke.)

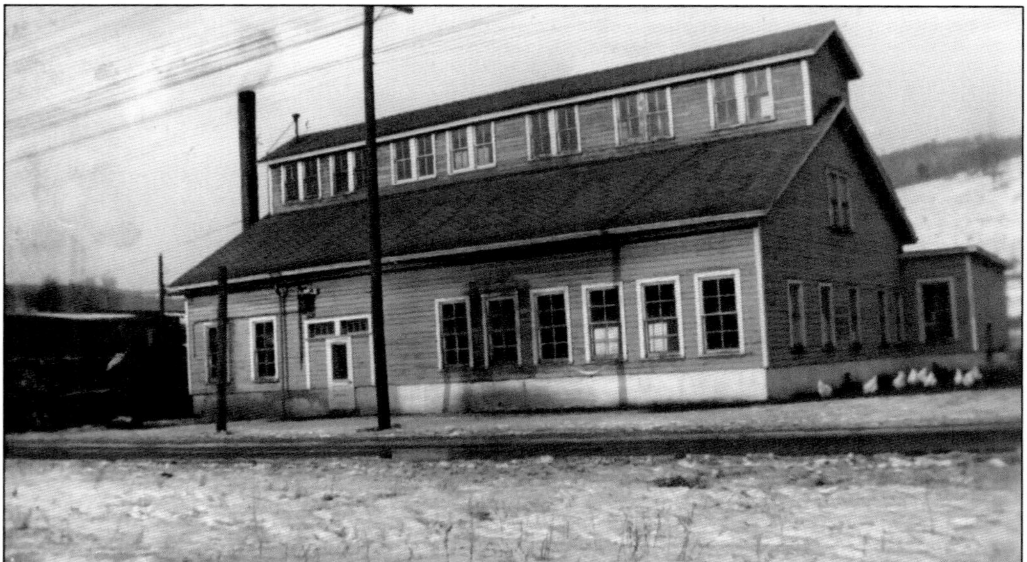

The Borden Company purchased land on Railroad Avenue to build a milk-receiving plant in 1916. Tensions were high between Borden and dairy farmers at that time, with the dairymen uniting to fight a perceived lack of control over their product. It was not until 1923 that Borden erected the Wellsville Receiving and Cooling Plant. This plant collected milk and sent it via train to Belmont for processing there. In 1951, James Gardner of the Gardner Pattern Works purchased this property, and the building housed his business for many years.

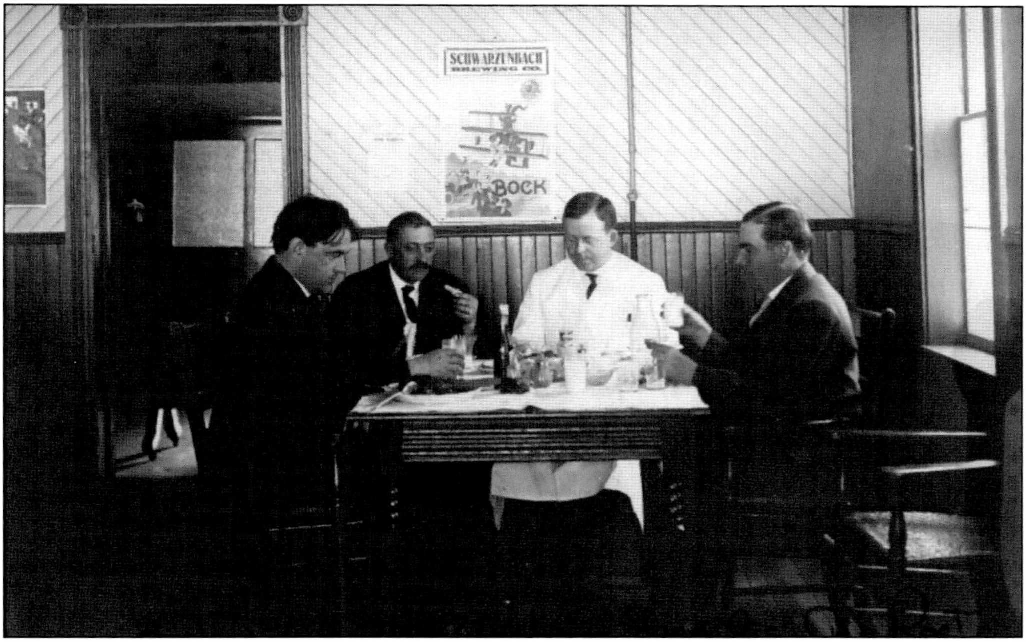

Friends meet for an informal lunch in a back room of the Fassett Hotel on North Main Street. Shown, from left to right, are Bayard C. Tullar, Midge Williams of Bolivar, Farnum Gee, and Asa W. Root of Bolivar. Gee, whose parents owned a hotel in Willing, New York, was associated with the Fassett Hotel for many years, becoming owner of the building in 1919 and retiring from the business in the mid-1940s. (James Dello.)

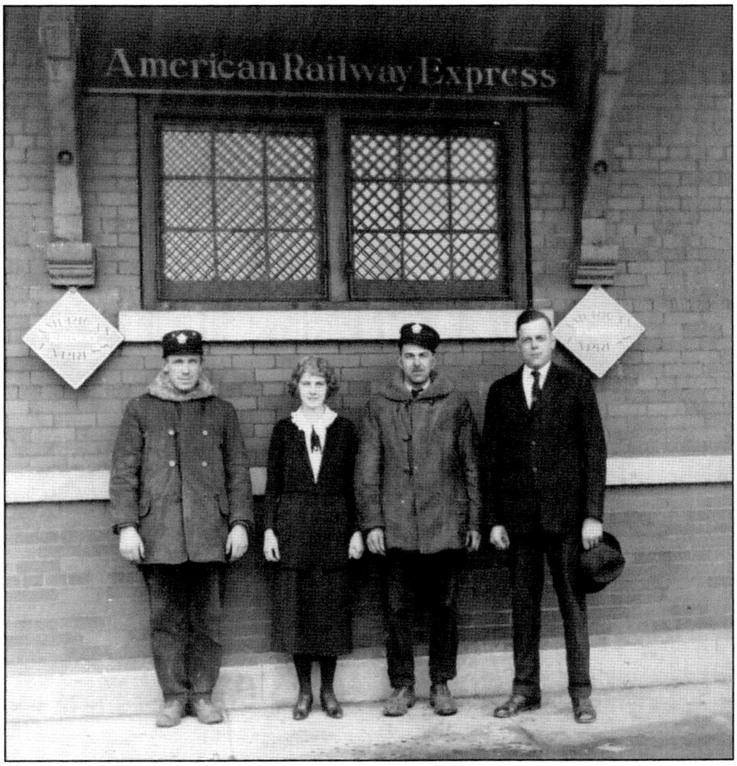

Wells Fargo Express became known as American Railway Express in 1918. Joe Kralinger, a longtime employee of Wells Fargo, was named manager of the Wellsville office. All express delivery services were handled from the Erie Station. This photograph shows employees of the American Railway Express in Wellsville on the south side of the Erie Station. They are, from left to right, are Merl Bissell, Genevieve Andrews, Charles Frank, and Joseph Kralinger. (Mather Homestead.)

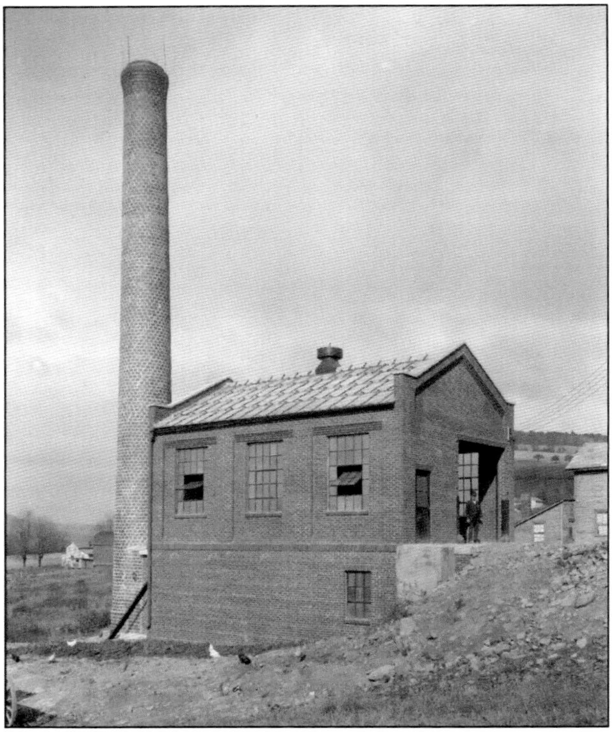

The Wellsville Incinerator was built in 1926 to accommodate the growing disposal needs of the village. Located at 475 Scott Avenue, the incinerator was constructed by the Dayton Corporation and operated until the 1960s. (Kristin Kruger.)

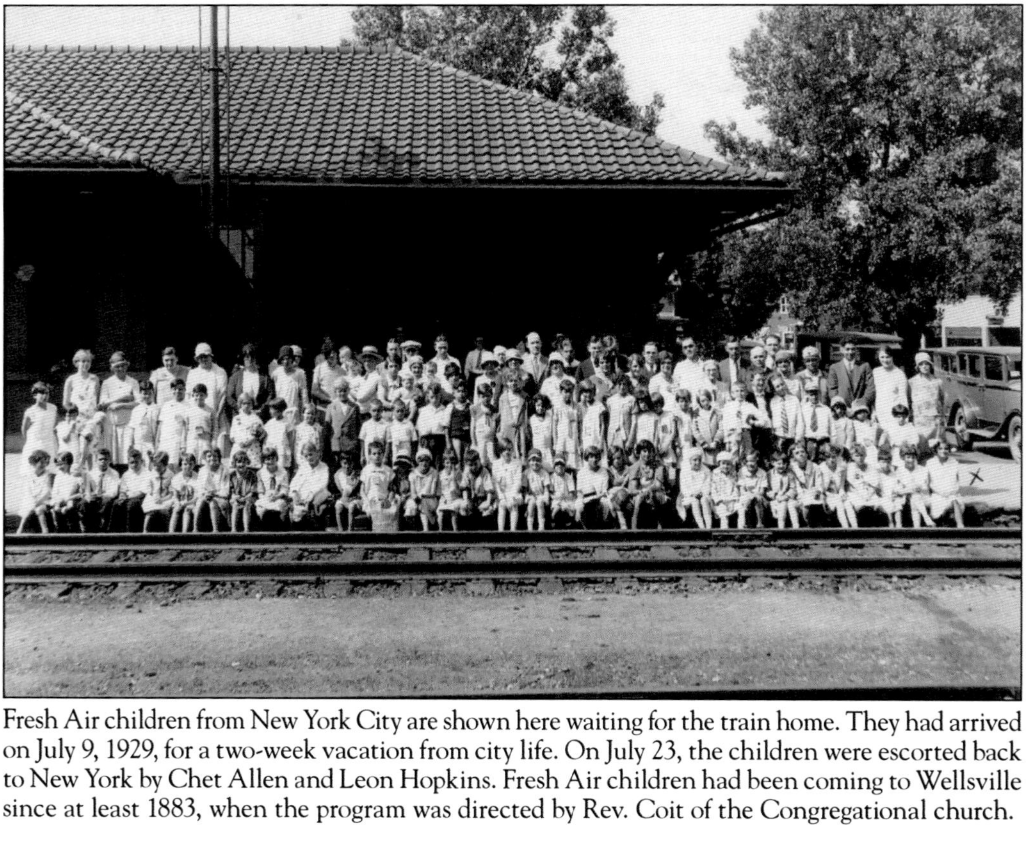

Fresh Air children from New York City are shown here waiting for the train home. They had arrived on July 9, 1929, for a two-week vacation from city life. On July 23, the children were escorted back to New York by Chet Allen and Leon Hopkins. Fresh Air children had been coming to Wellsville since at least 1883, when the program was directed by Rev. Coit of the Congregational church.

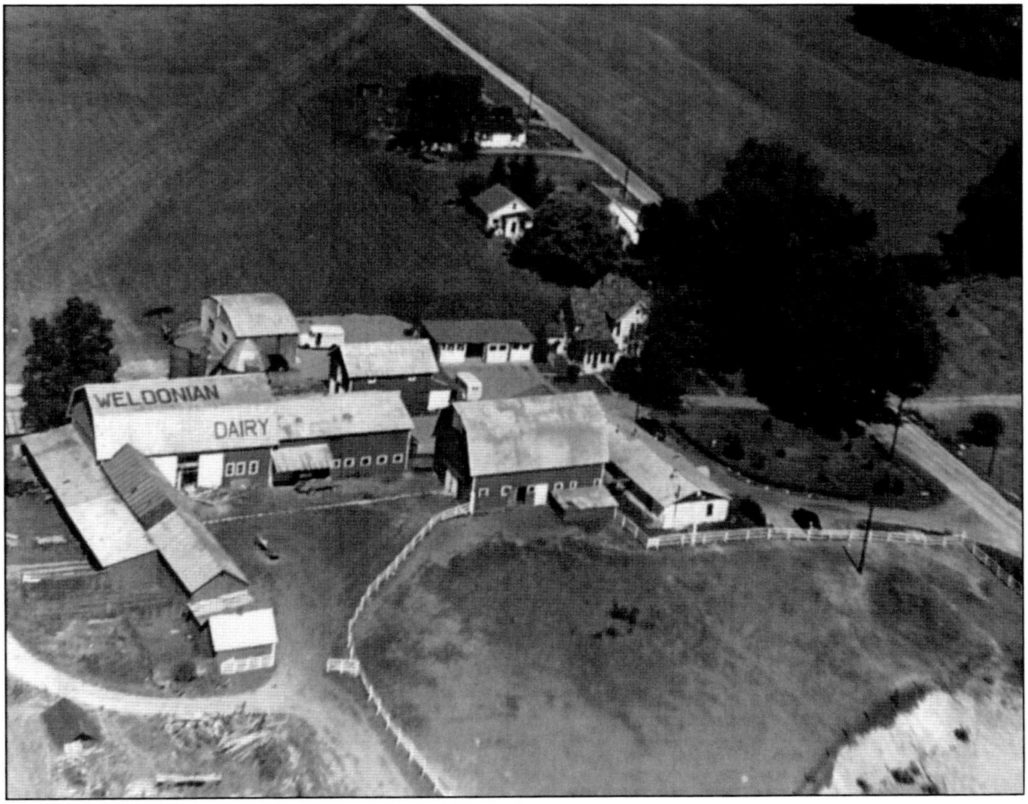

John and Jennie Phillips purchased the Charles Vincent farm on the Brimmer Brook Road (Phillips Road) and established the Weldonian Dairy, named for their home in Weldon, England. The Weldonian Dairy merged with the Minges Dairy in 1967 and ceased operations here shortly after that time. The undated photograph below shows a Weldonian Dairy Truck and unidentified driver around 1935. (Below, Nancy Crowell Cotoia.)

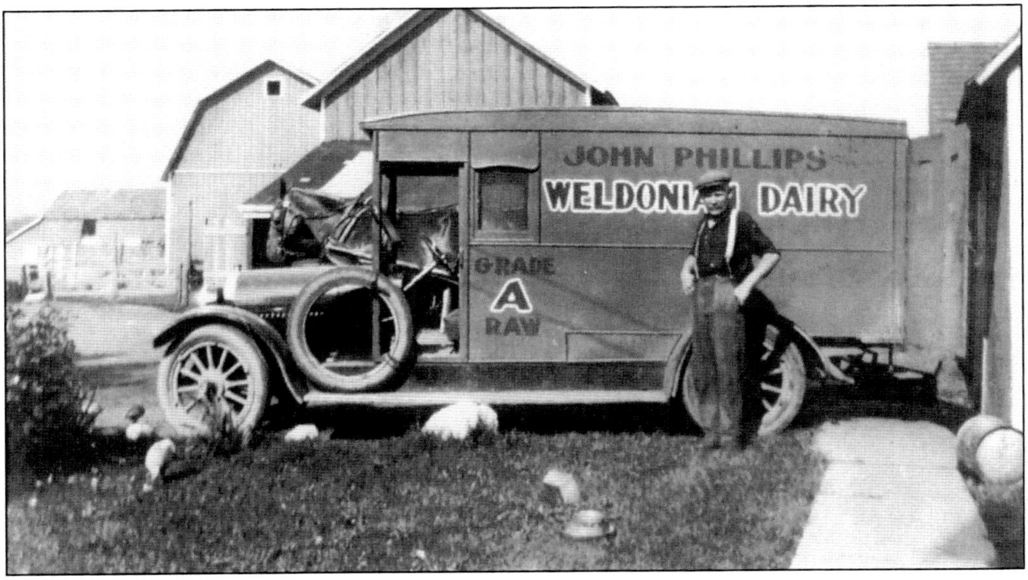

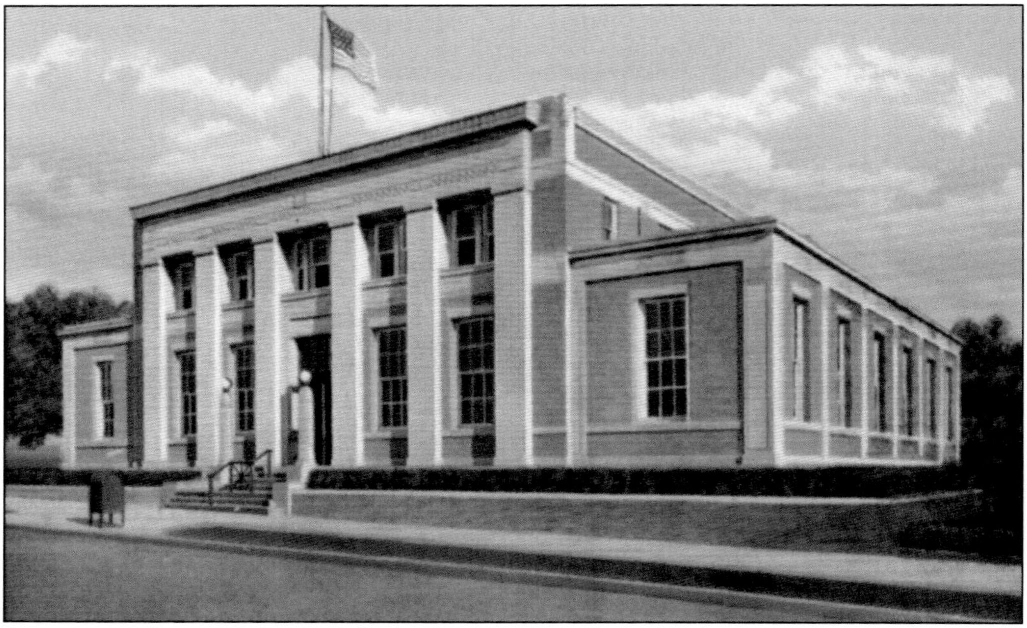

Postmaster Julius H. Fisher had the honor of overseeing Wellsville's first federal building. The structure was designed by architect Walter B. Olmsted and constructed during the Depression through a public works initiative. The building contains beautiful bas-relief panels and furniture designed by sculptor H.K. Bush-Brown. In 1989, the Wellsville Post Office, along with 143 other post offices across the state of New York, was named to the National Register of Historic Places.

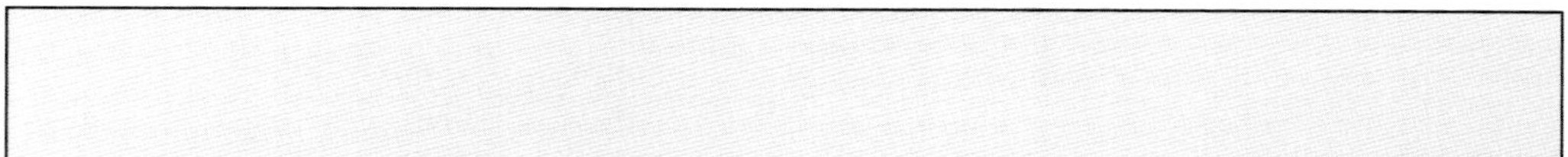

Wellsville postmaster Carl N. Marshall participated in National Air Mail Week in May 1938 when he prepared almost 2,000 letters for air transport to Buffalo by Wellsville pilot George A. Harris. The trip was sponsored by the Wellsville Philatelic Society. Pilot Harris left Wellsville at 12:22 p.m. during a light rain and landed at Buffalo 53 minutes later, completing the delivery of Wellsville's first airmail. (Kristin Kruger.)

The Bradley Producing Company conducted oil operations in the area for many years. Floyd Crowner worked for Bradley Producing in the maintenance and repair of oil wells. Crowner (fourth from the left in white sleeves) poses here with a crew in this 1936 photograph by Al Nordin.

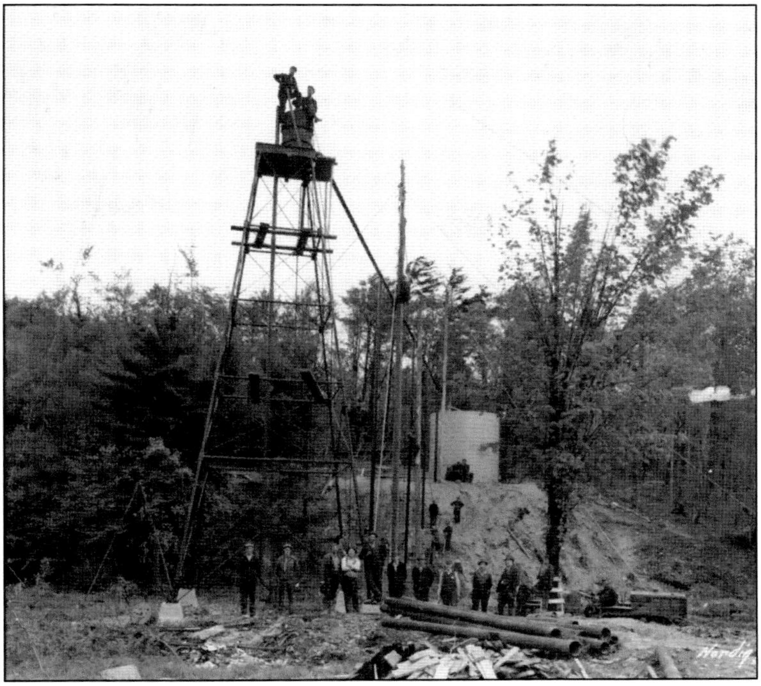

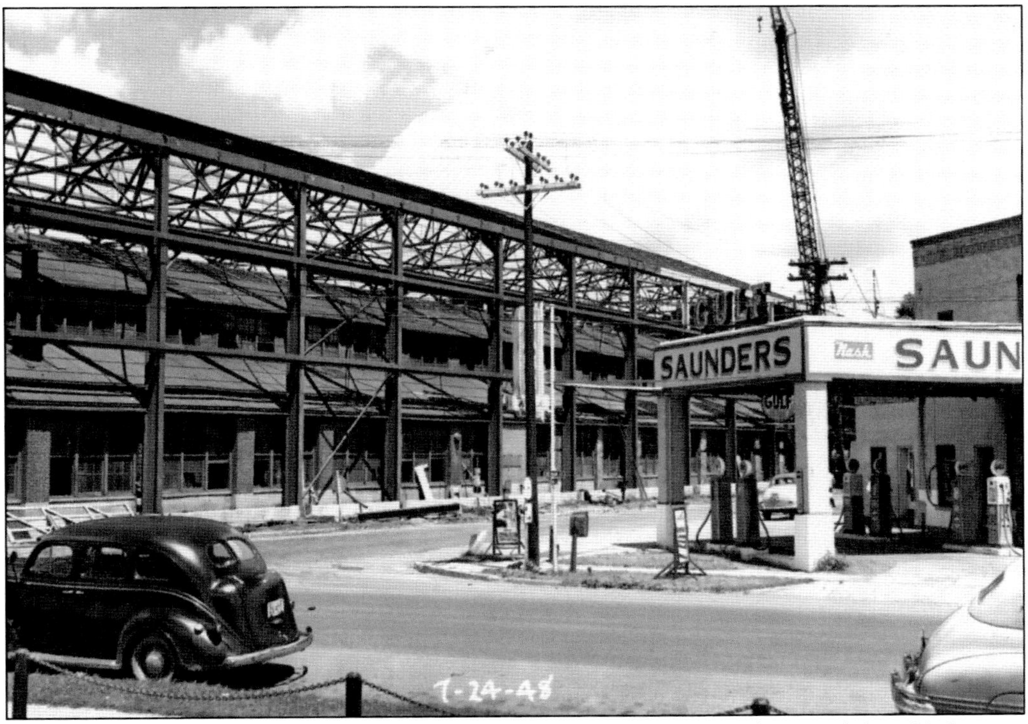

The Air Preheater Corporation erected a new building to replace and expand the old shop on the corner of East Dyke Street and South Main Street in 1947. Steel framing was built around the existing shop and offices, then metal siding was installed to close in the building. When the new structure was completed, the old shop building was then taken down. The heavy workload in the shop was not interrupted during the construction and demolition.

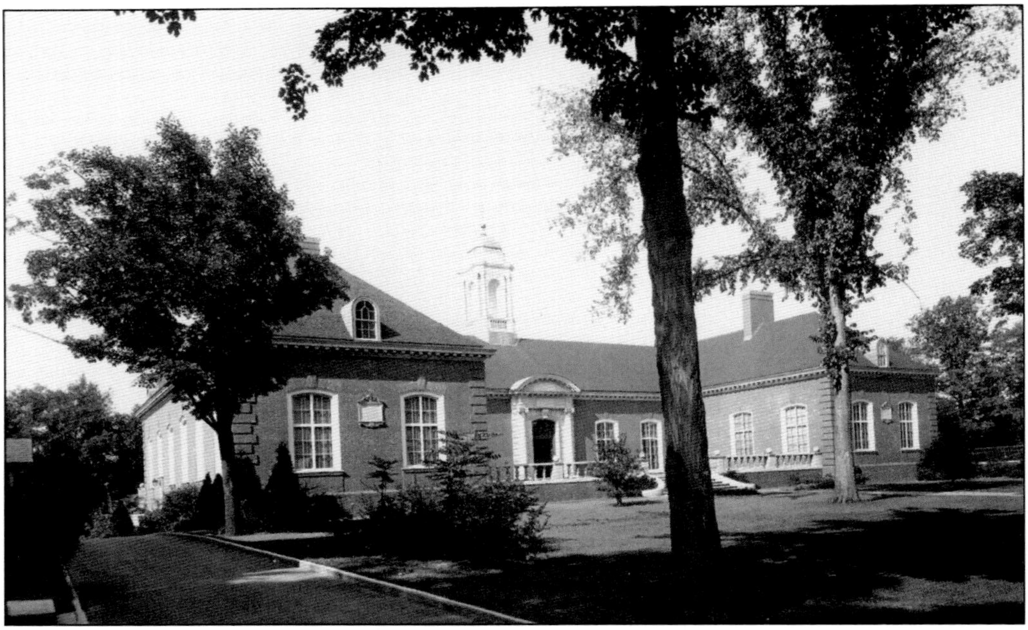

David A. Howe, benefactor of Wellsville's first library, planned another gift for Wellsville. He kept an eye on the old library, quietly funding it when necessary, and understood that a larger facility was needed. Upon his death in 1925, it was announced that he had left another generous donation to Wellsville, which would allow a larger David A. Howe Library to be built. The new library was constructed across the street from the old facility and was dedicated in 1937.

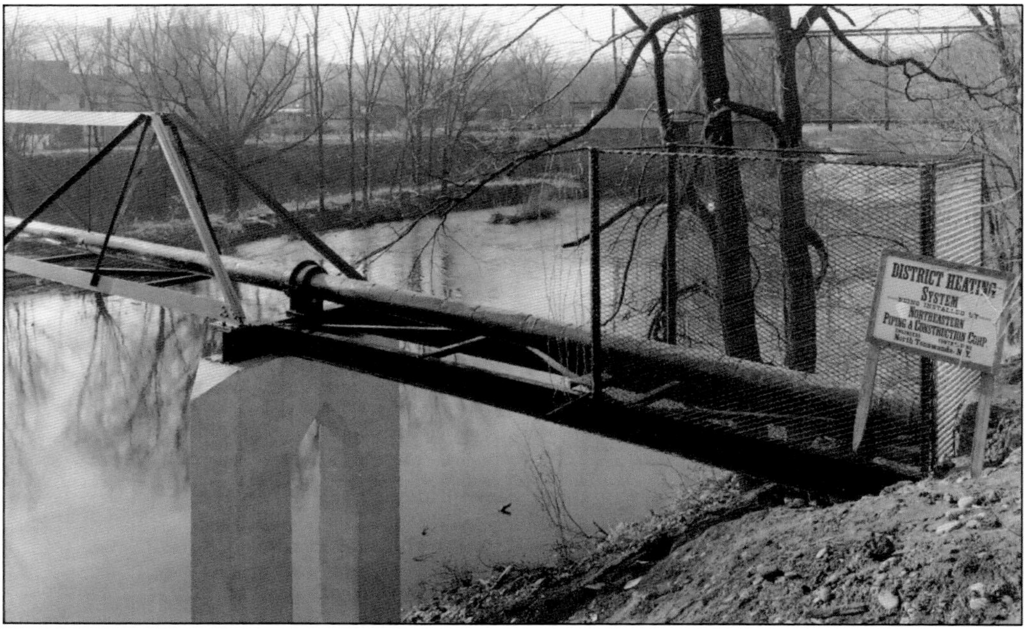

Steam lines were laid from the water-and-light facility to a few public institutions in 1927 to use the excess steam the plant was producing. The new high school was heated with steam, as were the hospital and the old Congregational church. In 1937, the new David A. Howe Library was supplied with steam heat. Steam lines to the library crossed the river just south of the old Pearl Street bridge, which can be seen in the background. (Christina Wightman.)

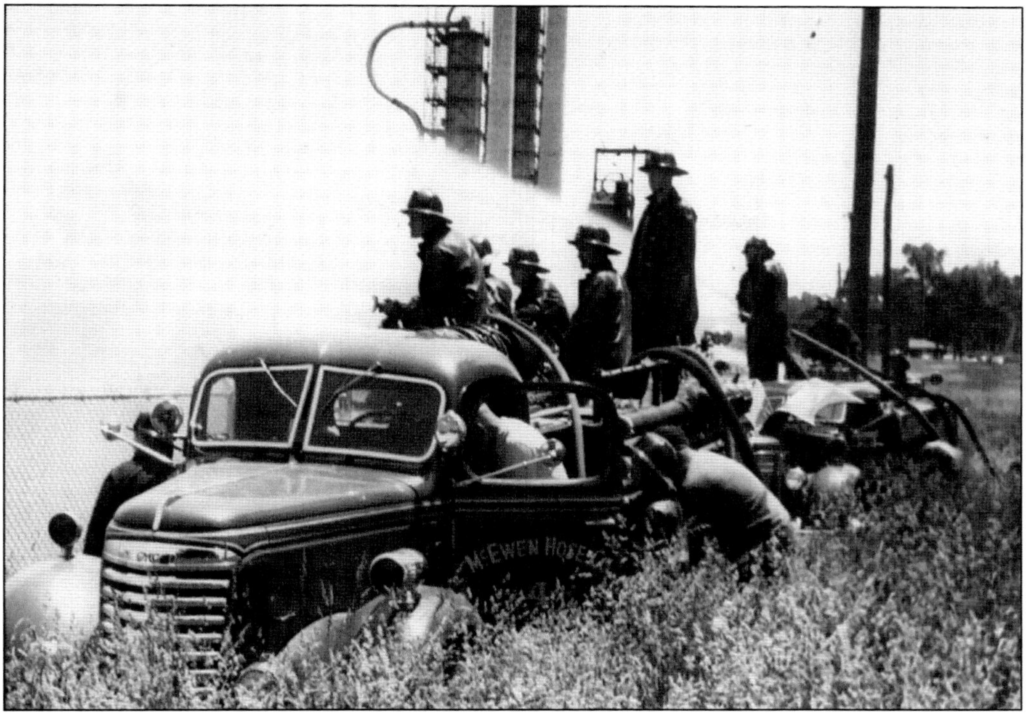

Just after 4:00 p.m. on July 17, 1938, a mechanical failure caused a fire in the centrifuge plant of the Sinclair Refinery and began 48 hours that villagers will never forget. Wellsville volunteer firemen set to work immediately with Sinclair personnel to contain the inferno, and units were called in from many towns in western New York and Pennsylvania. A large tank exploded, killing three spectators as it was blown across the Genesee River. The fire was finally contained by 6:00 p.m. on July 19. The great tragedy of the fire was the loss of the three spectators—Robert C. Powers, 38, Eugene F. McCormick, 37, and Walter Maeder, 44, all of Wellsville. The photograph below was taken moments after the tank exploded, sending spectators running for their lives. (Above, Wellsville Volunteer Fire Department.)

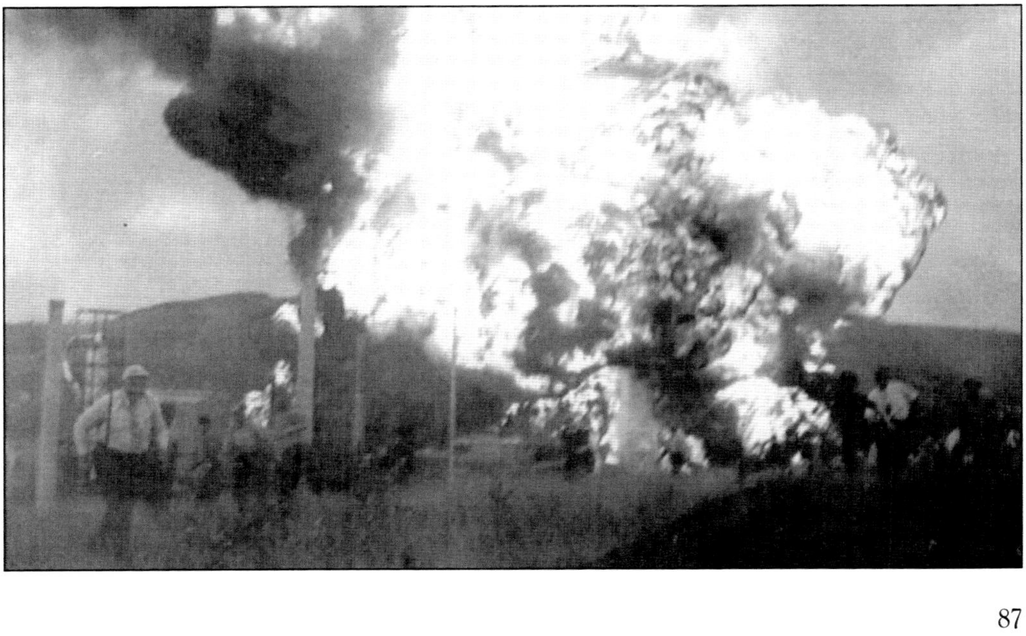

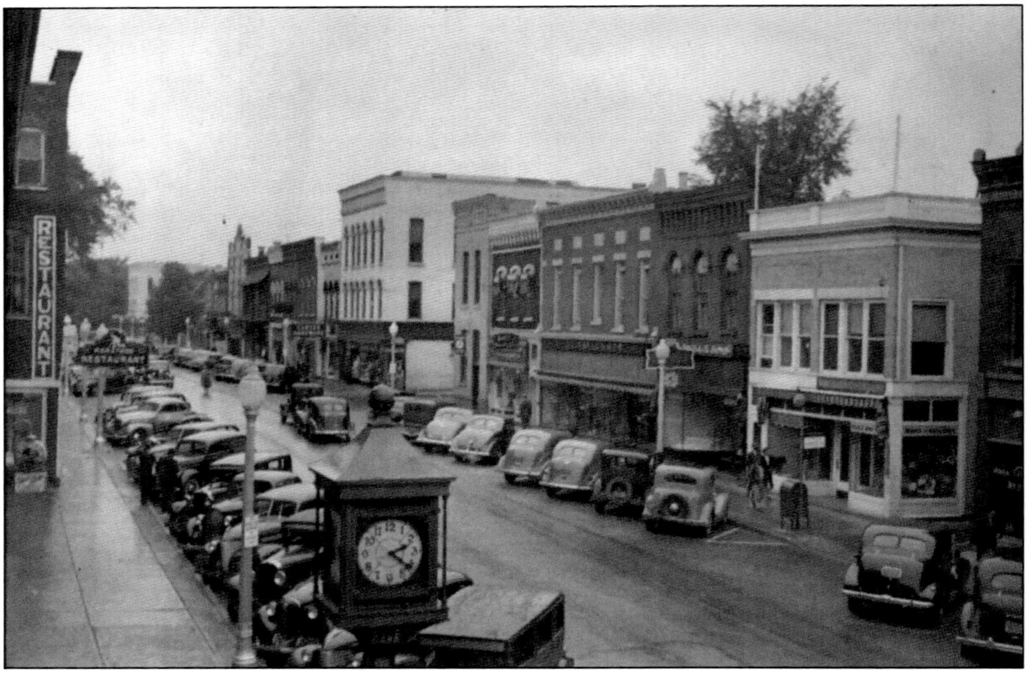

Diagonal parking was the only way to park on North Main Street in Wellsville, at least in the late 1930s. This view from the Thornton Building shows a nice wide street and a glimpse of how the village looks today.

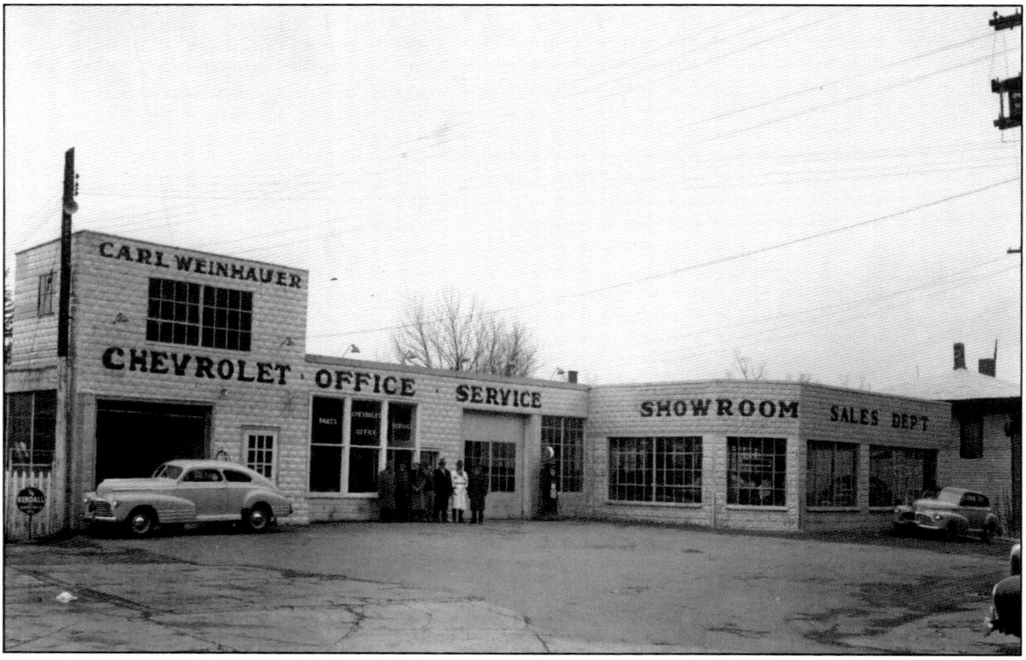

Carl Weinhauer started his career in car sales with his Chevrolet and Durant agency at 79 South Main Street in 1922. After a fire destroyed his garage in 1938, he relocated that part of his business to the old Moogn Livery building at the rear of Weinhauer's North Main Street salesroom. The business was purchased by Pat Lester in 1945. (Donald Baldwin.)

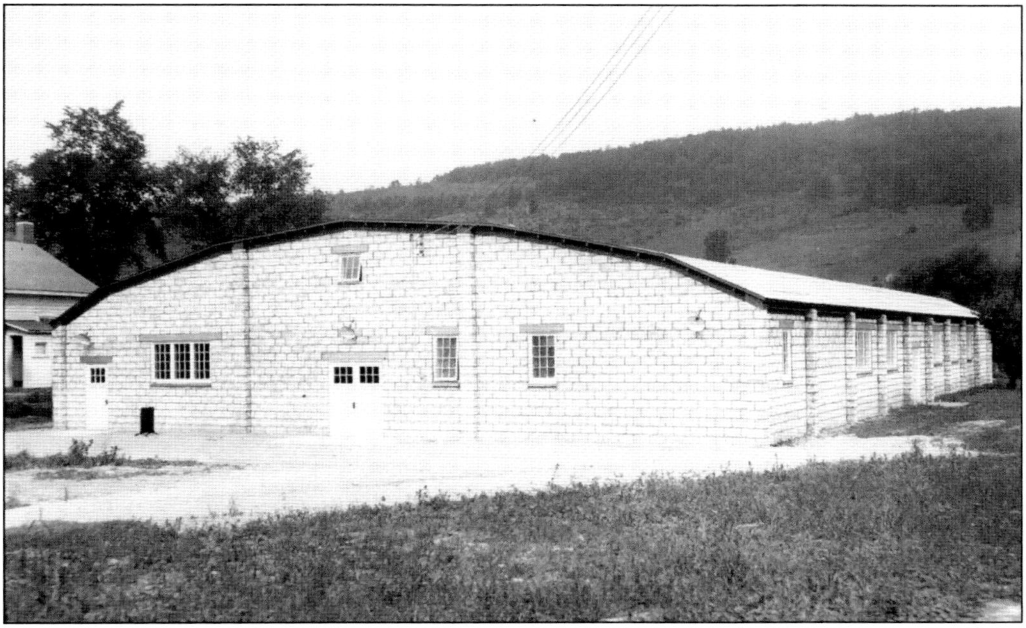

Sloan's Funcrest opened in 1938 on Baldwin Road, just a little outside the village. Harry Sloan was the owner/operator of Funcrest until his death in 1951. Sloan's children Woodrow Sloan and Onalee Sloan Dwyer took over rink management. The rink employed a skating professional for many years and sent several people on to various skating championships. In 1969, Eileen and Jack Evans became owner/operators and renamed it Funland. Below, Skaters from Wellsville and Elmira pose at one of the many skating programs sponsored by Funcrest in the early 1950s. (Both, Ann Comstock.)

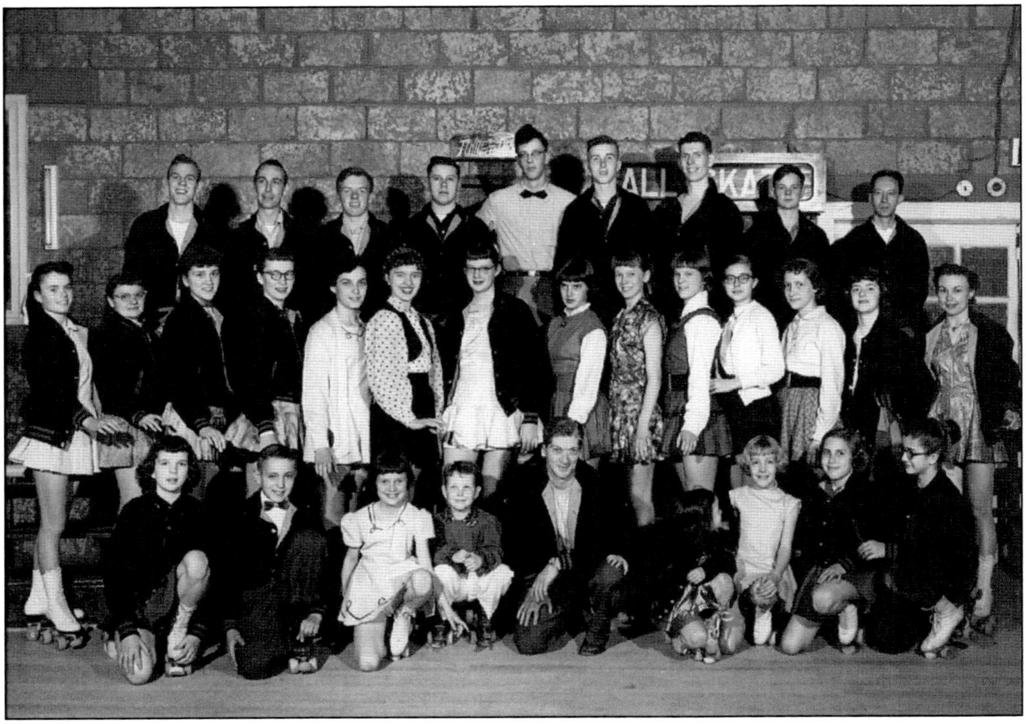

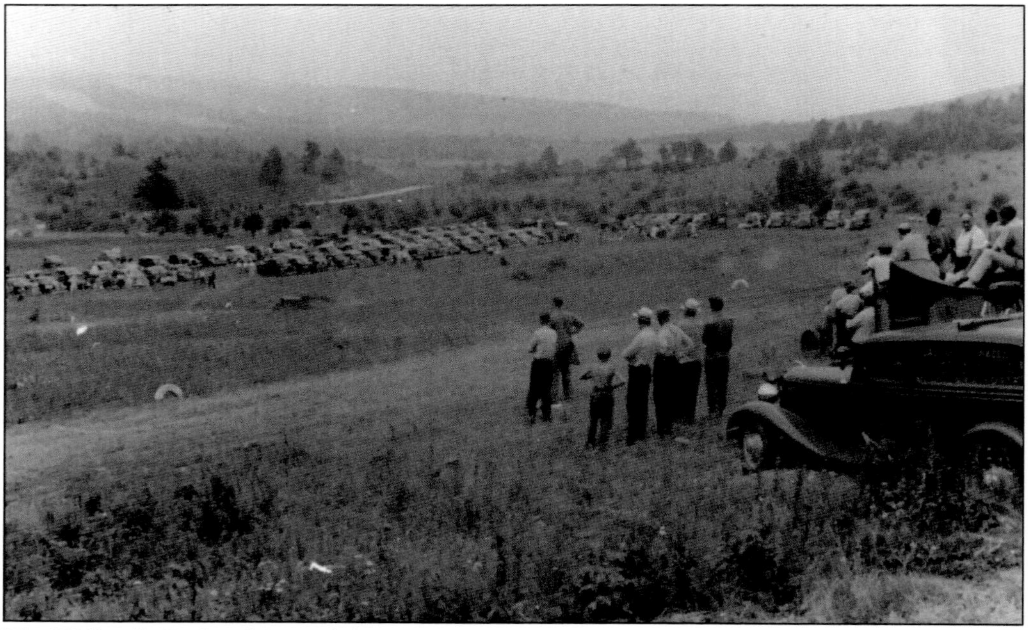

The Wellsville Rod and Gun Club ran a fundraiser to benefit the club during the summer of 1940. The club advertised jalopy races at Steeplechase Race Track on the Wellsville-Genesee Highway. The car at the far right has writing on the window promoting the event, which was held every Sunday at 2:30, at least until the government prohibited jalopy races due to gas shortages prior to World War II. (Christina Wightman.)

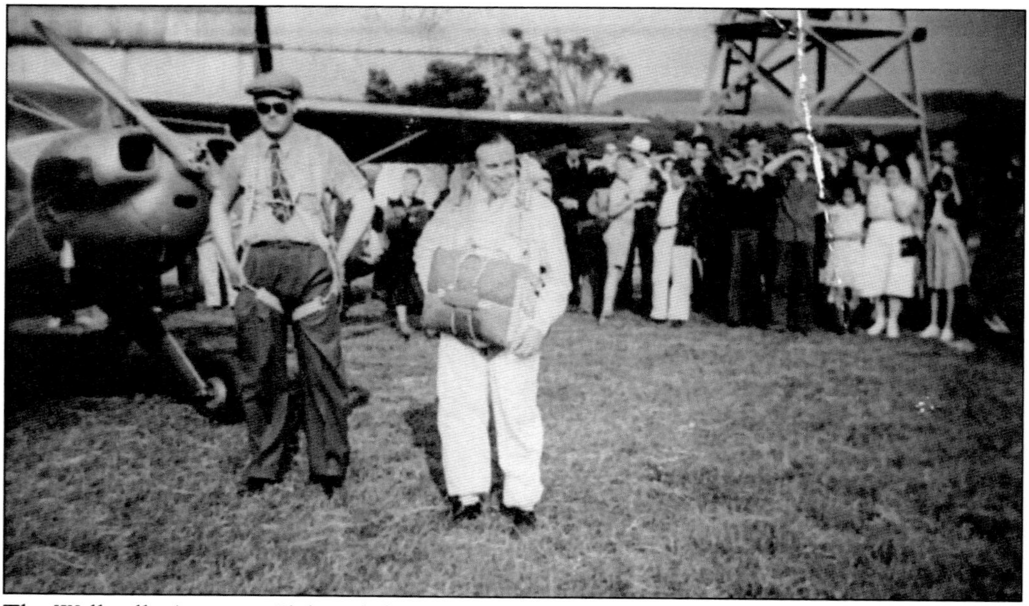

The Wellsville Aviation Club and the American Legion sponsored an Aviation Meet on July 4, 1940. During the event, 25 planes flew into Crowner Field, where an air race was held, aviation aerobatics were exhibited, and rides were sold to the public. Earl "Rip" Cline (right) made a parachute jump at the field from a plane piloted by Francis "Stretch" Kane (left) of the Aviation Club. The meet took place just a week before Wellsville voters went to the polls to approve the purchase of Crowner Field for a municipal airport. (Barbara Tarantine Hulbert.)

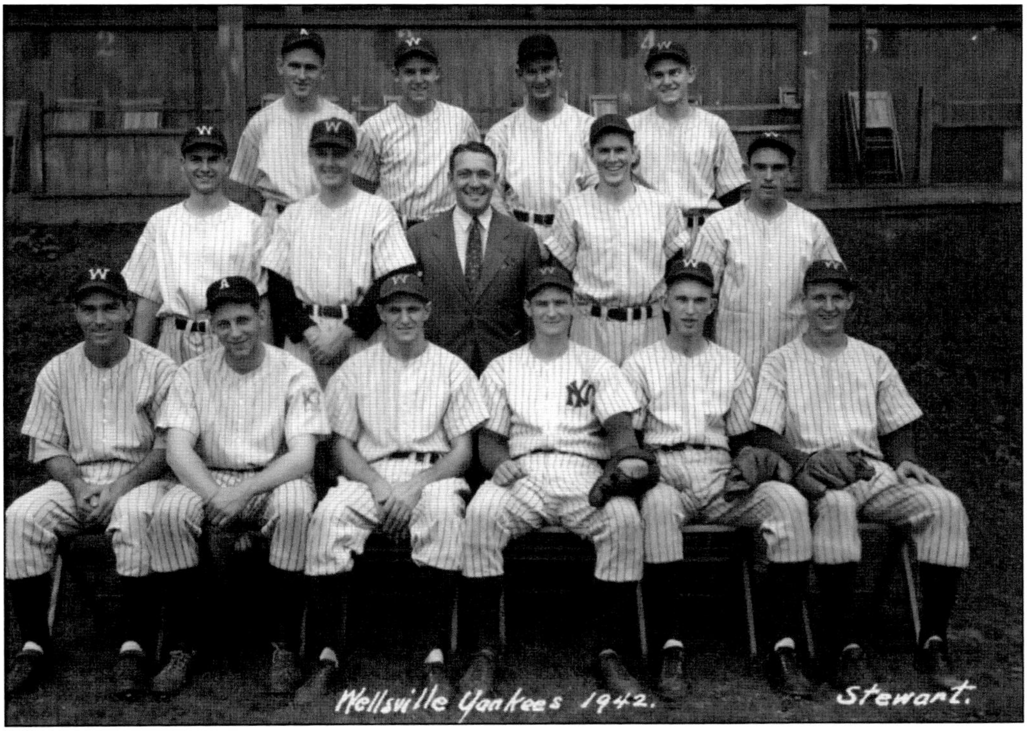

The Wellsville Yankees made their debut in the Pennsylvania–Ontario–New York (PONY) league on April 30, 1942, in a game against the Hornell Pirates at Tullar Field. Local people were delighted that professional baseball had returned to Wellsville after a 27-year absence. The team was managed by player Walter Van Grofski. Pictured, from left to right, are (first row) Greenwald, Woop, Van Grofski, Revels, Prahm, and Och; (second row) Coleman, Cherry, Brandenburg, Hallford, and Moore; (third row) Mahon, Kirchoff, Ross, and Silvera. The Yankees franchise in Wellsville ended the popular run of the Sinclair Baseball Club.

In 1903, a ball field was built on property owned by Mary Gordon. When Gordon passed away in 1910, ballplayers and fans realized that their field might be sold out from under them. Angie Tullar, coached by her baseball-playing son Bayard, acted quickly to purchase the old lot from Gordon's estate. By spring 1911, the new Tullar Athletic Field was ready for games. This aerial photograph of Tullar Field was taken around 1955.

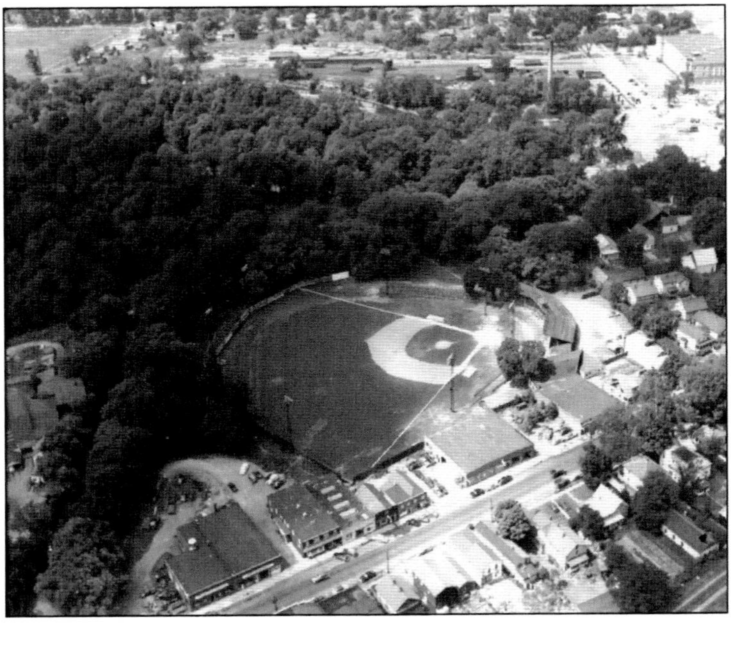

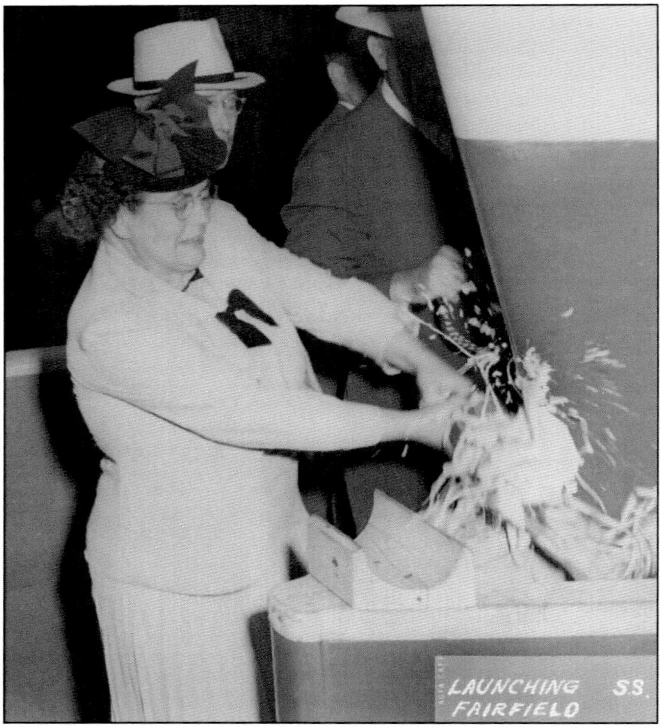

A call went out during World War II from the US Maritime Commission to help name some of the hundreds of Liberty ships produced for the war effort. John Herrick, publisher of the Bolivar Breeze, proposed four names for Liberty ships—*Edwin L. Drake*, *Orville P. Taylor*, *Lewis Emery Jr.*, and *Patrick C. Boyle*, all of which were accepted and commissioned. All ships were named after pioneers in the oil business. The SS *Orville P. Taylor* was launched September 3, 1943, at the Bethlehem Fairfield Shipyard in Baltimore, Maryland. Florence Taylor Maddren, granddaughter of O.P. Taylor, had the honor of christening the ship and sending it off to duty.

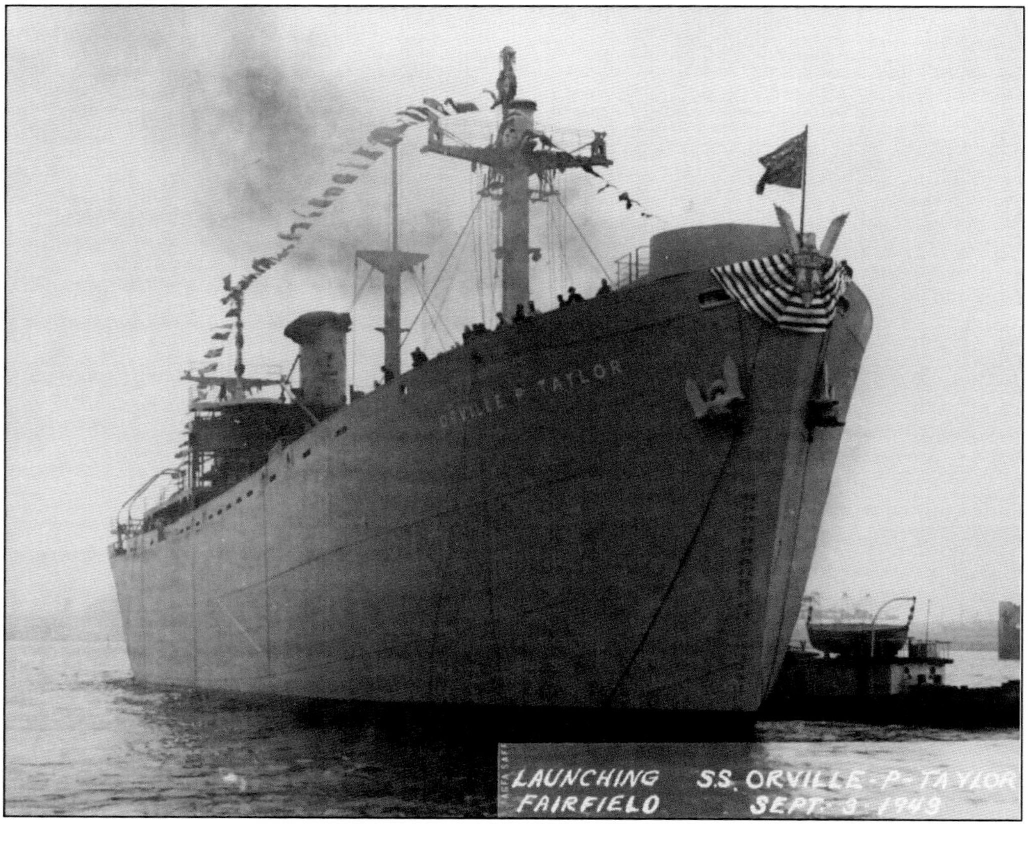

During World War II, the American Legion erected a wall of honor listing the names of the men and women from Wellsville who were serving in the armed forces. The final wall contained 934 names, 22 of whom were killed in action. The wall was set on the lawn of the David A Howe Library and remained there until after the end of the war. This photograph depicts an incomplete wall of honor. (Town of Wellsville.)

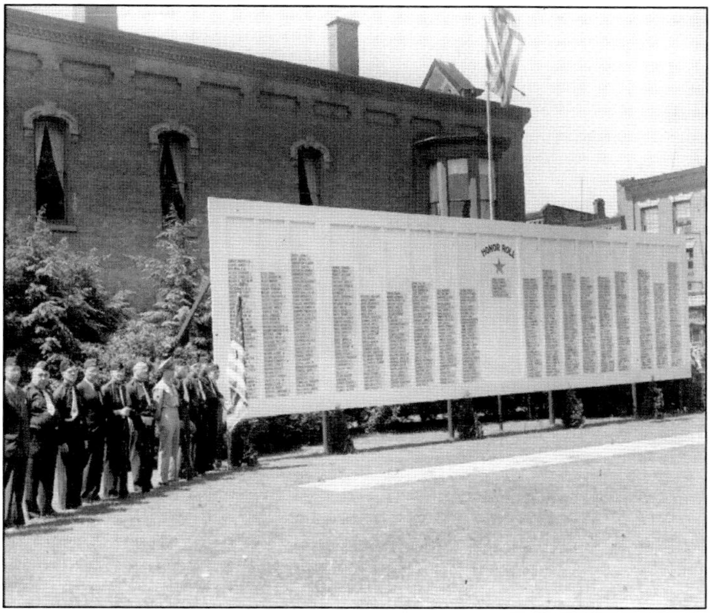

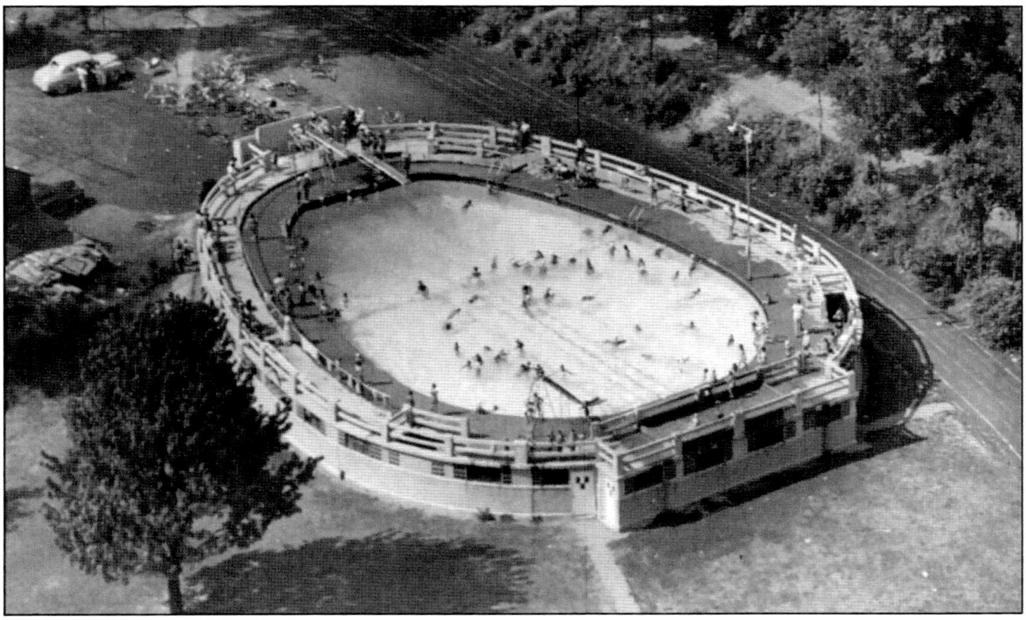

The Wellsville War Service Tribute Association Incorporated and initiated a $50,000 campaign in 1945 to raise funds for a civic swimming pool to honor Wellsville's servicemen and servicewomen. The L.C. Whitford Company won the contract to build a Bintz Ovoid Pool, which contained all the necessary pool equipment. The pool was opened in 1947 and was enjoyed by townspeople for years. It was demolished in 1973 for the construction of the Route 17/19 bypass.

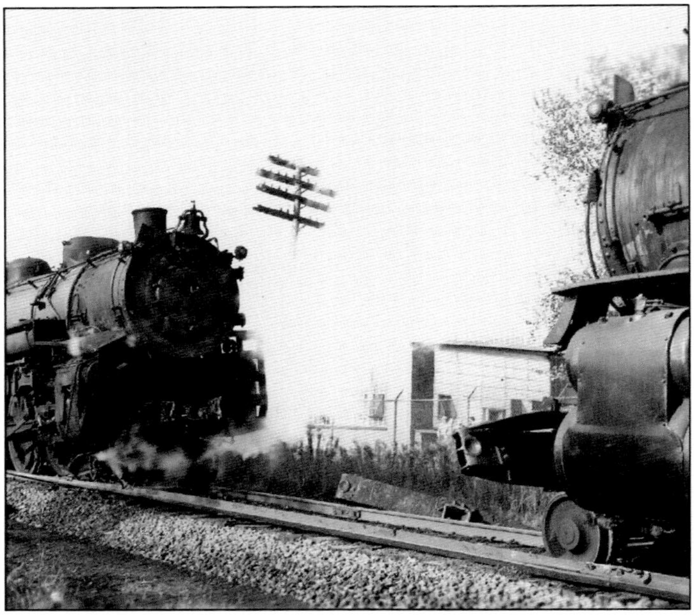

Workers at Worthington got a surprise on October 15, 1945, when two trains collided head-on in front of the plant on Coats Street. An eastbound milk train consisting of a locomotive, three milk cars, and a caboose met a freight locomotive working in Wellsville. The engineer of the freight train tried to back up but could not build speed fast enough, and the milk train also tried to slow down. Two railroad men were hurt, and the trains suffered damage in their front ends. (James Dello.)

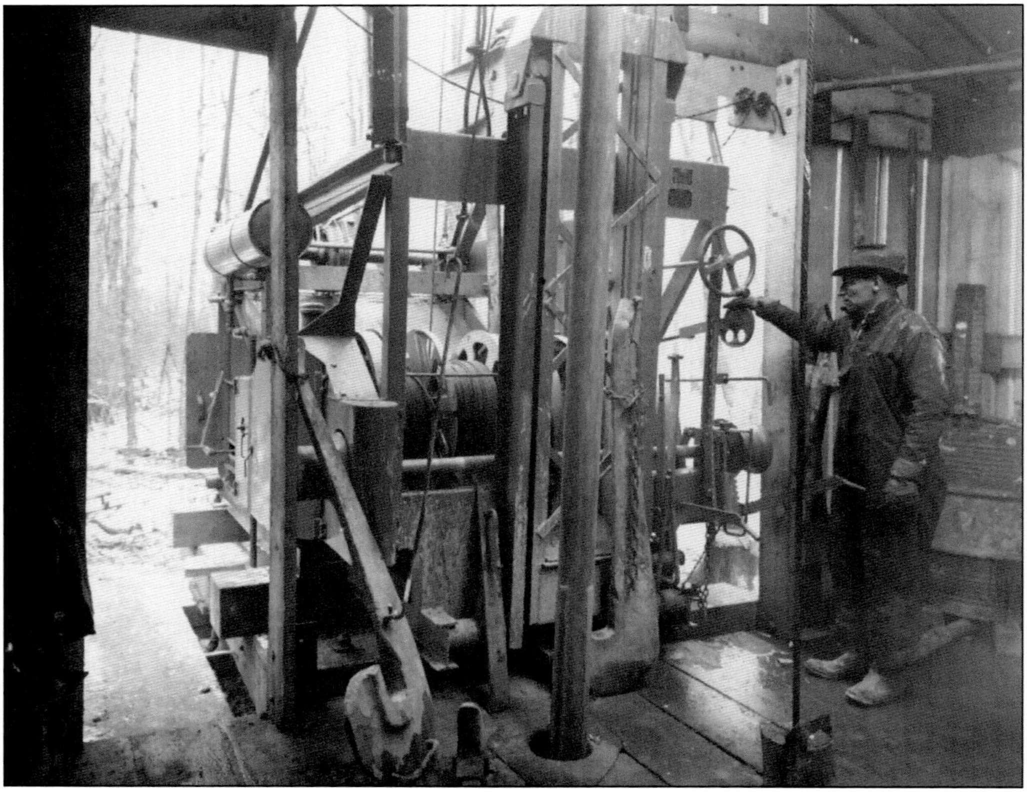

In the early 1940s, drillers William and Henry Bohne were approached by the Bucyrus Erie Company to help design a spudder (a portable drilling rig) that would meet the drilling demands of the New York, Pennsylvania, and Ohio oil fields. The first Bucyrus Erie 28-L spudder was delivered to them shortly thereafter and proved very successful. William is shown in their rig shanty with the 28-L in the late 1940s. (Joel and Mary Bohne Havens.)

Five

Some Local Churches and Schools

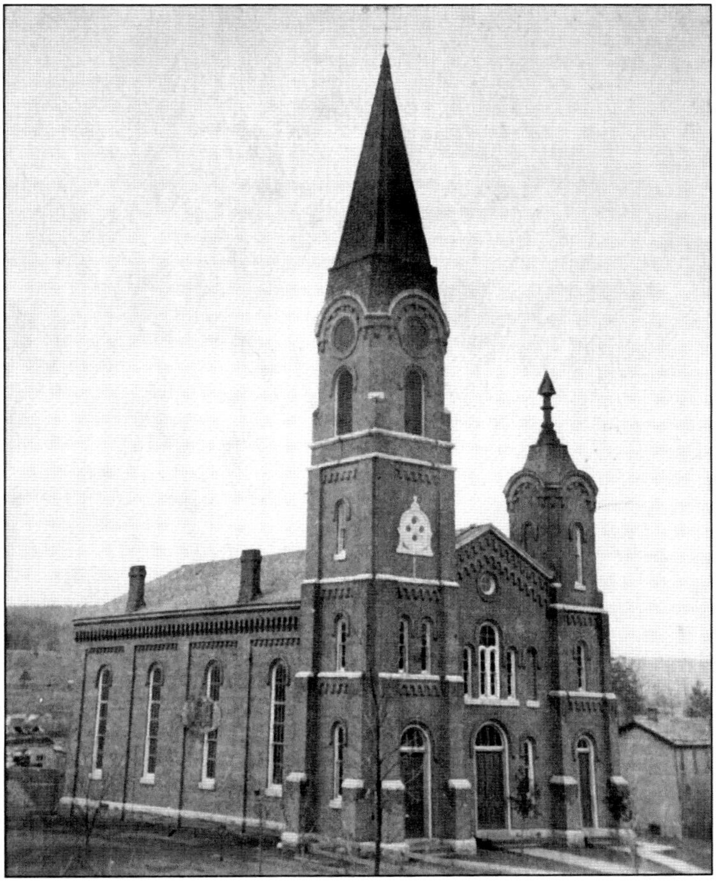

The Baptist congregation built its original wooden church at this site on North Main Street in 1856. That structure was destroyed in the fire in 1867, and the church was rebuilt with brick. Due to a dwindling congregation, the Baptist society of Wellsville was disbanded, and the property was given to the New York State Baptist Convention in 1932. The David A. Howe Public Library is now located on this site. (David Hornburg.)

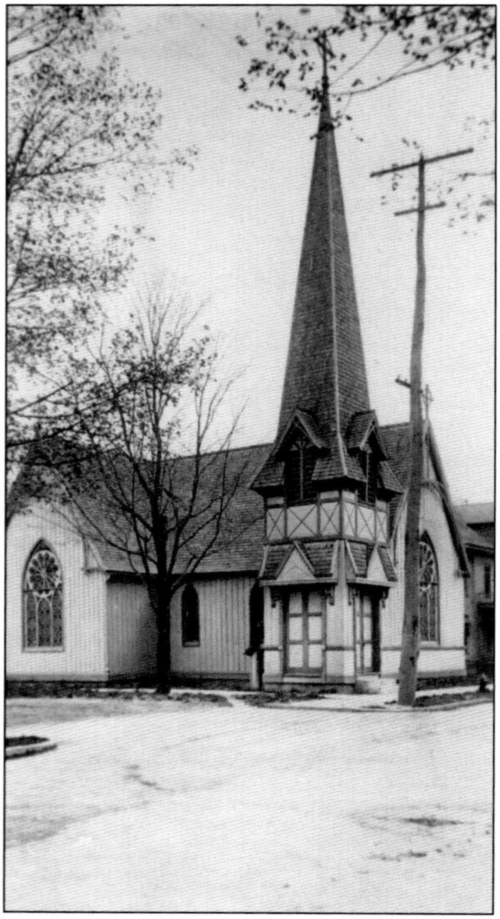

This pretty church (left) is the original St. John's Episcopal Church in Wellsville. It was built on upper Jefferson Street in the late 1860s. The congregation wanted to be in a more central location and, in 1872, moved the building to the corner of North Main Street and East Genesee Street. A fire destroyed the church in 1907, and the new St. John's Episcopal Church (below) was built in the same location. (Left, Craig Braack.)

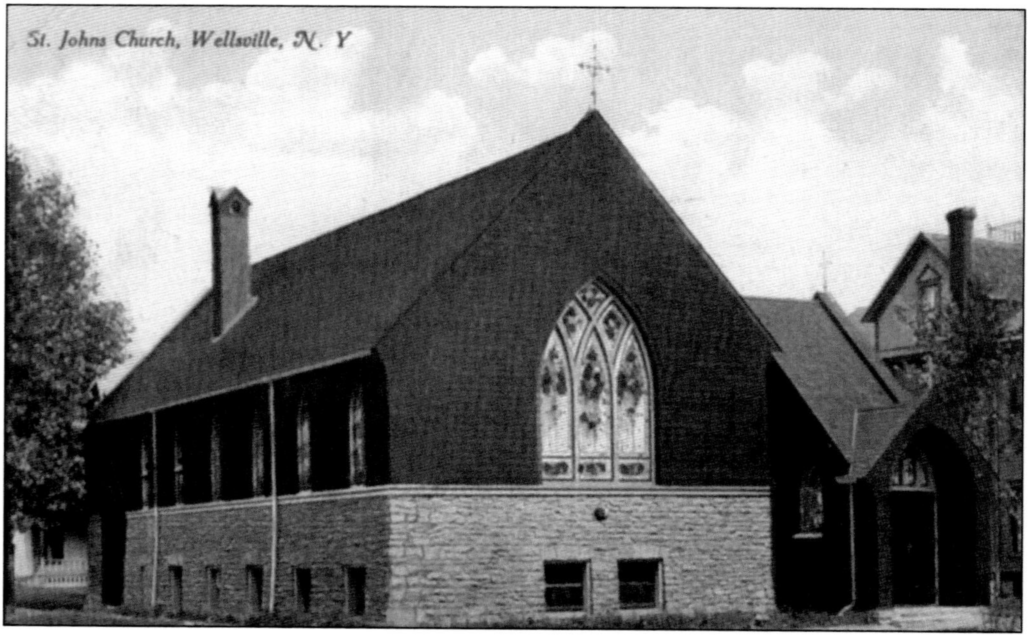

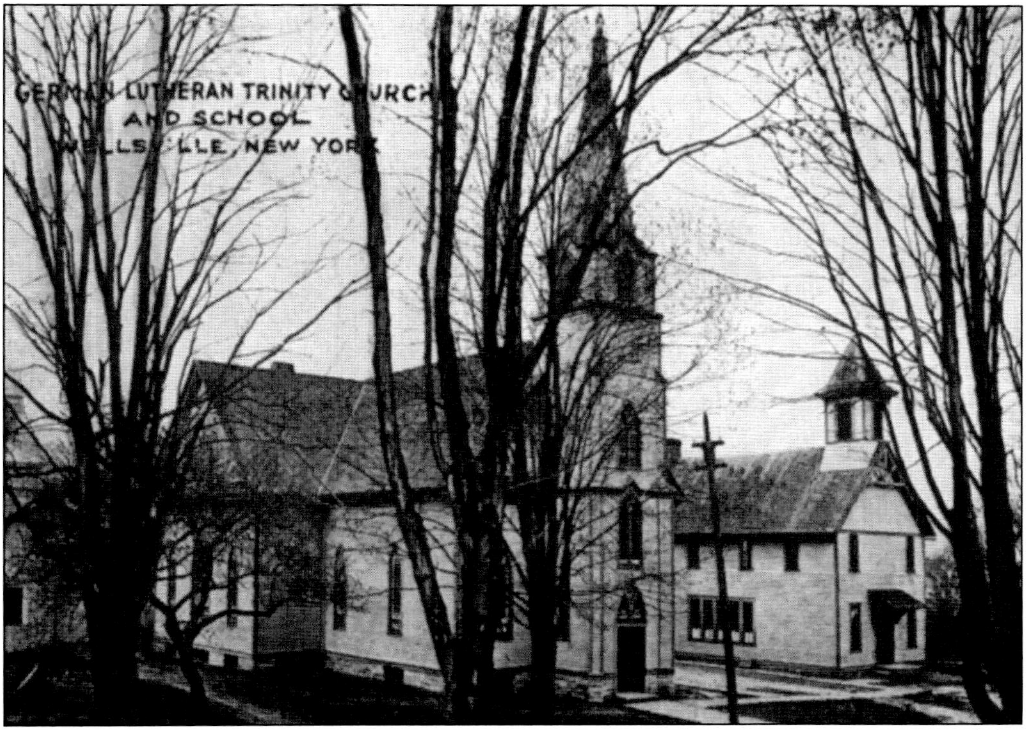

The parishioners of the Lutheran church met in a remodeled house on Martin Street until the Congregationalists built their new church in 1873. The Lutherans purchased the old Congregational church on West Genesee Street, taking formal possession in November 1873. The members enlarged the church and built a schoolhouse, which was replaced in 1954 by a brick parish hall. The 1972 flood destroyed the parish hall and took enough property that the church was unable to rebuild it. The congregation of the First Trinity Evangelical Church acquired the property of the old Wellsville Hotel on North Main Street and constructed their new church there in 1974.

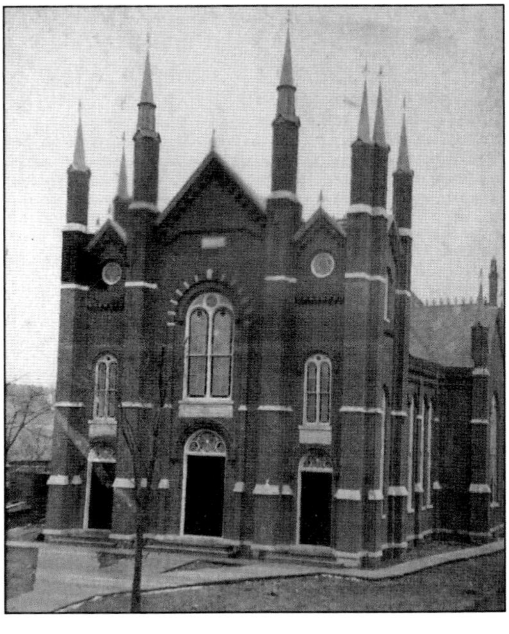

The members of the Congregational church conducted a cornerstone ceremony for their new building on North Main Street in August 1872. When the church was opened in 1873, it was dedicated completely free of debt on the $27,000 building cost. The brick church was originally 100 feet by 50 feet and had a very distinctive design with several spires at the top. Critical structural issues were discovered in 1966, which compelled the congregation to build a new church farther north on Main Street. The new building was completed in 1969, in time for Easter services.

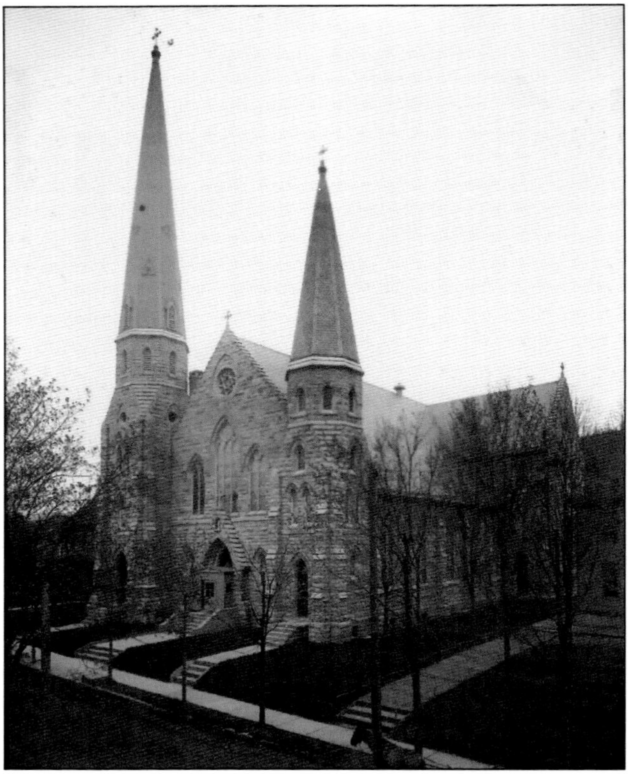

Fr. Dean Leddy led the drive to build the beautiful Immaculate Conception Church, and parishioners made many generous donations to the building fund. Plans for the church were drawn by architect Michael C. Sheehan of Buffalo, and work commenced in July 1895 and took only two years to complete. Bishop Quigley of Buffalo conducted the dedication service in October 1897. (Donald Baldwin.)

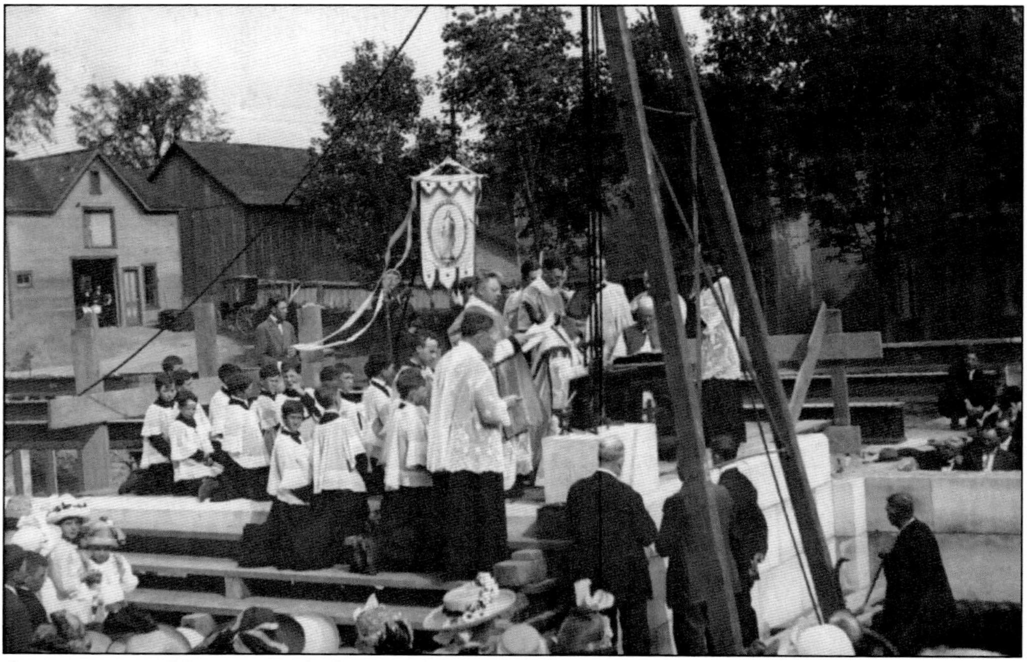

Construction of the new Catholic parochial school was started in 1911 by moving the old wooden lyceum building from this site to the rear of the property. In June 1912, William Stokes & Sons of Buffalo began construction of the new school. Here, Bishop Colton of Buffalo conducts the cornerstone ceremony in August 1912.

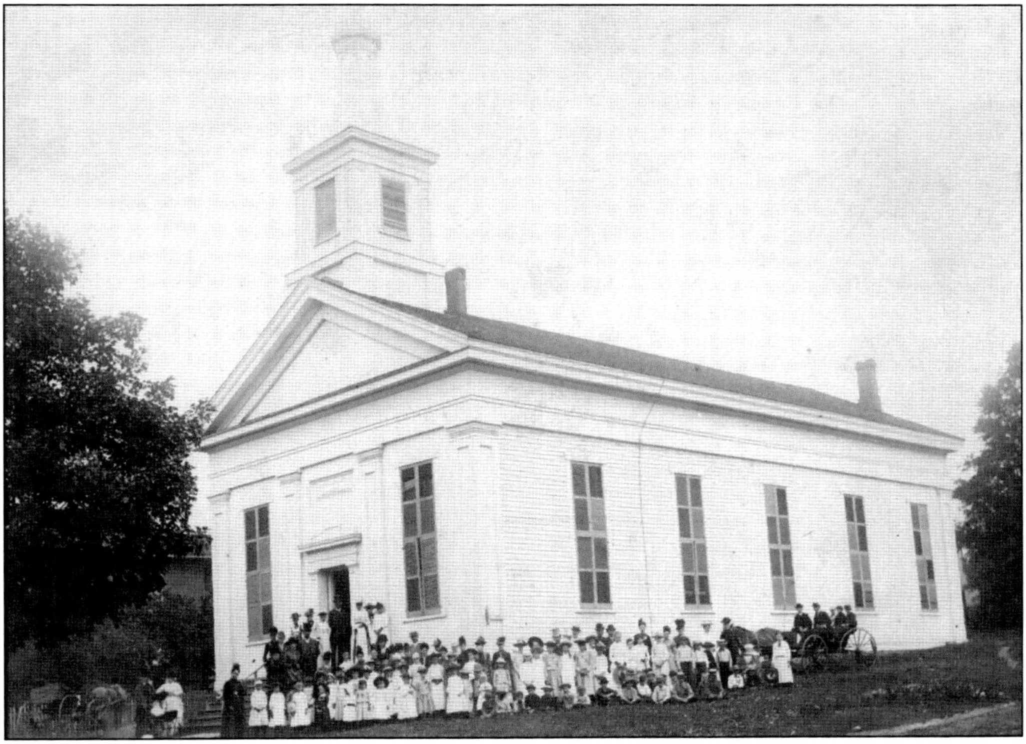

The first Methodist Episcopal church (above) was a large wooden structure on Harrison Avenue (Maple Avenue) and was built in 1853. The building was remodeled and used as a parsonage after the new church was constructed. It is now a private residence. A new church (below) was constructed of stone on the corner of Madison Avenue and Maple Avenue and was dedicated in April 1893 by Bishop Vincent of Buffalo.

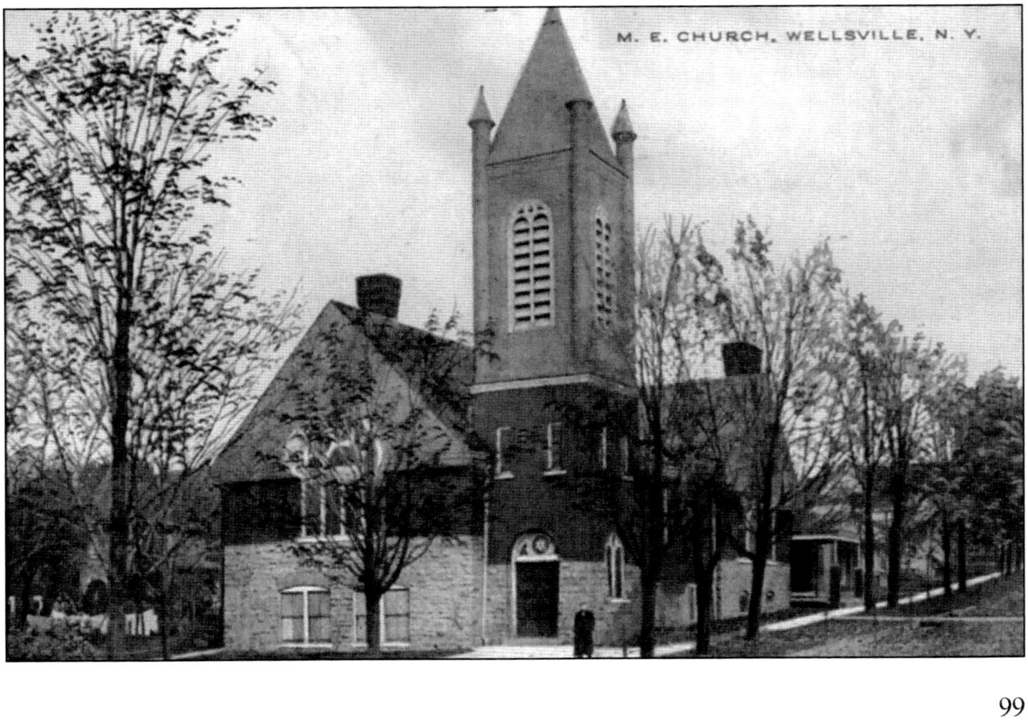

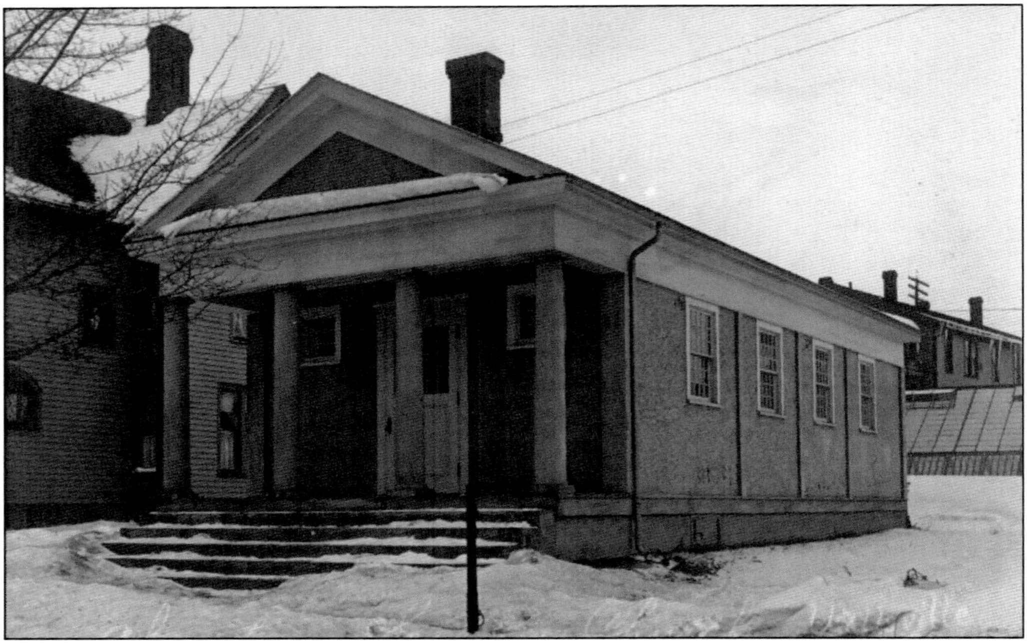

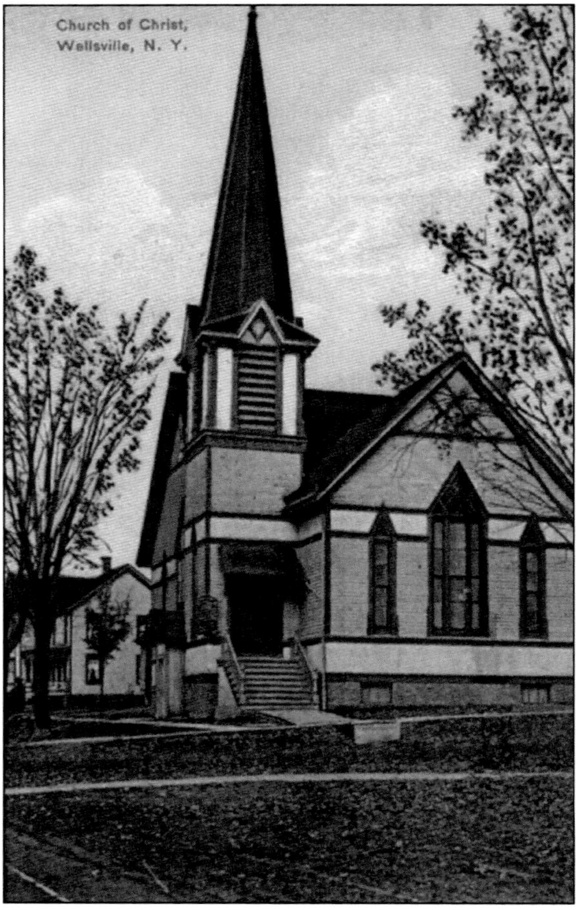

The Christian Science congregation began meeting in this little building at 28 Jefferson Street in 1909. A reading room was opened for the general public to use at that time. By the 1930s, the Christian Scientists had moved their reading room to 322 North Main Street. The Wesleyan Methodist church held services here in the 1930s before it moved to an old candy factory building on West State Street. That congregation is now the Brookside Wesleyan Church on the east side of the village.

The Broad Street Church of Christ was spun off from the Church of Christ in Scio, thanks largely to the efforts of deacon Andrew Applebee. This little church was built in 1889 and enlarged shortly after, but the small building could not keep up with the growing church population. The congregation built a new Christian temple in 1913. This building, minus its steeple, is now an apartment house just behind the newer church.

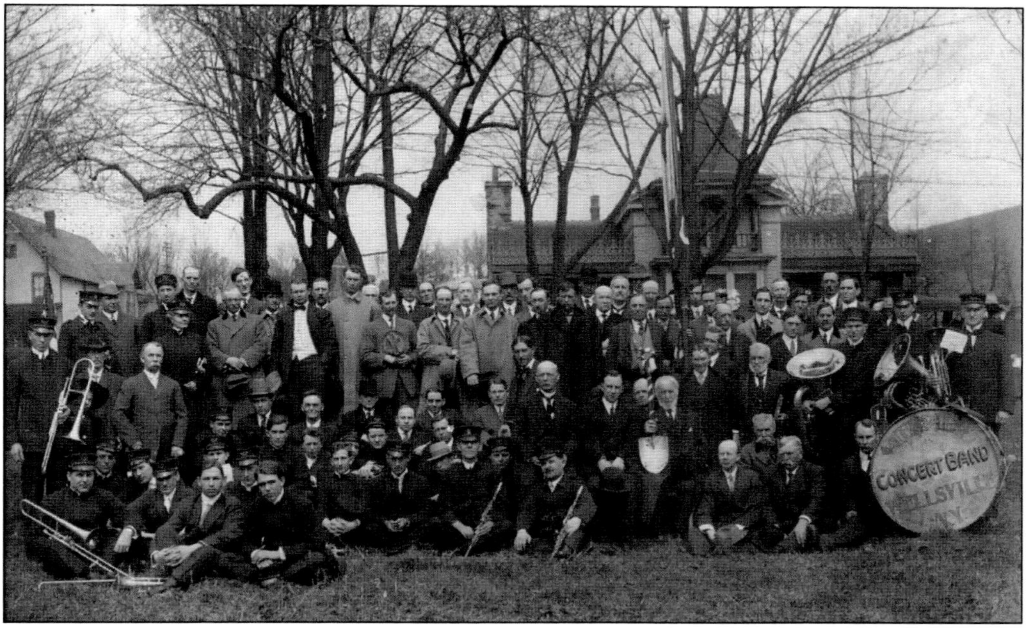

Thomas J. Applebee (shown holding a shovel), as the oldest member of the church, had the honor of formally breaking ground for the new Christian temple. The Temple Concert Band turned out to enliven the ceremonies on the corner of Maple Avenue and West Fassett Street in April 1913. This photograph shows only the men of the church; the ladies were waiting for their turn to be photographed.

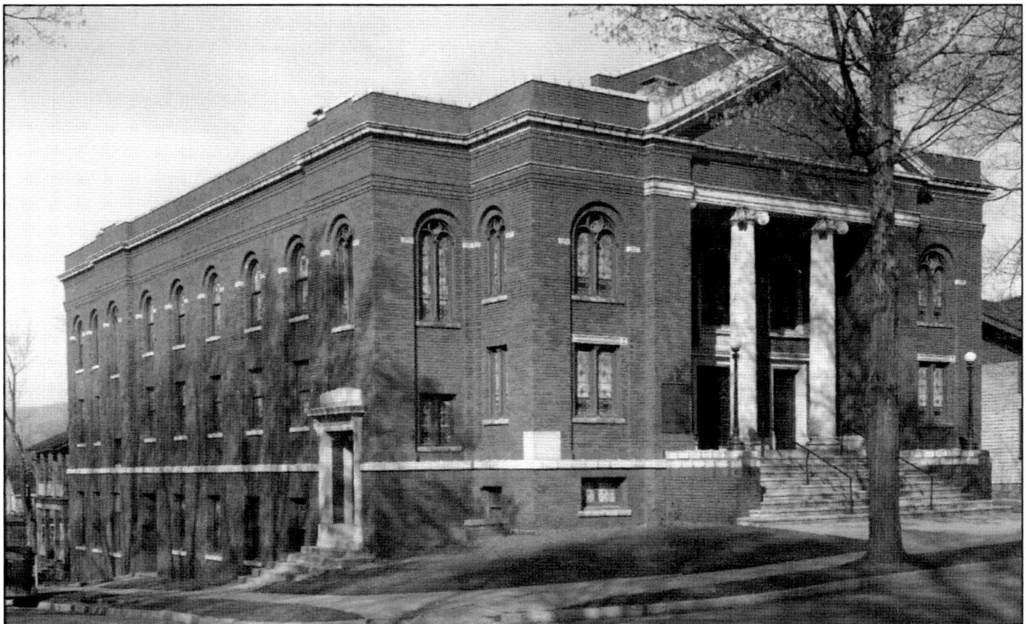

Members of the Broad Street Church of Christ began building their new Christian temple in 1913 and occupied it in 1914. It was constructed in a very different style from other churches in the area, and members hoped it would act as a community center as well as a church. Many organizations have used the facility to meet, play basketball, or have an informal meal.

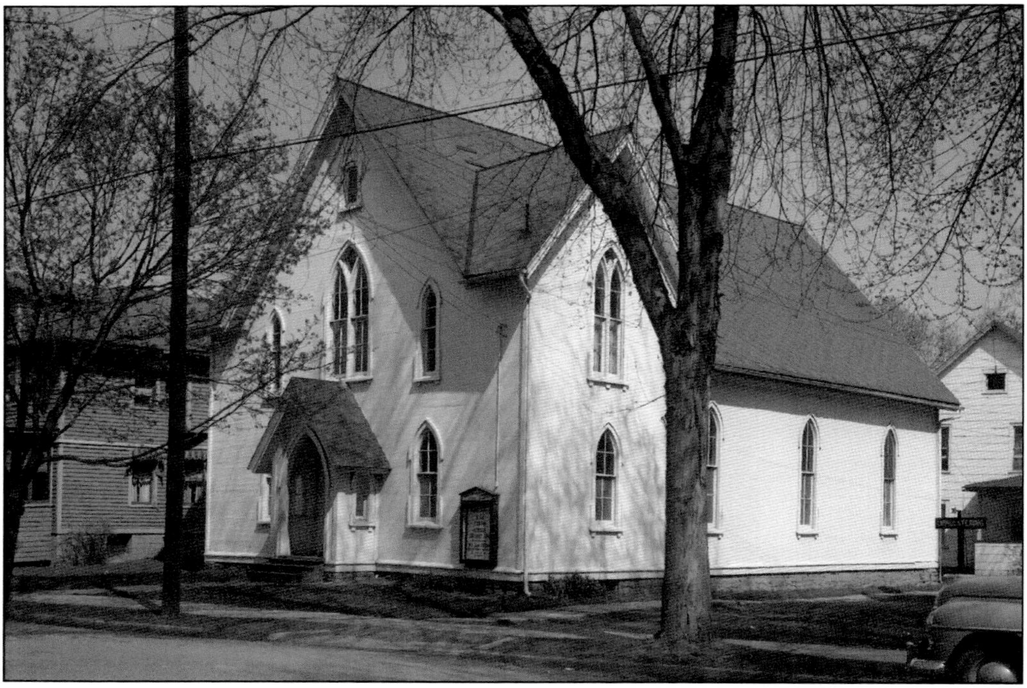

A German Methodist congregation built this church on West Pearl Street in 1875. The building was badly damaged during a 1914 fire at the Aluminum Company just across the street, but it was quickly repaired. In 1914, the church was sold to the Christian and Missionary Alliance Church, which owned it until 1965.

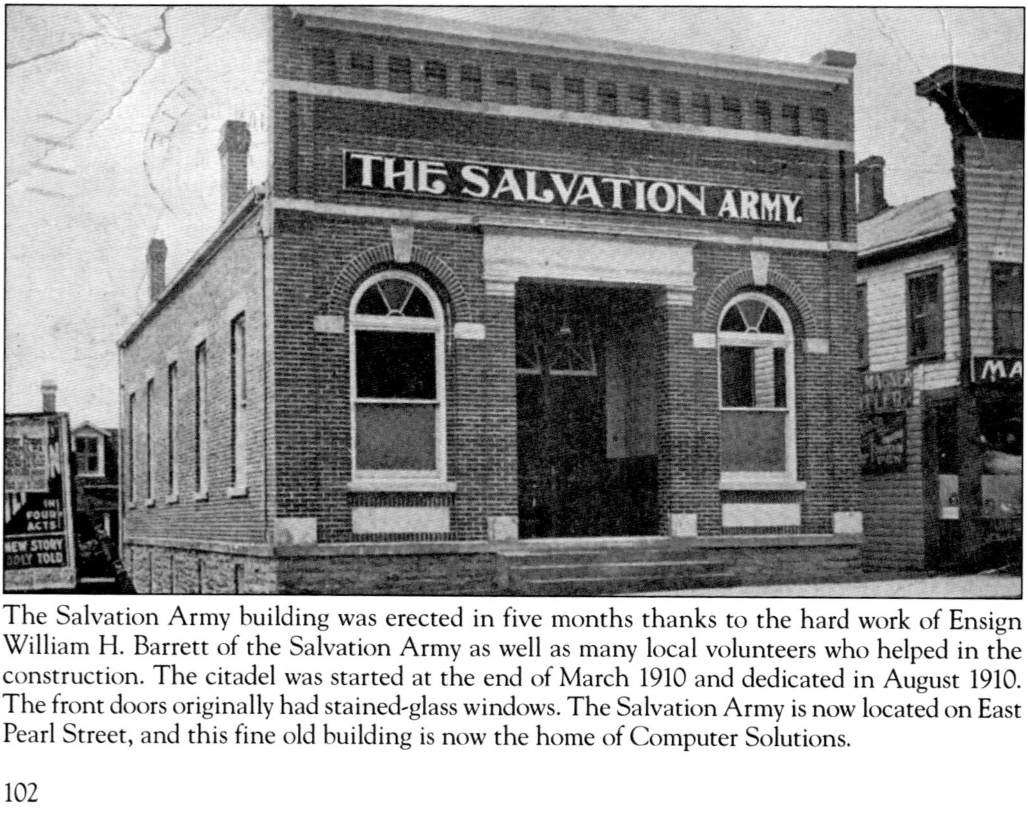

The Salvation Army building was erected in five months thanks to the hard work of Ensign William H. Barrett of the Salvation Army as well as many local volunteers who helped in the construction. The citadel was started at the end of March 1910 and dedicated in August 1910. The front doors originally had stained-glass windows. The Salvation Army is now located on East Pearl Street, and this fine old building is now the home of Computer Solutions.

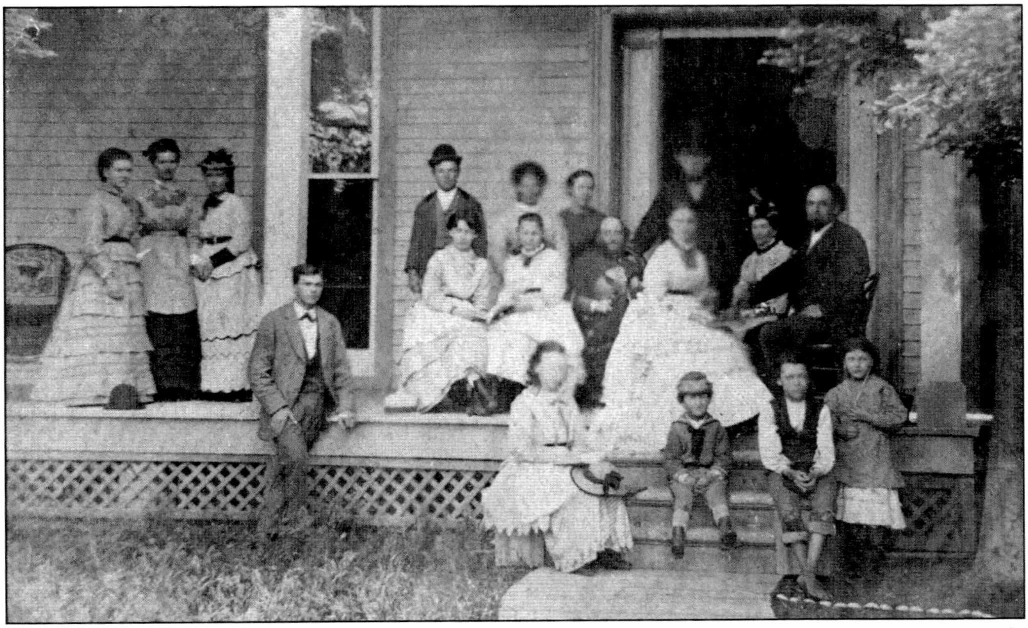

Charles Simmons's grand plan for the development of the Riverside area included the Riverside Collegiate Institute. Rev. J.S. Bingham was the headmaster from 1873 to 1877. In 1877, Rev. A.W. Cummings purchased the school and renamed it the Wellsville Riverside Seminary. Classes were taught in preparation for a college education. The school suffered a fire in 1882, after which it was repaired, but it burned again in 1888 and was never rebuilt. This photograph shows faculty and students on the porch of the dormitory next to the school; Reverend Bingham is shown seated at the far right.

This wooden schoolhouse was called the Union School and was located on North Main Street where the library now stands. The school opened in January 1860, with Prof. A.C. Spicer serving as principal of the Higher and Academic Departments. There were four departments—Primary, Intermediate, Higher, and Academic—and tuition ranged from $1.50 to $5 per term. The first high school graduation from the Union School was in 1863. This was the second school to be built on this site, and it was destroyed by fire in 1876.

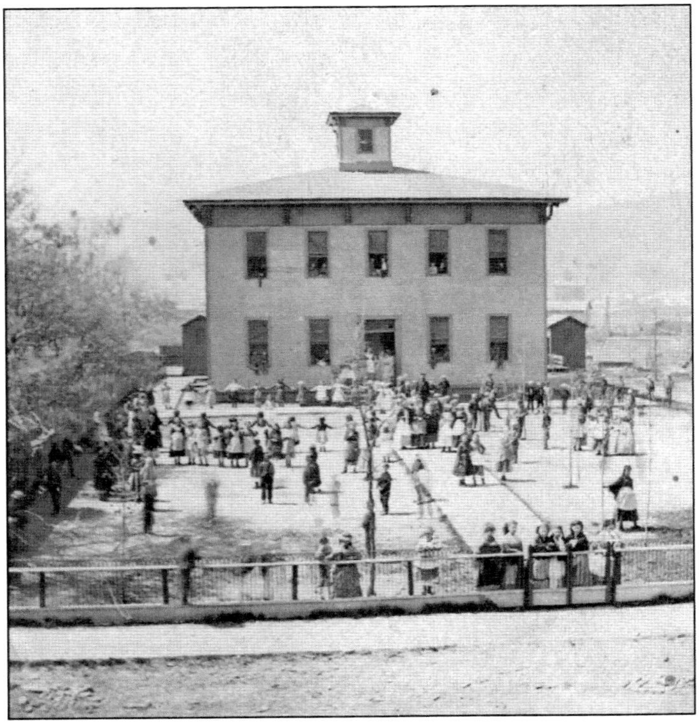

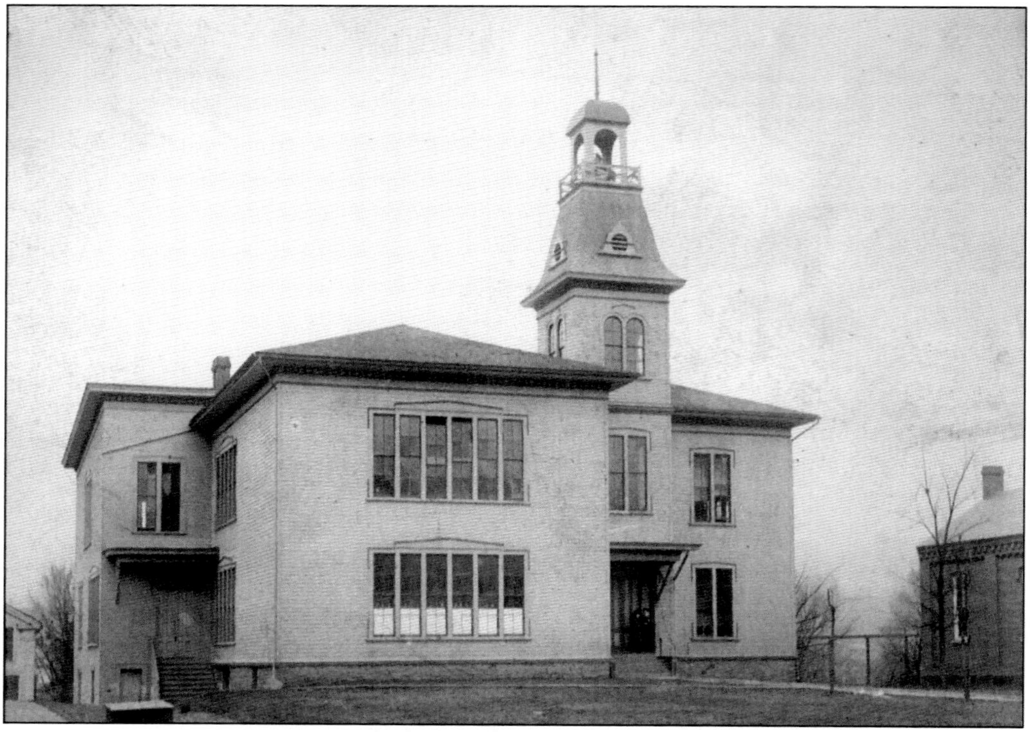

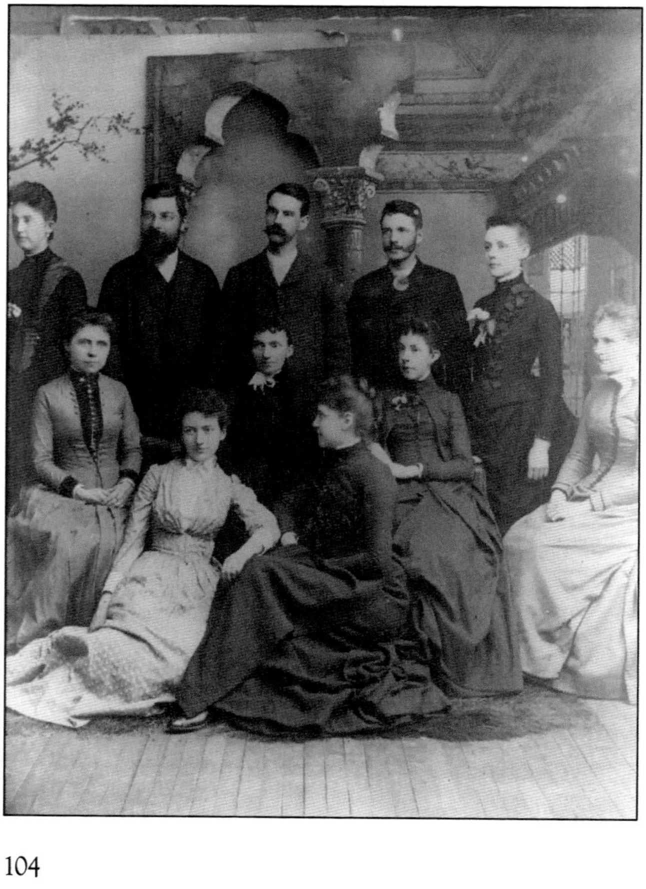

The Wellsville Free Academy was built immediately after the old Union School burned in February 1876. The new school was occupied in November of that year. Chauncey B. Macken was the principal for this school, which was destroyed in a fast-moving fire in 1891. School was held in the Lincoln Block on North Main Street for the next year.

The faculty of the Wellsville Free Academy pose for a photograph around 1890. From left to right are (first row) Fanny York and Laura McDowell; (second row) Adelle Fuller, Addie T. Elwell, Nellie Devore, and Bridget Shaughnessy; (third row) May Moore, Rev. George Buch (part-time Latin and French teacher), Prof. C.M. Harding, William C. Noll (assistant principal), and Theresa Hildrith. (DAHPL.)

This is the fourth school to be built on the North Main Street site. The new high school was constructed of brick, but in October 1909, it was also badly damaged by fire. Students were again quartered in various buildings all over the village as work commenced to repair, remodel, and enlarge the school.

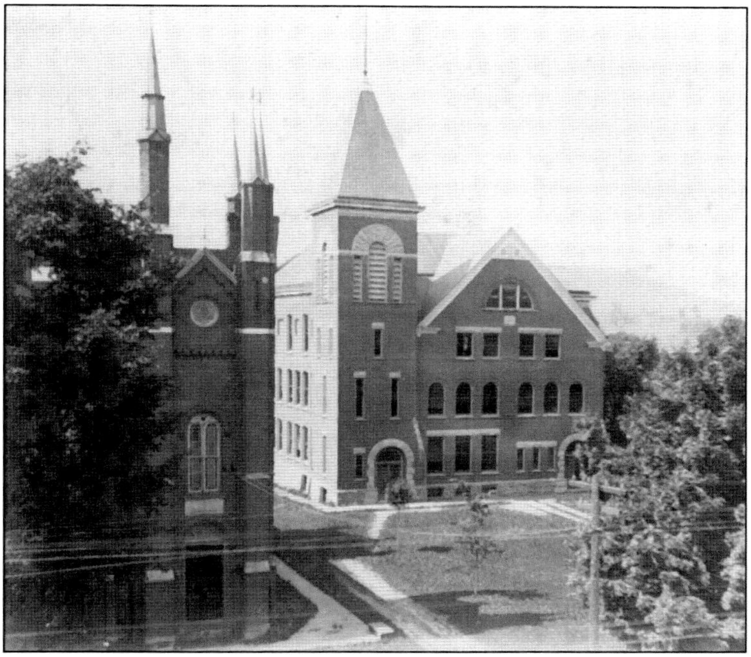

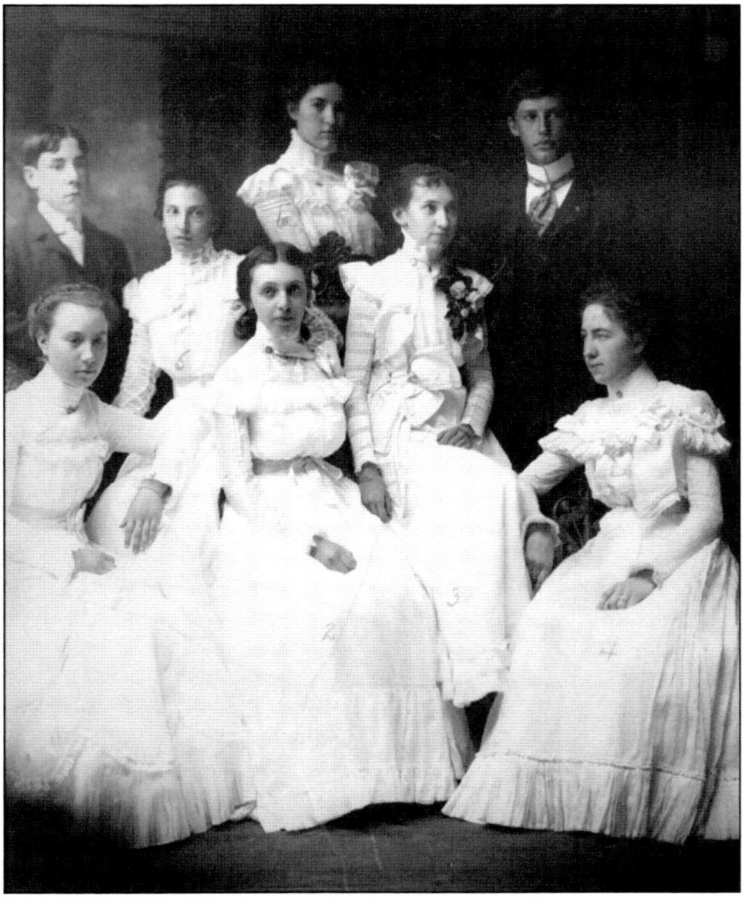

Wellsville High School graduated nine students in June 1900, but only eight of them posed for their class photograph. They are, from left to right, (first row) Ethel Barnes, Maude Osborne, and Elizabeth Yates; (second row) Helena Fulmer and Bernice Furman; (third row) William Duke Jr., Gertrude Richards, and Paul D. Jump. Irene Mills is not in the photograph. (DAHPL.)

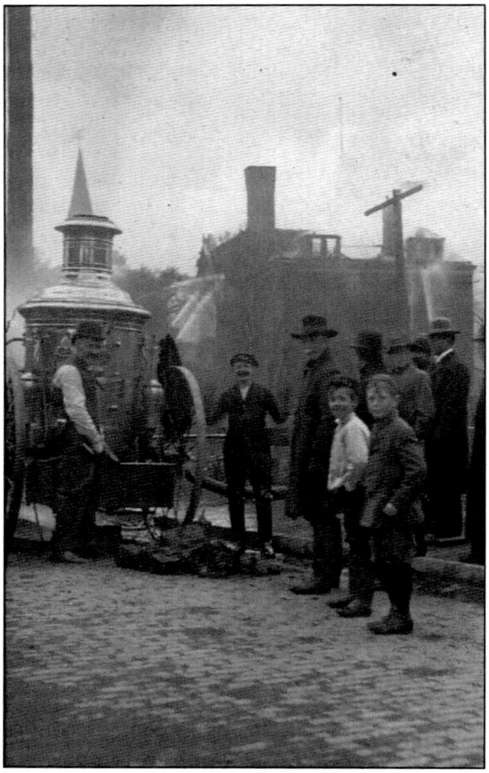

The steamer was called out during the October 17, 1909, high school fire. Shown here, in one of the few photographs existing of firemen at work during a fire, are Joe Leonard (to the left of the steamer) and Engineer Ed Rice (to the right of it). Three of the spectators shown are Elbert Foster (in the dark hat looking at the camera), young John Slough (in the white shirt), and his friend Arthur Junker (on the right).

This is the 1892 high school building on North Main Street as it appeared in 1910 after being remodeled and enlarged following the 1909 fire. This school remained opened until 1924.

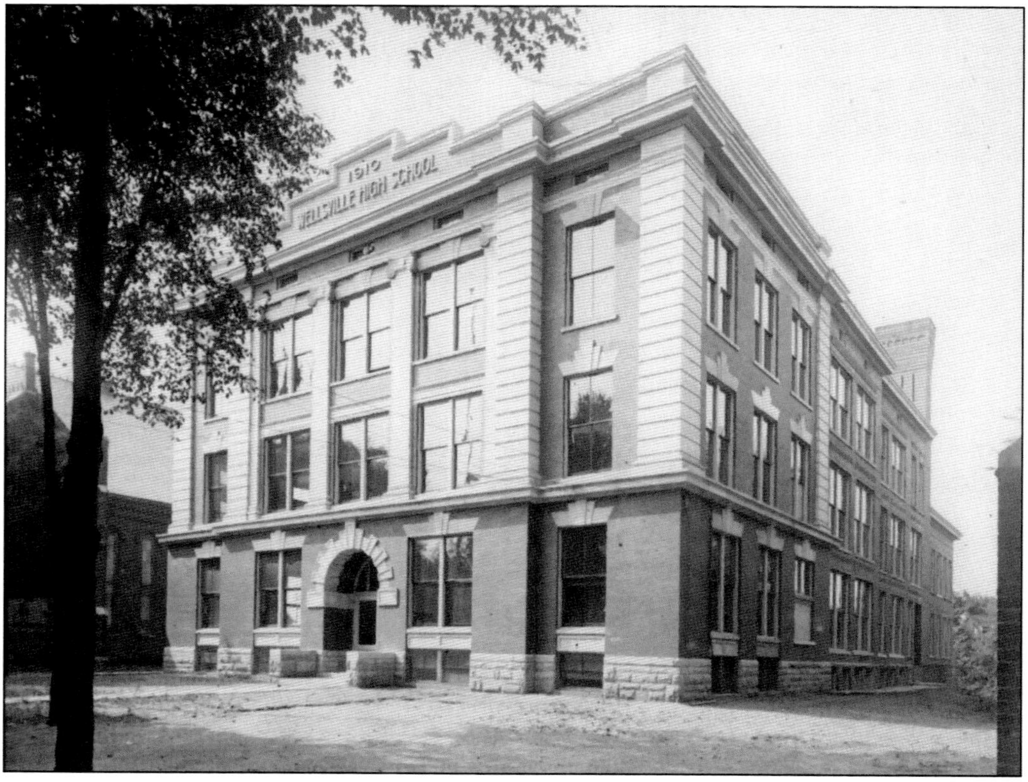

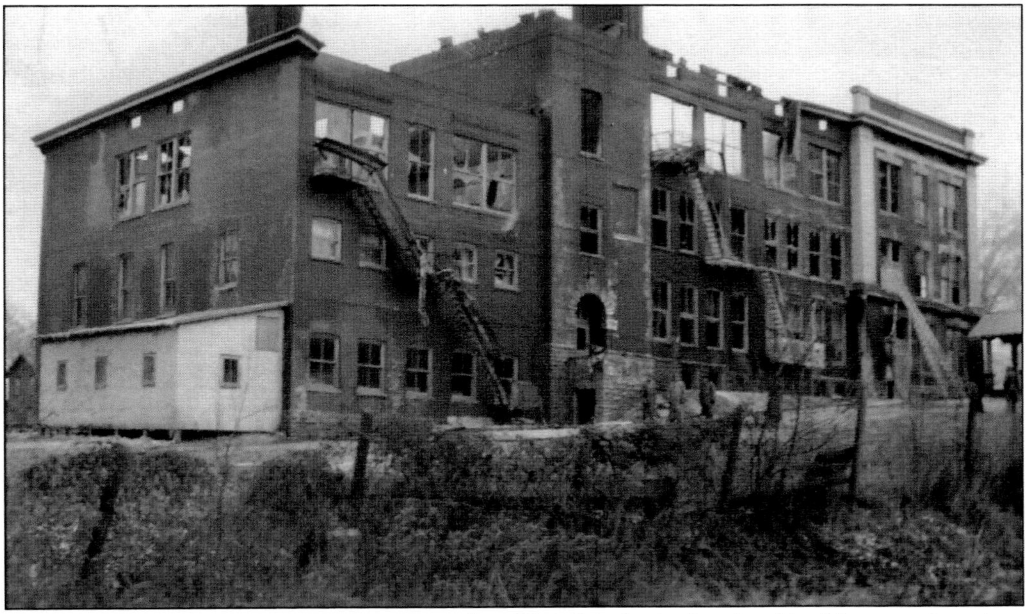

The fire alarm rang at 1:20 a.m. on November 25, 1924; the high school building was burning. Firemen worked to save the Baptist and Congregational churches on either side of the structure, but they could not save the school. The building was a loss. From the start, the fire was thought to be an arsonist's work. Classes were again spread all over the village for the next few years. It was the fifth and final time that a school at this location had been struck by fire. A school was not rebuilt on this site.

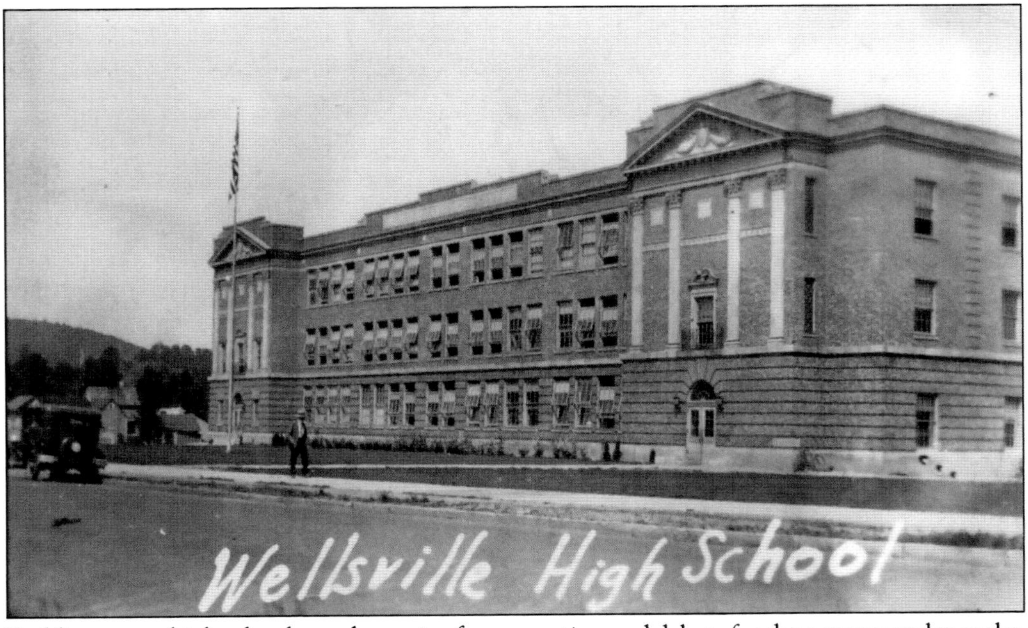

Building a new high school was the topic of conversation and debate for the next several months. Property was finally secured on West State Street for the new Wellsville High School. The school was occupied in 1927, and has been expanded and reconfigured at least twice since then. (James Dello.)

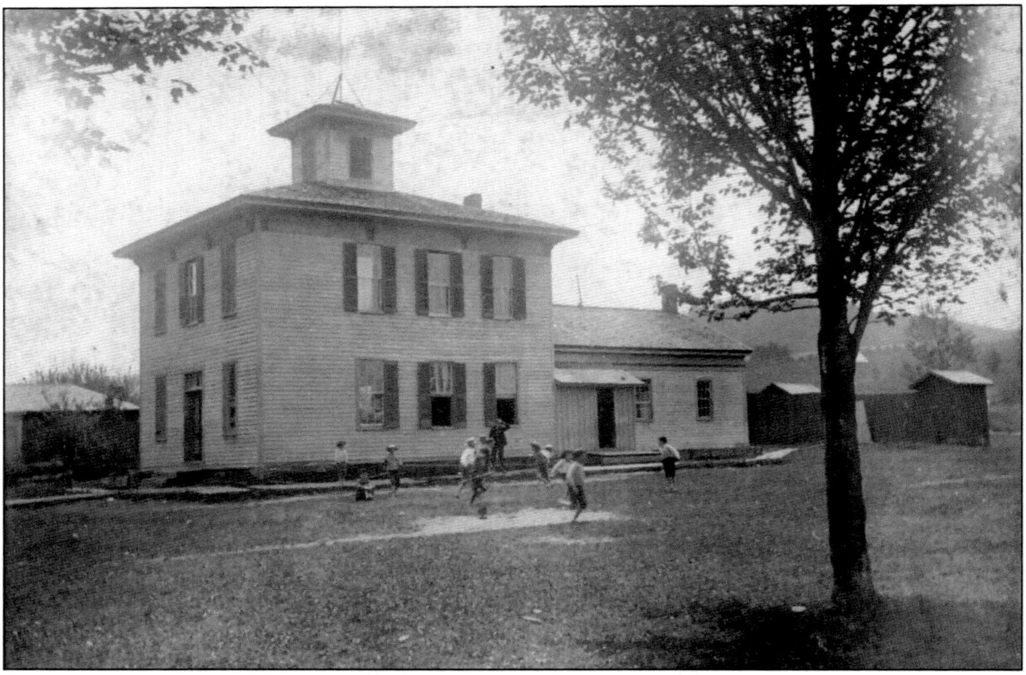

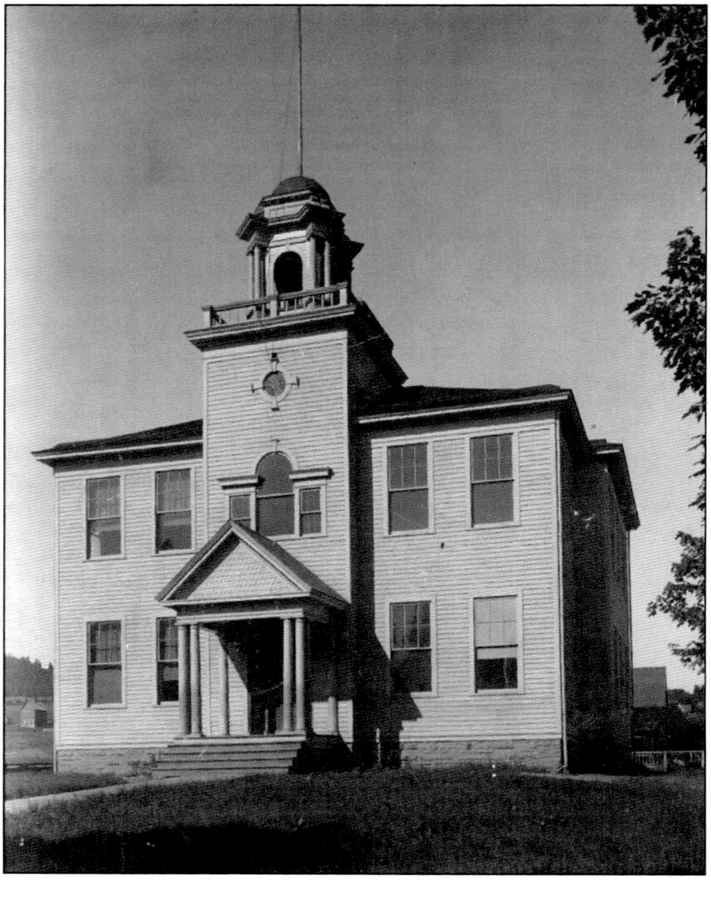

The Brooklyn School at the corner of Brooklyn Avenue and Pine Street was at one time an entirely separate school district founded in the late 1850s. This schoolhouse served well for many years, but by 1894, overcrowding forced the school board to authorize a new building. The second school to occupy the site on Brooklyn Avenue and Pine Street was opened in 1897. This school was built just a little closer to the corner of Pine Street and Brooklyn Avenue, so the children could continue classes in the old school while the new one was erected. Classes were conducted here until 1927, when they were moved to the new high school on West State Street. (Left, Erin O'Connor.)

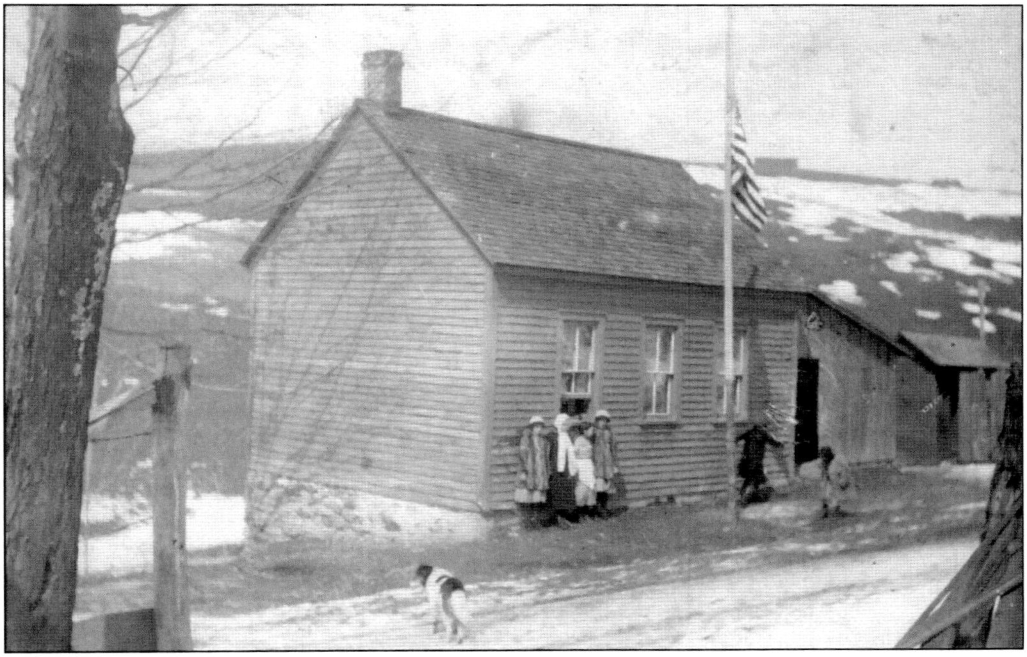

A school was organized on Hanover Hill in November 1857, and a schoolhouse was built on the Grastorf property there in 1859. The first teacher in this new building was Maria Nobles, who later married James T. Covel. Maria lived past her 100th birthday and was the grandmother of Daisie Covel Grastorf and Fern Covel Rixford, who both taught at the Hanover Hill School. When the school consolidated with Wellsville District No. 1, the land reverted to Walter Grastorf, who bought the building and converted it into a dwelling. (Donald Baldwin.)

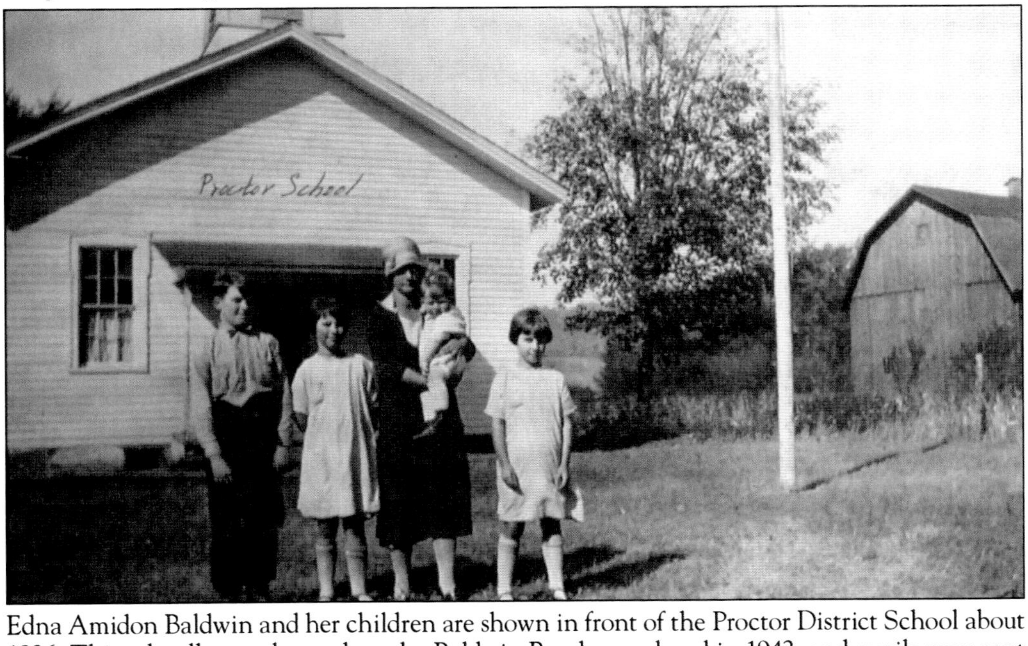

Edna Amidon Baldwin and her children are shown in front of the Proctor District School about 1926. This schoolhouse, located on the Baldwin Road, was closed in 1942, and pupils were sent to the village to school. Shown in this photograph are, from left to right, Donald, Louise, Edna (holding little Leo), and Pearl. (Pearl Baldwin Schultz.)

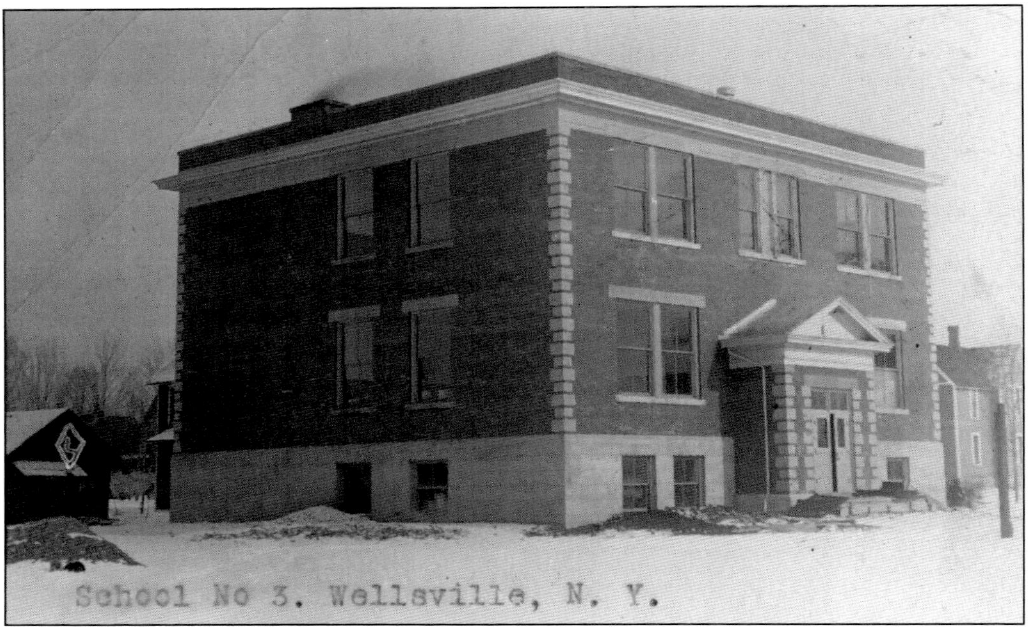

The Washington School on the corner of Osborne and Hanover Streets was built in 1909. The new school consolidated several smaller districts into this one structure, which was called School District 3. This facility closed upon the opening of the new elementary school on School Street in 1961, and the building was sold to the Dyke Street Engine Co. No 2, which erected a new fire hall on its foundation.

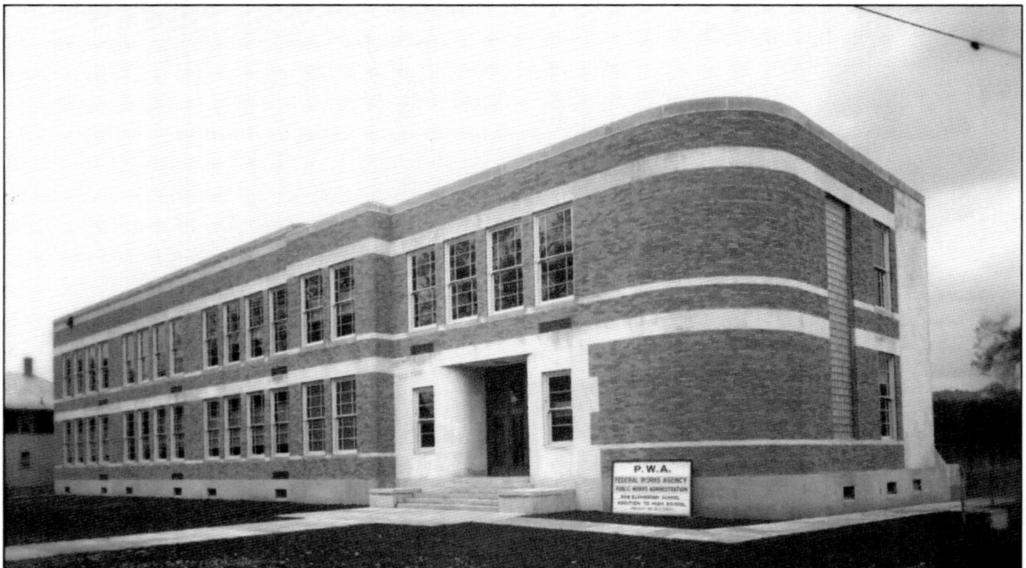

A new Brooklyn Avenue School was authorized in 1938, and funding was provided by a Public Works Administration grant. The new school was built near the high school and contained only 13 classrooms. It was expanded in 1948 with 12 more classrooms and a cafeteria. In its later years, it was used exclusively as a middle school. Classes were recently transferred to the high school building after a remodeling program allowed the consolidation of both institutions. (Donald Baldwin.)

Six

1950 TO 1980

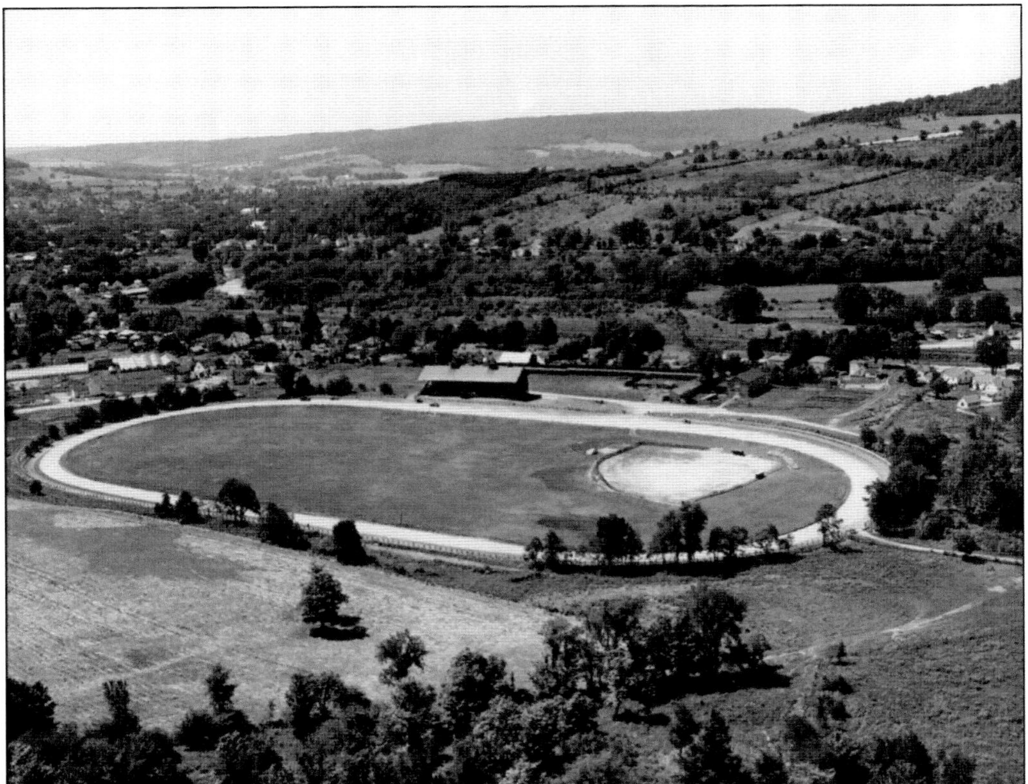

The old track for the defunct Wellsville Fair began to see new life during the 1950s with the advent of stock car racing. The Wellsville Raceway opened in August 1950 and closed in 1955. The Wellsville Elementary School is now located on this site.

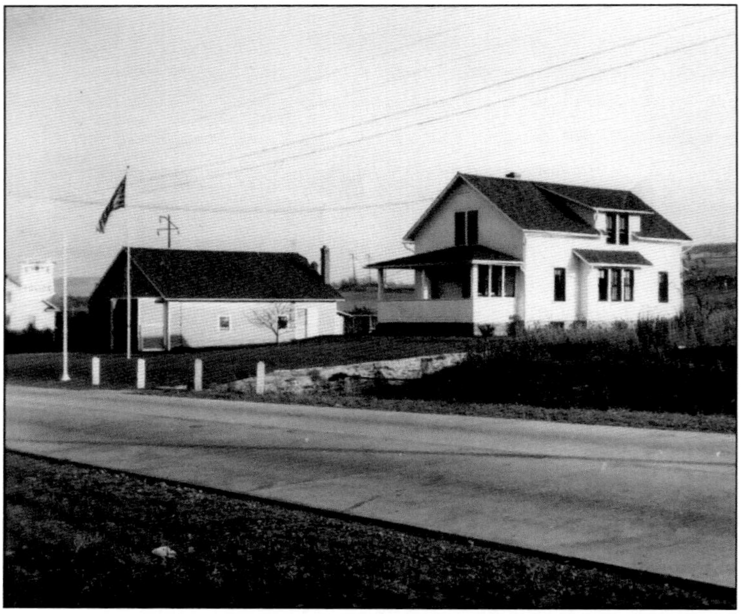

The New York State Police barracks at Wellsville opened in 1945 using a house on Bolivar Road as the office. In 1955, Eddie Schiavi purchased a portion of the property for his business called the House of Glass. A new building for the state police was erected in 1966 just a little farther west on Bolivar Road. (James Dello.)

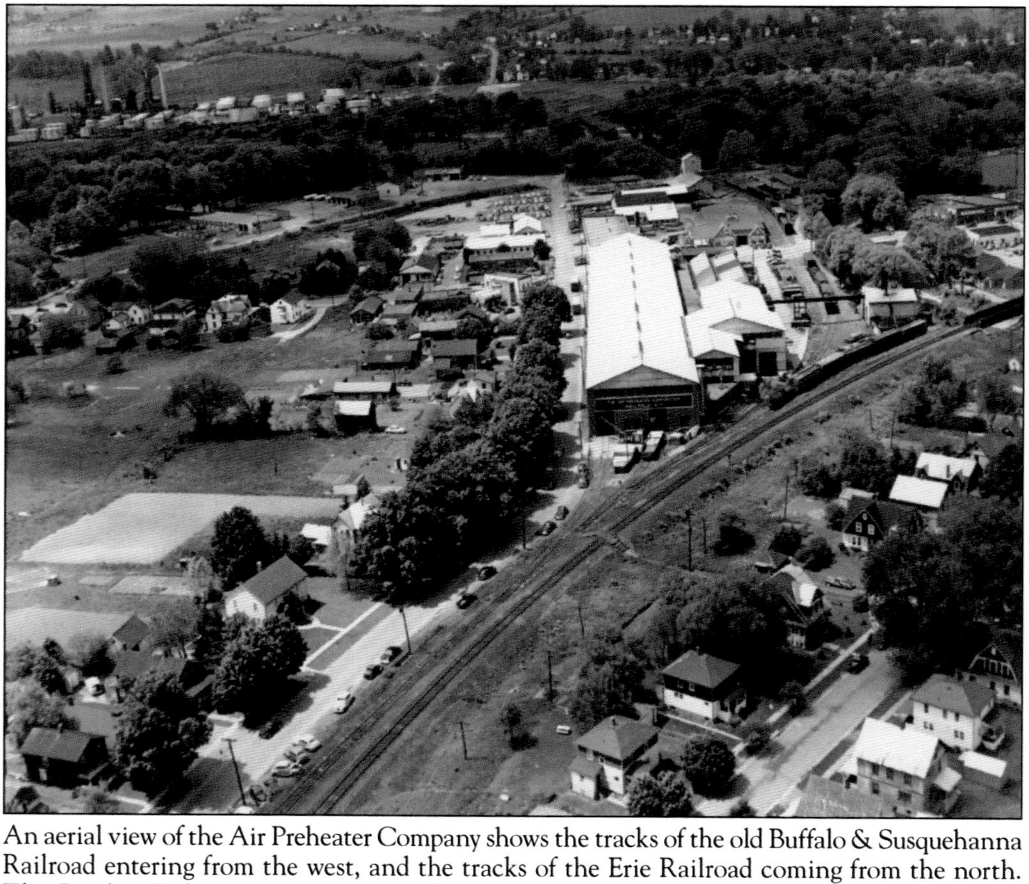

An aerial view of the Air Preheater Company shows the tracks of the old Buffalo & Susquehanna Railroad entering from the west, and the tracks of the Erie Railroad coming from the north. The Sinclair Refinery can be seen in the background in this mid-20th-century photograph. (James Dello.)

Fire started in the upper rooms of the old city hall in the mid-morning of April 1, 1954. City hall was state-of-the-art when it was built in 1895, but by 1954, it was showing its shortcomings. As the fire was contained in the upper floors, firemen were able to remove their equipment from the lower floors of the building. The upper two floors were destroyed by the flames, and the structure was considered a complete loss. The removal of the old building allowed the opening of Madison Street to Park Place by 1956.

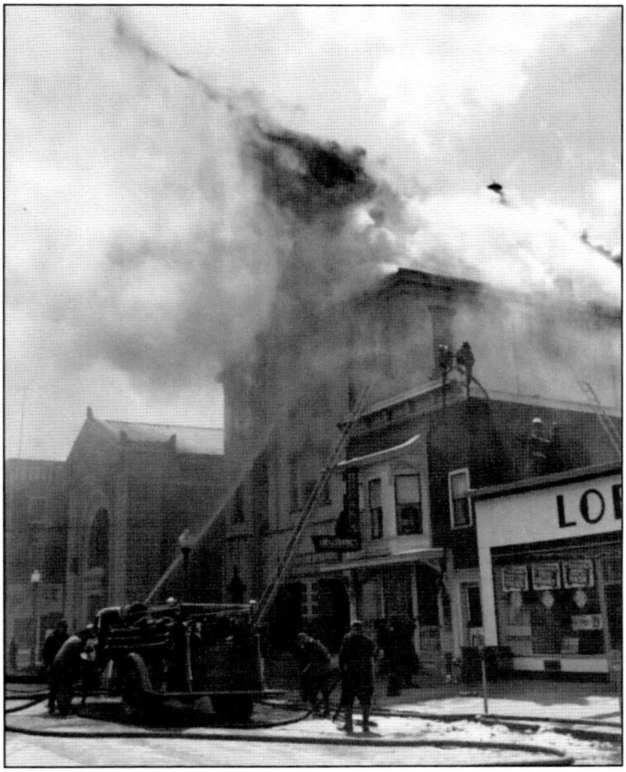

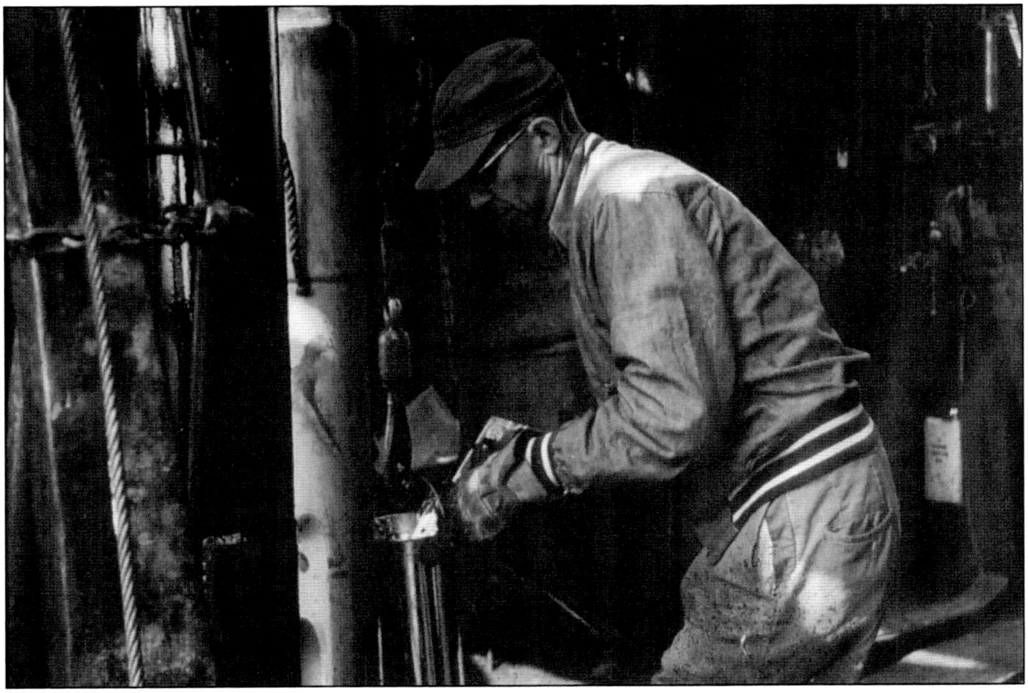

This photograph shows Vern Marsh preparing to shoot an oil well. Marsh is seen pouring nitroglycerin into a shell that will be lowered to oil-sand depth. Shooting a well with nitroglycerin improved the oil and gas recovery from the well. (Dan Nicholson.)

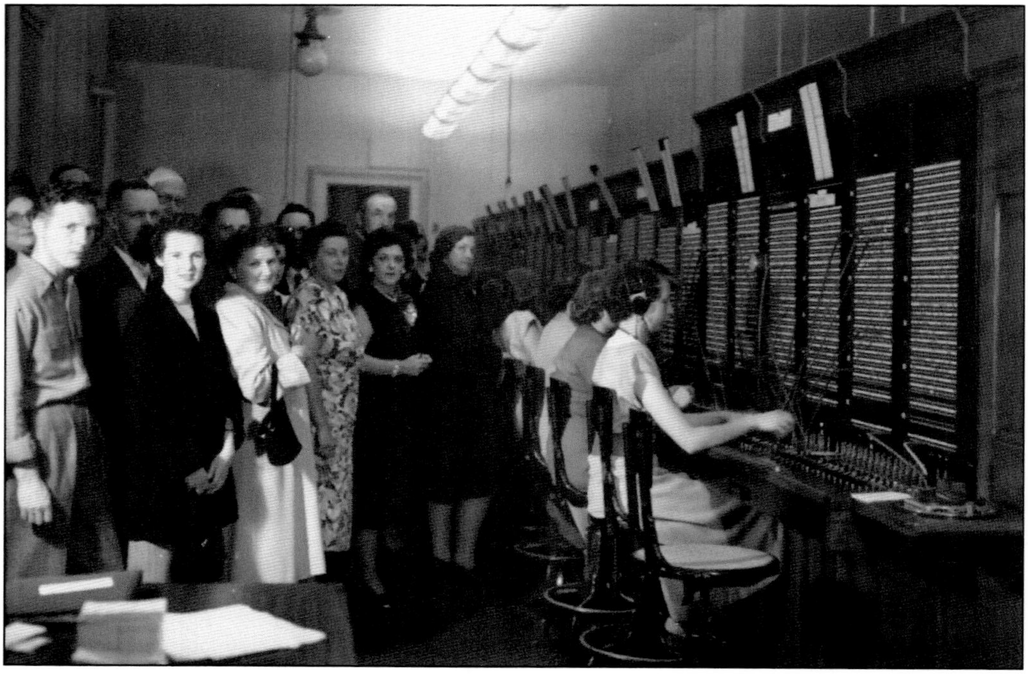

The New York Telephone Company switchboard was located on the second floor at 120 North Main Street. This photograph shows a group of men and women viewing an area that was normally very restricted to outsiders. Jane Aiken joined the telephone company in 1946 and is shown here as the closest operator to the camera. (Jane Aiken.)

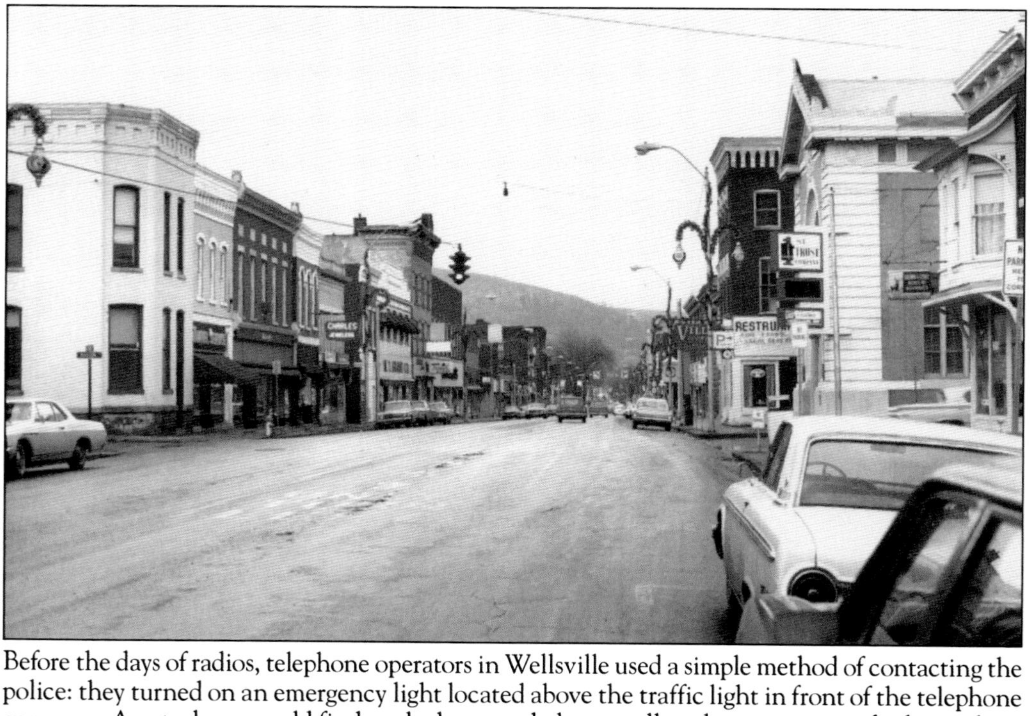

Before the days of radios, telephone operators in Wellsville used a simple method of contacting the police: they turned on an emergency light located above the traffic light in front of the telephone company. A patrolman could find a telephone and place a call to the operators to find out where he was needed. The emergency light looks like a small dot in this photograph.

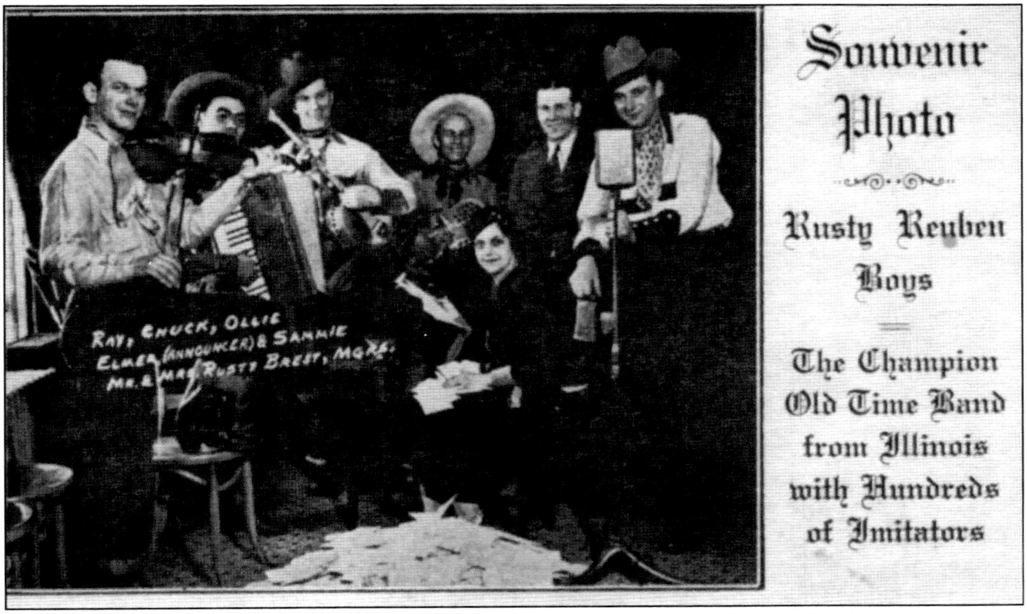

Ed "Rusty" Brest met his wife, Genevieve Baldwin, in 1931 when he and his band, the Rusty Reubens, were broke and stranded in Wellsville. Married in 1932, the Brests managed and traveled with the Rusty Reubens until 1939. The band played hillbilly-style music in dance halls and theaters all over the United States.

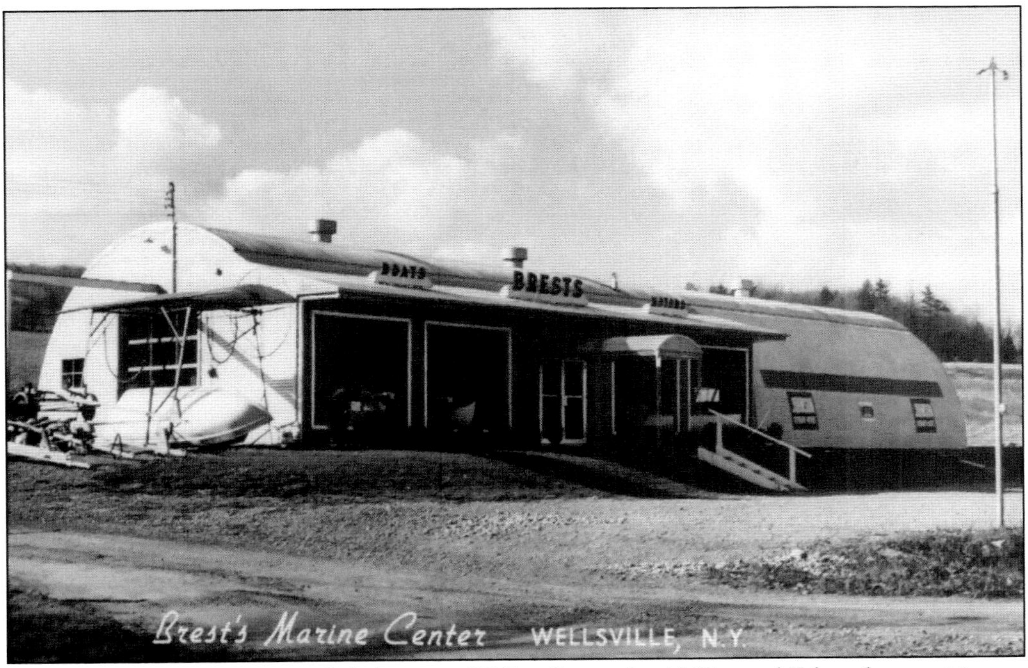

Ed and Genevieve Brest settled down in Wellsville in the 1940s, and Ed took a position at Worthington Pump. They operated a marine-supply business out of their basement for years until they built this Quonset hut–type structure in 1955. The building has since been home to car dealerships, an Italian restaurant, an outdoor store, and, most recently, an antique cooperative. (Craig Braack.)

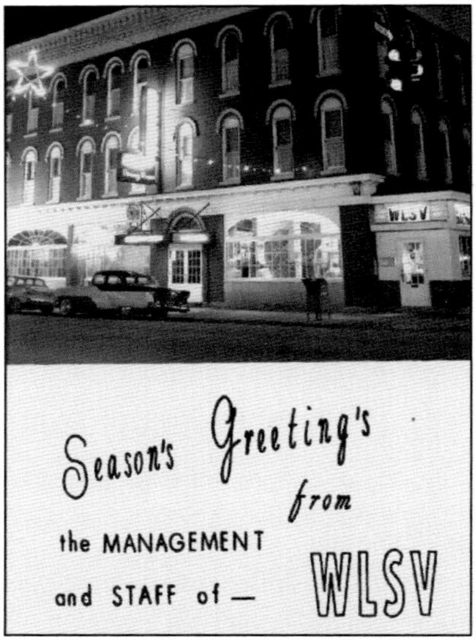

Wellsville's first radio station, WLSV 790 AM, premiered on October 31, 1955. The first location of the station was in the former barbershop of the Fassett Hotel, as shown here in this Christmas postcard. The station now operates in conjunction with 103.5 WJQZ FM radio and is located on Railroad Avenue. (Donald Baldwin.)

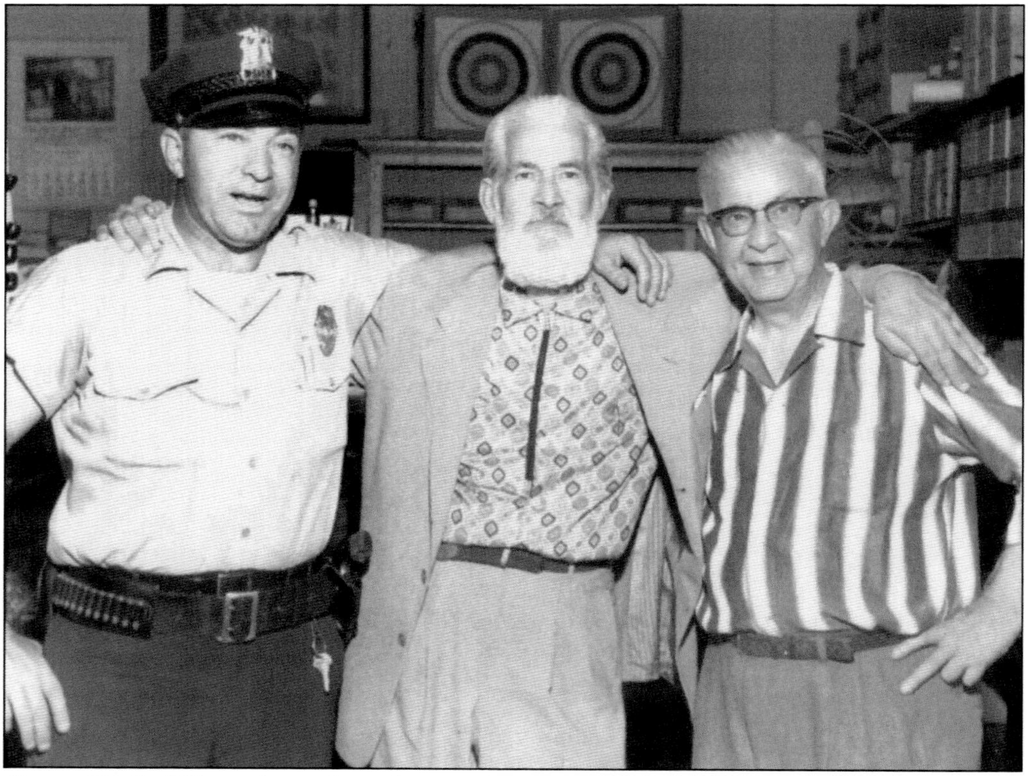

George "Gabby" Hayes (center) was born in the town of Willing. The Hayes family later moved to Wellsville, and George was educated in Wellsville schools. He was always interested in the stage, performing in school as well as in community productions. After he left Wellsville, Hayes had a successful career in vaudeville, and he later garnered more recognition for his movie roles as a cowboy sidekick. He returned to Wellsville often to visit relatives and friends, as shown here in a picture with Wellsville police officer Richard McNulty (left) and George Debarbieri (right). The men are standing in the Debarbieri store on North Main Street in this undated photograph. (Timothy McNulty.)

The village of Wellsville celebrated its centennial during the week of June 30–July 6, 1957. It was a tremendous undertaking, employing more than 400 volunteers. There were window displays, beard-growing contests, kangaroo courts, concerts, dances, tractor-driving contests, fireworks, pageants, tours, parades, and much more. This photograph shows Dela Horn (left) in her "Most Authentic Costume," and Alyce Hopkins in her "Best Reproduction Costume," as they pose for centennial advertising.

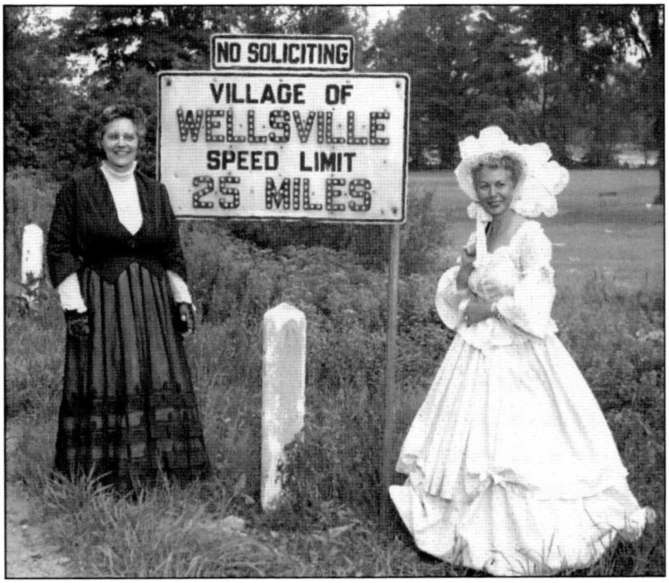

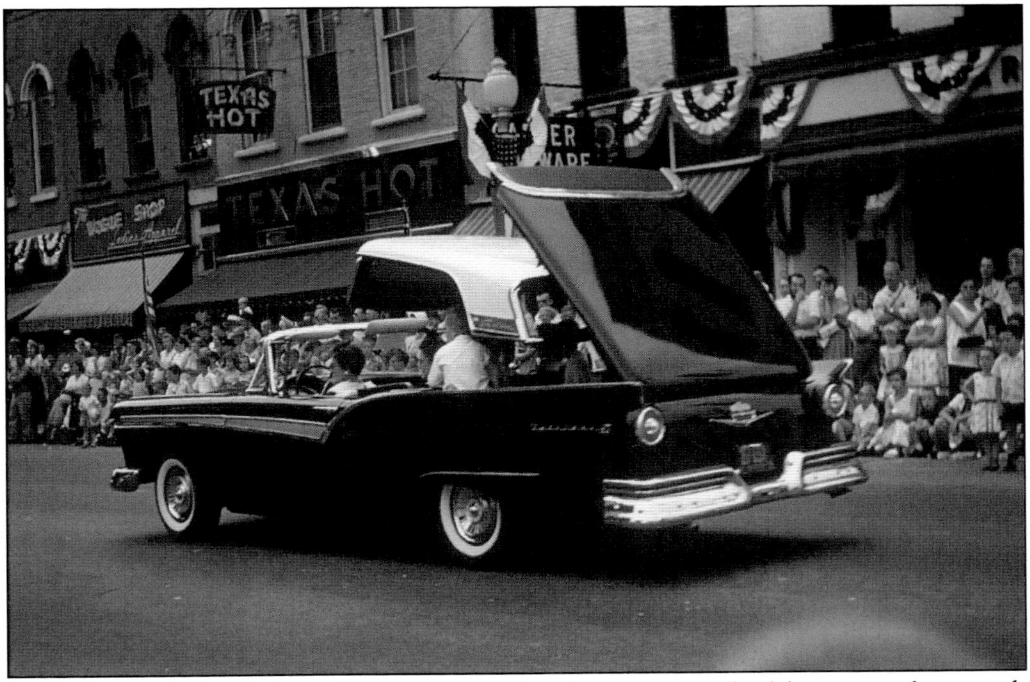

There were well-attended parades almost every day of the centennial celebration, each one with a different theme. This car is part of the transportation-themed parade as it rolls down North Main Street almost in front of the Texas Hot.

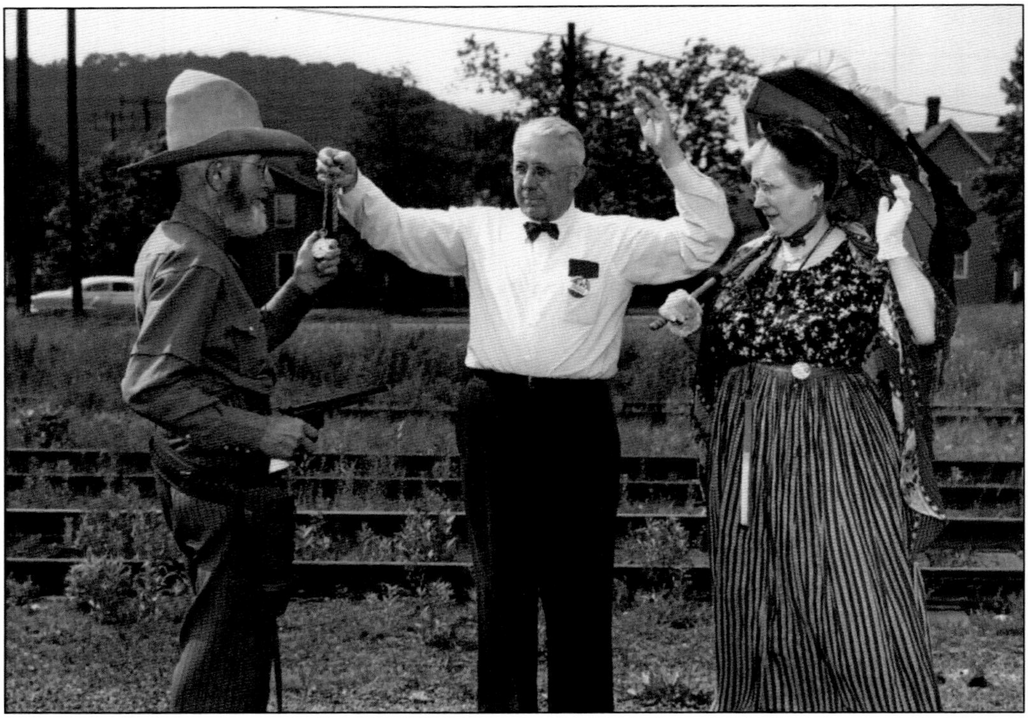

Martha and Albert Howe are confronted by "gun-toting badman" David Rogers in this posed photograph for the centennial celebration. Martha was Wellsville town historian for many years and wrote a very popular history book called *A History of The Town of Wellsville, New York*, published in 1963.

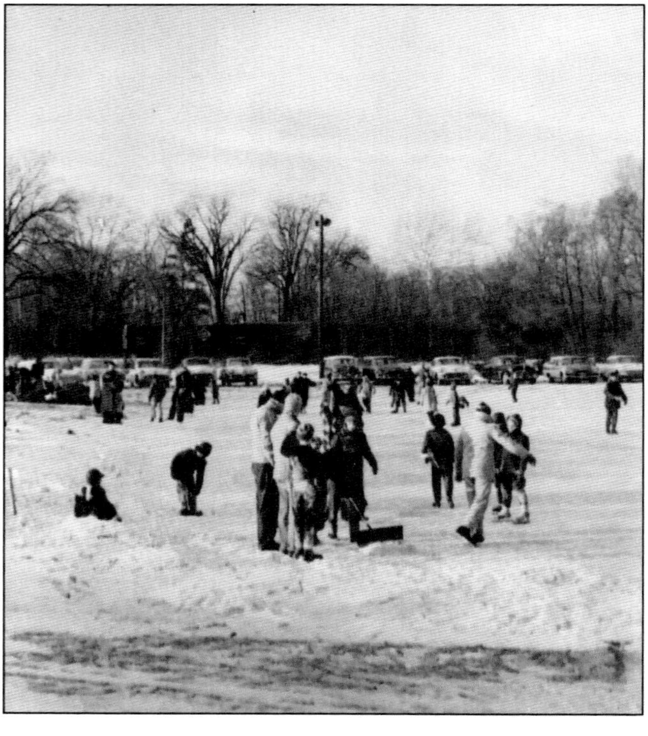

The village approved an ice-skating rink late in 1956 on property located behind Woodlawn cemetery. Built by town workers during lulls in their normal schedule, the Ice Skating and Canoe Lagoon was opened for skating in early 1957. While the skaters enjoyed the rink immensely, the village and recreation department had a difficult time funding supervisory personnel, and the rink was eventually drained. (Christina Wightman.)

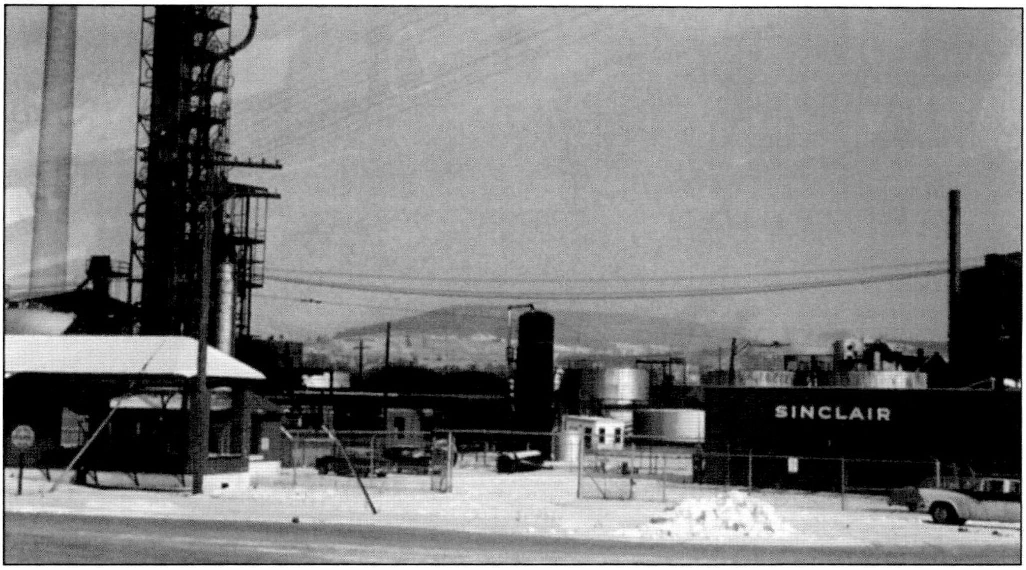

Sinclair Refining dealt a devastating blow to Wellsville in 1958 with the closing of the refinery. The diminishing supply of Pennsylvania crude oil and a large fire the refinery had just suffered were cited as major factors in the decision. Some employees were offered the chance to move to other Sinclair locations, and some lost their jobs. The refinery property was given to the town and village. In 1966, Alfred State College made part of the old refinery its Wellsville Vocational School campus.

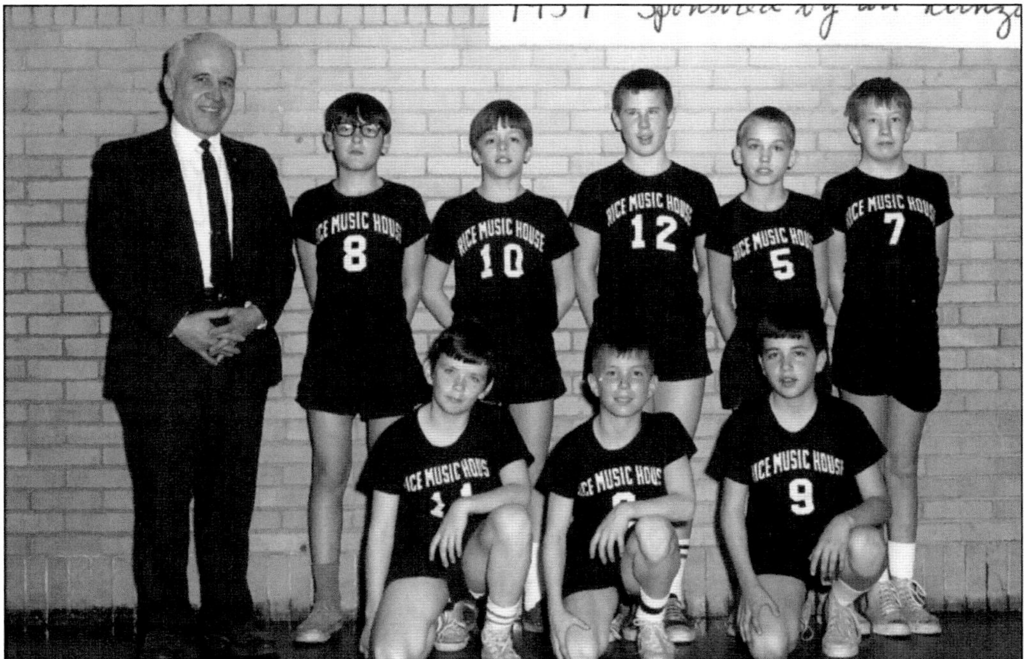

Arthur Runzo, owner of Rice Music Store, sponsored a small-court basketball team around 1969. Shown in this photograph, from left to right, are (first row) Mike Ryan (11), Craig Kephart (6), and Bob Sobeck (9); (second row) Runzo, Mike Zentz (8), Paul Forhan (10), Joe Hennessey (12), Steve Midgely (5), and Marvin Stebbins (7).

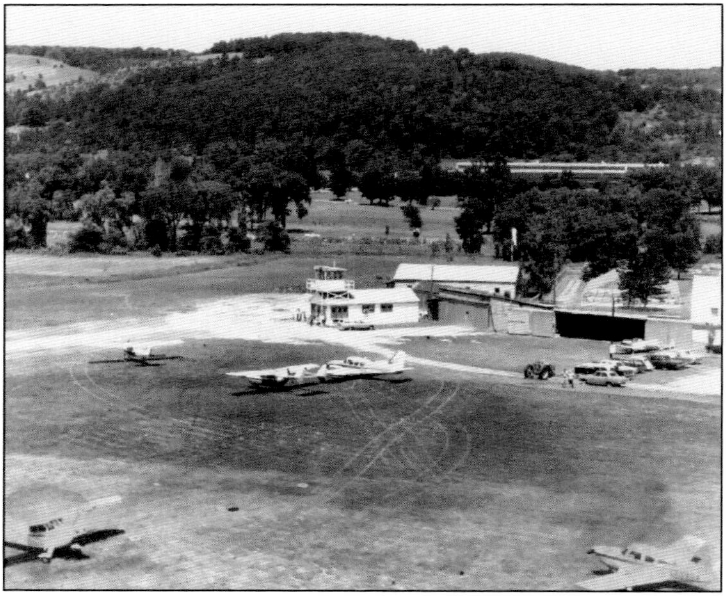

The citizens of Wellsville voted to purchase the Crowner farm on the Bolivar Road in 1940 for use as a municipal airport. This photograph dates to the early 1960s and shows a sweeping view over the airport toward Turbodyne Steam Turbine Company. Modesto "Mote" Tarantine began his long association with the airport after his service in World War II. (Barbara Tarantine Hulbert.)

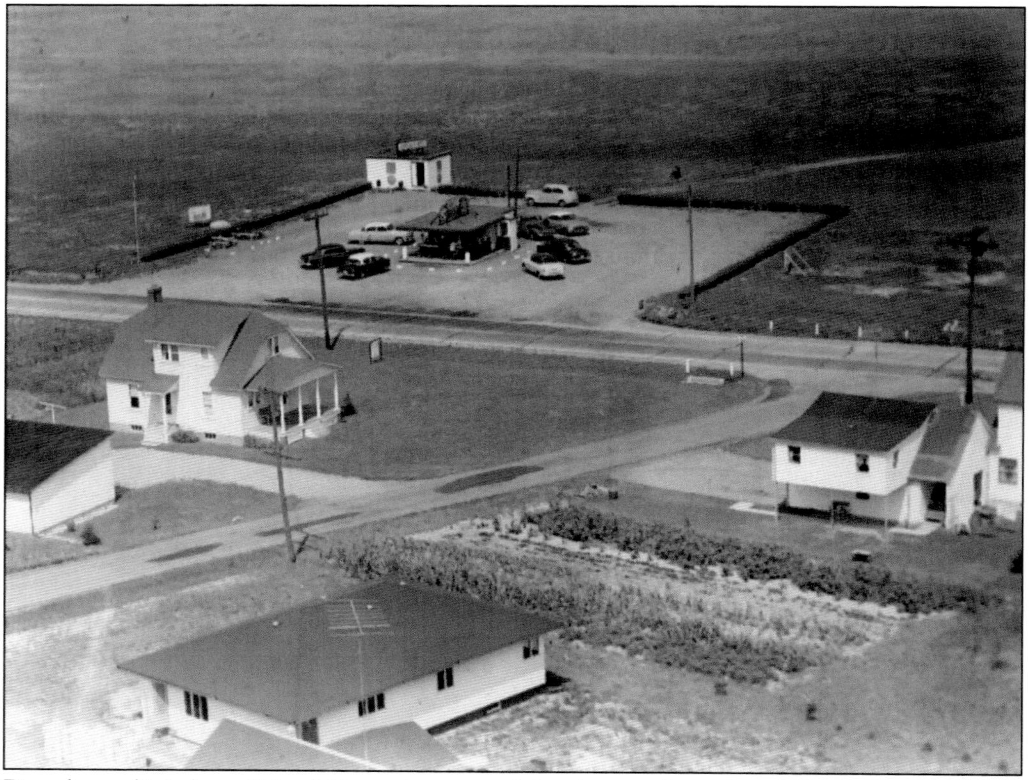

Dorothy and Modesto "Mote" Tarantine opened the Airport Drive In on Bolivar Road in 1951. The establishment was located on town property at the edge of the Crowner Field Municipal Airport, which was managed by Tarantine. In 1964, the Tarantines sold the business to Frank and Alfred Gomez, who ran the restaurant for several years. This aerial photograph was taken around 1957 almost above the intersection of Florida Avenue and Bolivar Road. (Barbara Tarantine Hulbert.)

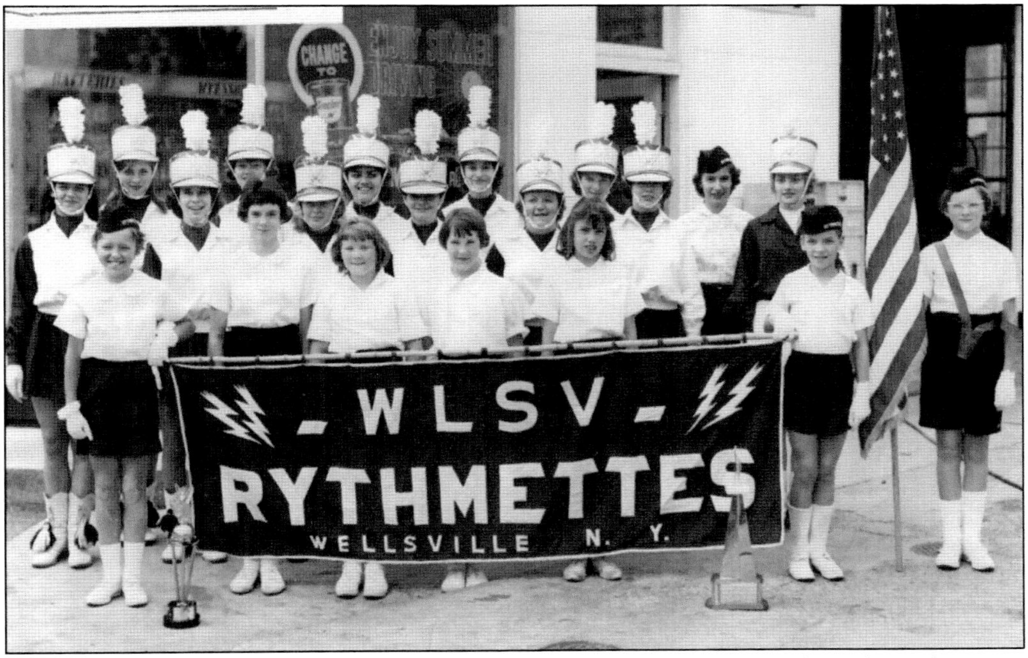

The Wellsville Rythmettes was a girls' drill team that was formed in 1958. The girls are shown on opening day of Terry Cook's new Sinclair station on the corner of North Main and West State Streets in 1962. Between 1958 and 1963, the girls had a very active summer schedule, appearing in parades and competitions, but they did not regroup after 1964.

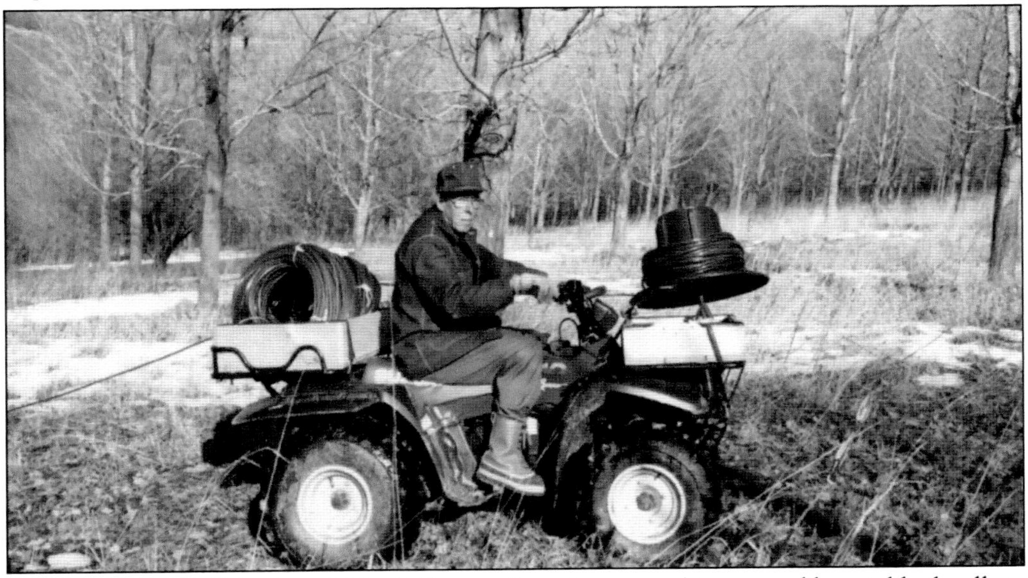

Merritt and Richard Vossler of Niles Hill were oil producers, working several low-yield oil wells in the area. Their wells only produced about 10 barrels a day, not enough to fully support their growing families, so Merritt turned to maple syrup to supplement his income. In 1956, he won first place for maple cream and second place for maple sugar at the New York State Maple Festival in Cooperstown. Over time, Merritt went from being an oil producer to being a maple syrup producer. Merritt's grandsons now run the operation. Merritt Vossler is shown stringing plastic tubing to his maple trees around 1991. (Vossler family.)

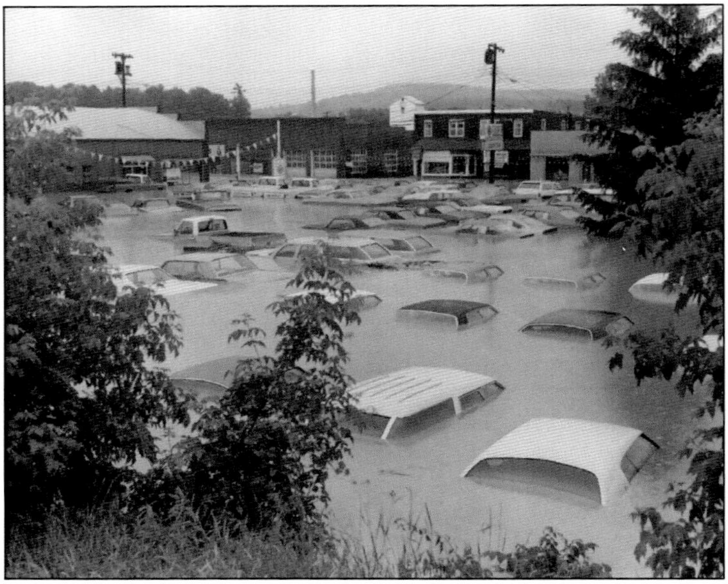

In June 1972, as Hurricane Agnes blew through the area, a storm considered an offshoot of the hurricane dumped over nine inches of rain upon the streets, homes, and fields of Wellsville. It was the worst flooding in Wellsville since 1916. This Richard Neal photograph shows the Lester Chevrolet dealership on South Main Street underwater. (Allegany County Historical Society.)

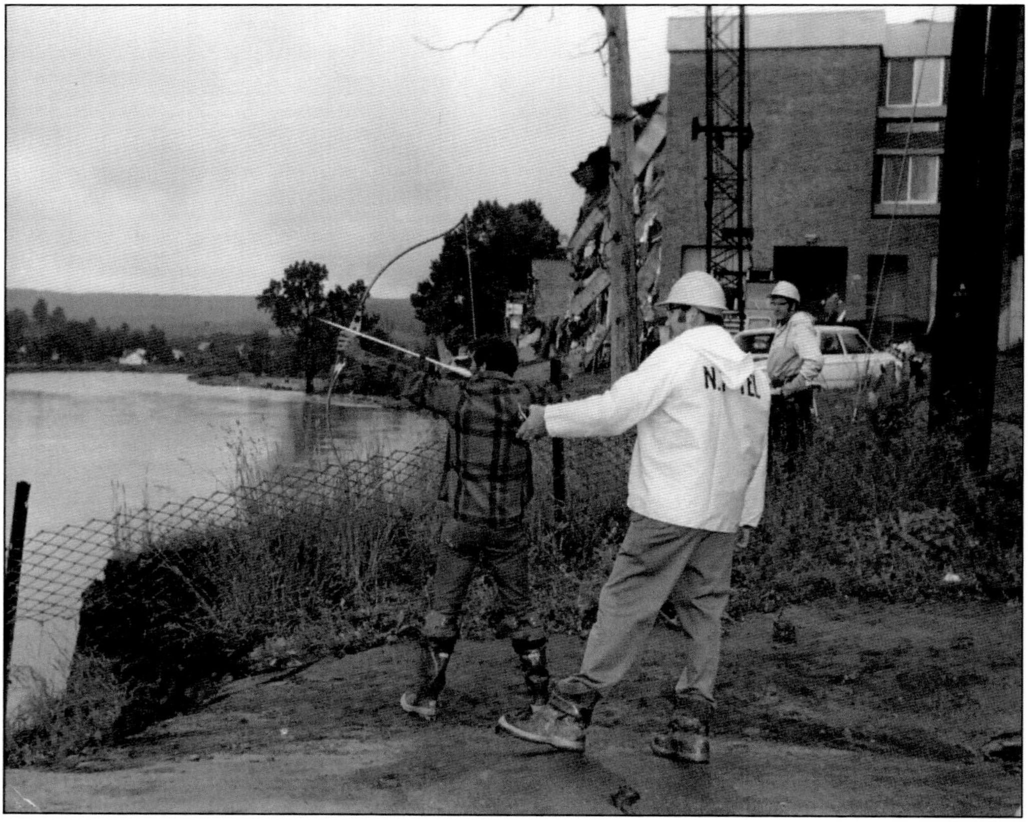

The floodwaters in June 1972 undermined a new, unfinished wing of the Jones Memorial Hospital, which tumbled into the Genesee River, taking vital cable that connected Wellsville to the rest of the world. With bridges out or unsafe, telephone lineman Rollin Colegrove used a bow and arrow to shoot a fishing line across the river to connect to a heavier rope that could then haul a cable across the water. (Craig Braack.)

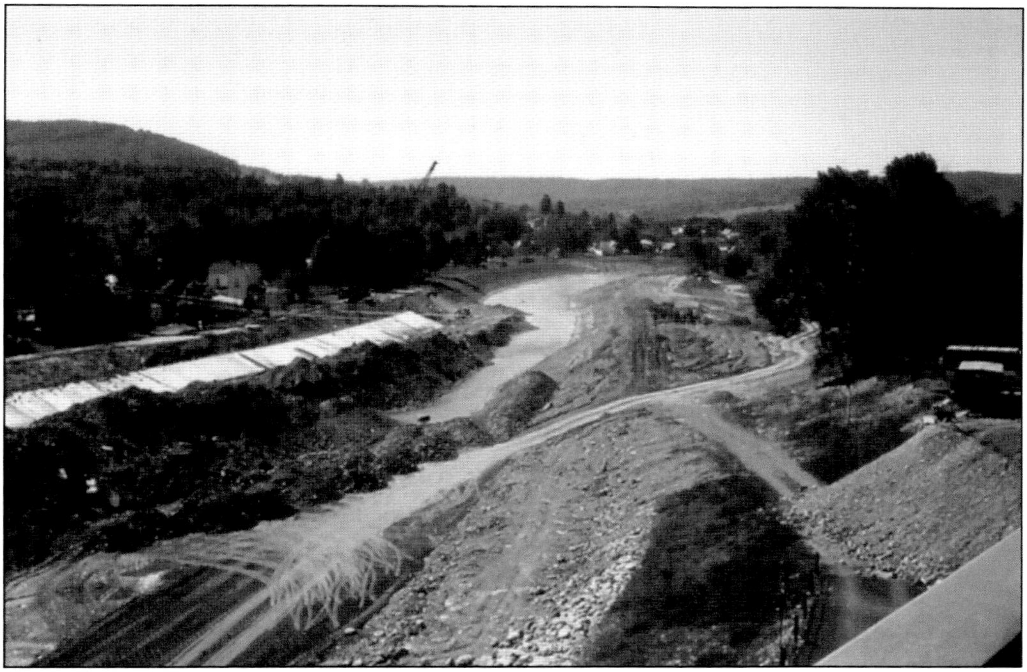

Village officials had been developing a plan with the New York State Highway Department to build a highway to take heavy traffic off Main Street. Part of that plan was to redirect the river and install flood control. The 1972 flood made that work essential. The Genesee River was moved slightly west, and its course was straightened. This photograph was taken from a window of Jones Memorial Hospital, with a view looking northwest. (Jones Memorial Hospital.)

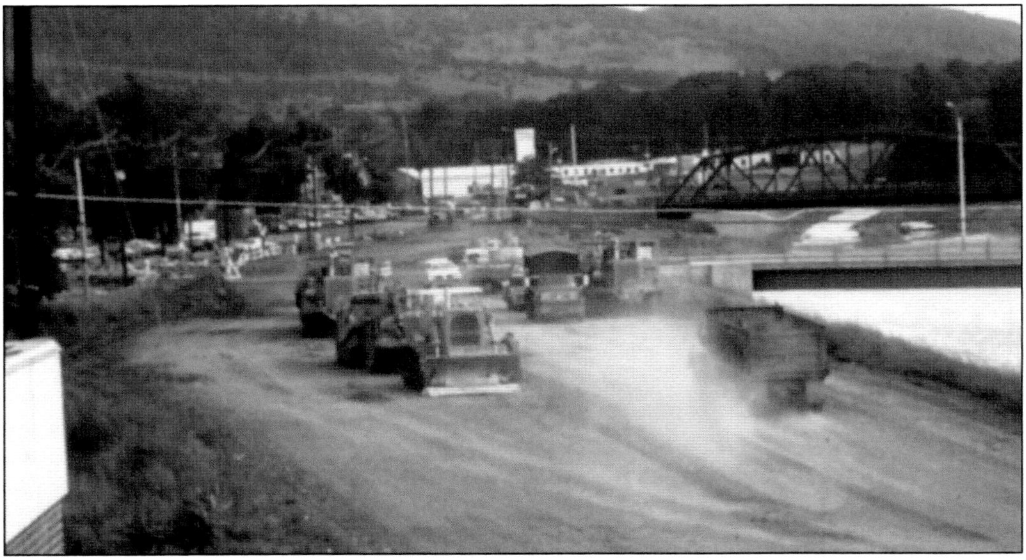

In its early days, the village was remodeled by fire. Later, the automobile did the same thing. The need to use automobiles has required the purposeful demolition of buildings to create empty places to park or drive cars. In the mid-1970s, the arterial was built to alleviate traffic, especially truck traffic, on Main Street. This photograph shows the new Madison Street bridge in the background as machines grade a path for the new highway. (Jones Memorial Hospital.)

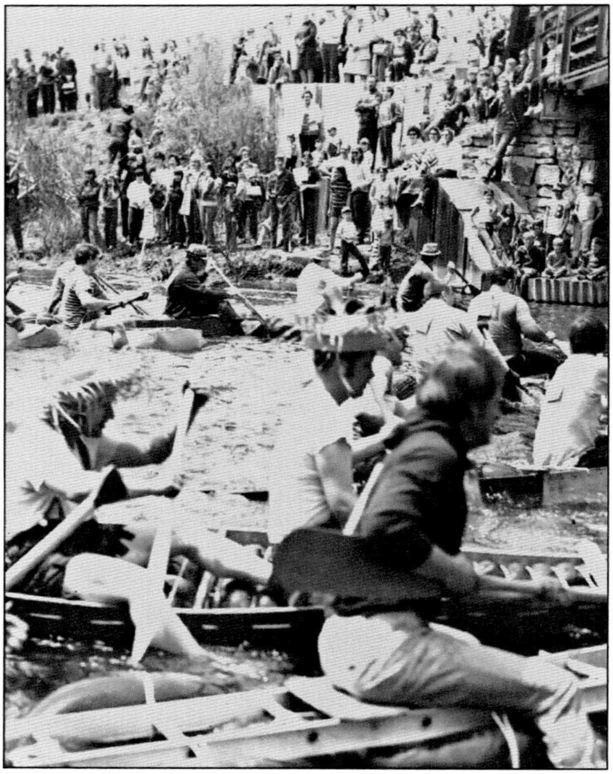

The Innertube Regatta was the creation of a group of Air Preheater employees in 1960. The goal was to create a vessel for two people using fewer than four inner tubes and keep it afloat on the Genesee River for three miles—from Hanks Crossing in Willing to Island Park in Wellsville. The regatta ran for two years, and resumed in 1967 to a field of 28 entrants. There were 190 registered entrants in 1976. Sponsored by Air Preheater and later by the Wellsville Lions Club, the Innertube Regatta has passed into fond memory. Contestants paddle down the river in this undated photograph. (Allegany County historian.)

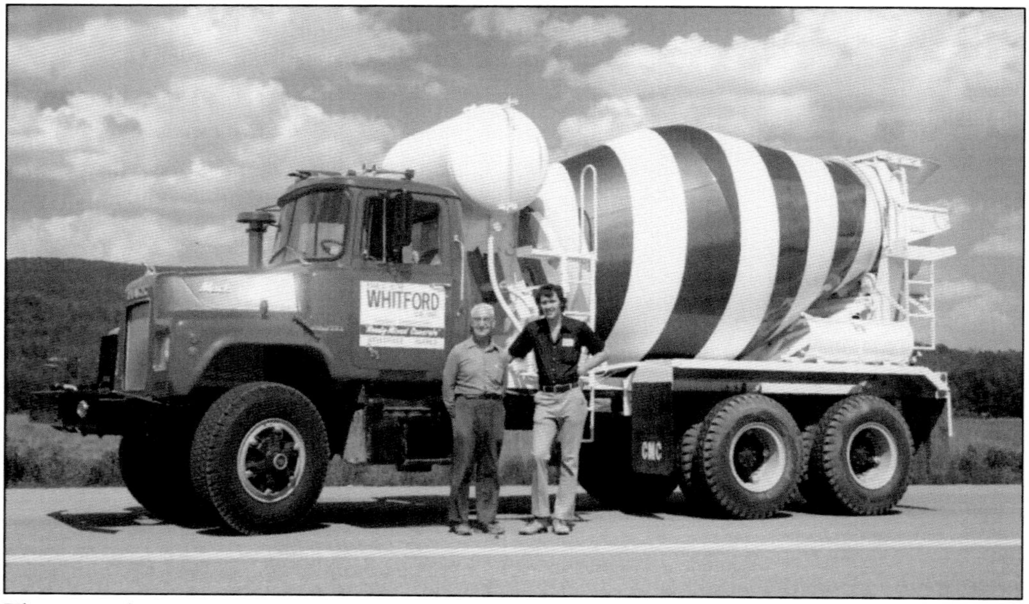

The general contracting company of Langford C. Whitford was started in 1922 and is credited with building many structures in Allegany County. L.C. Whitford built the beautiful David A. Howe Public Library, the Allegany County Courthouse, the Veterans Memorial Swimming Pool, the newest office building at Dresser Rand, and many more landmark buildings and bridges in and around the state of New York. Chan Whitford (left) and Homer Ingraham are shown with an addition to the Whitford fleet around 1972. (L.C. Whitford Company.)

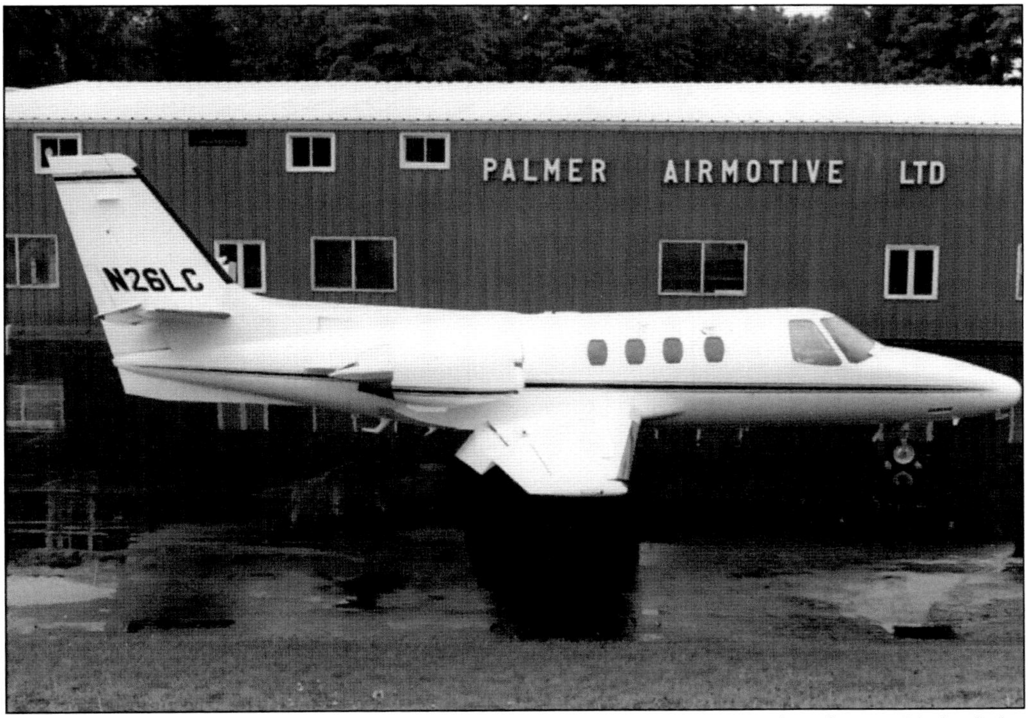

Jack Palmer's part-time hobby became his full-time business in 1963 when he established the Palmer Airmotive Company. The company developed a worldwide reputation for painting airplane exteriors and reconditioning their interiors. Palmer Airmotive was originally located in a hanger at the Crowner Field Airport and was moved to the new airport at Tarantine Field in 1970. (Jill Palmer.)

The Great Wellsville Balloon Rally was started in early 1976 as part of the Great Wellsville Air Show sponsored by the Wellsville Aviation Club and has grown into a huge event celebrated on the third weekend in July every year. This photograph captures the locally famous Carpet Town balloon around 1980 as it hovers over the Dough Box Coffee Shop near a new "Welcome to Wellsville" sign on Bolivar Road. (Marsha Sick.)

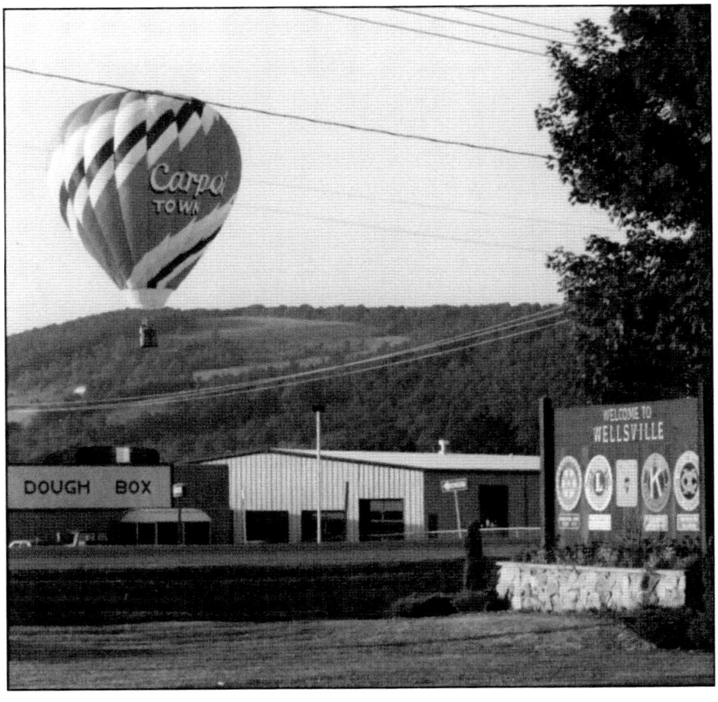

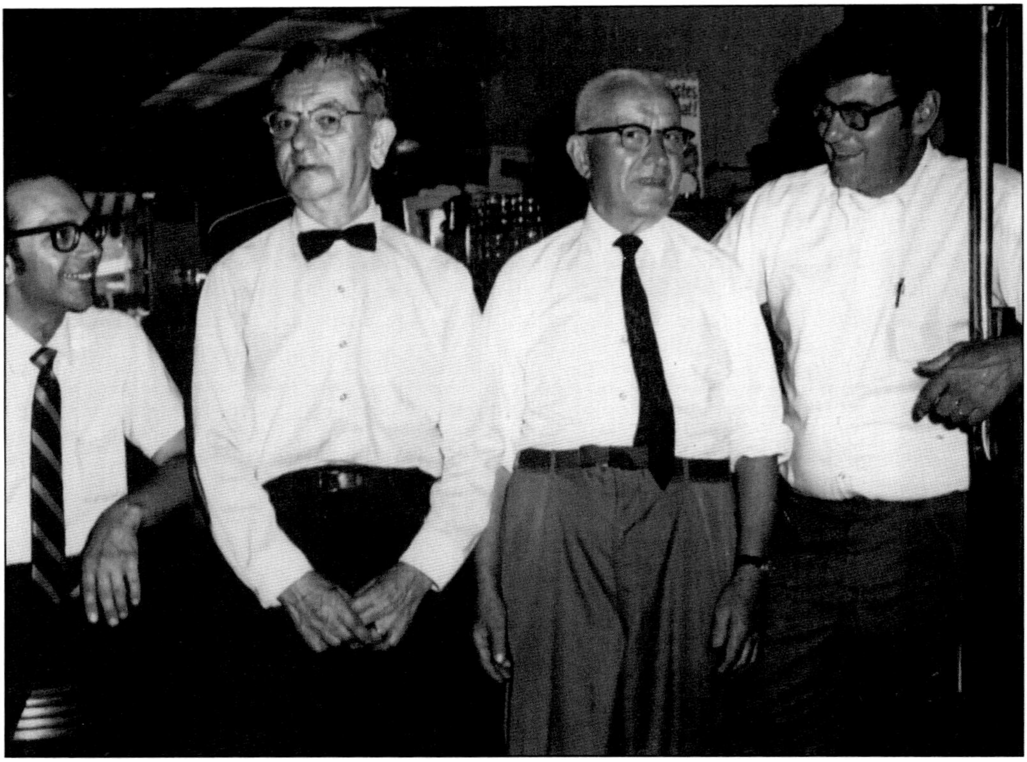

If there is one thing that says home to Wellsville residents more than anything, it would be the smell and the taste of a Texas Hot. James Rigas opened the Texas Hot at 132 North Main Street in 1921, and George Raptis joined him just a few weeks later. Gus Rigas and James Raptis took over management from their fathers in the 1950s; now their sons Christopher Rigas and Michael Raptis are the third generation to run the restaurant. The Rigas and Raptis families held huge celebrations for the 40th, 50th, and 75th anniversaries of the restaurant, and many residents look forward to its 100th anniversary in 2021. In the photograph above are, from left to right, James Raptis, George Raptis, James Rigas, and Gus Rigas in the restaurant about 1957. Below is a Texas Hot postcard from the late 1980s. (Both, James Raptis.)

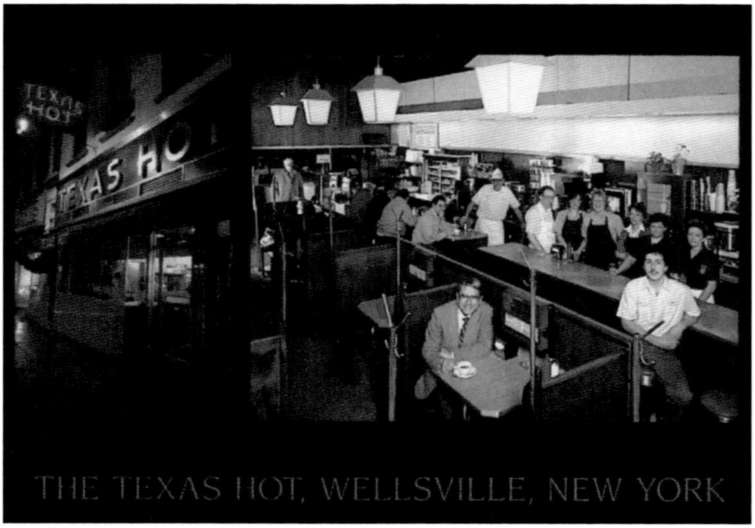

About the Thelma Rogers Genealogical and Historical Society

The Thelma Rogers Genealogical and Historical Society, the historical society for Wellsville, New York, was formed in 1959. The society can claim Hazel Shear, Robert and Virginia Macauley, Verna Willis, Ellis Hopkins, Martha Howe, Mary Rosa, Muriel Kruger, Mary Richards, and Hubert Bliss as a few of its founding members. Namesake Thelma Lewis Rogers had been urging her friends, who shared her love of history and genealogy, to form a local society in which historical and genealogical information could be shared with others. Unfortunately, Thelma passed away before her dream could be realized. The society's founders, Thelma's friends, decided to commemorate her name when they designated the new organization the Thelma Rogers Genealogical and Historical Society.

The mission of the society is to collect, preserve, and share the history of Wellsville and the surrounding area. This mission is achieved through presentations to schools and the community, the sharing of files, tours of the museum, and research on the growth and history of Wellsville. The society's files contain information on family names in and around the greater Wellsville area, as well as information on businesses, buildings, events, and schools in the village of Wellsville.

The society's museum, the Nathaniel Dyke Museum, is located at 118 East Dyke Street, Wellsville, New York. The museum is open on Wednesdays afternoons from May 1 until the end of October, from 1:00 to 4:00 p.m. The society can be contacted at its street address (zip code 14895) or through e-mail—thelmargh@gmail.com—and can be found on Facebook as the "Wellsville New York Historical Society."